AF754593

PROSPER OR PERISH

Prosper or Perish

Credit and Fiscal Systems in Rural China

Lynette H. Ong

CORNELL UNIVERSITY PRESS ITHACA AND LONDON

Cornell University Press gratefully acknowledges receipt of a Subsidy for Publication Grant from the Chiang Ching-Kuo Foundation for International Scholarly Exchange (USA), which generously assisted the publication of this book.

Cornell University Press gratefully acknowledges receipt of a grant from the Association of Asian Studies First Book Subvention Program, which aided in the publication of this book.

Copyright © 2012 by Cornell University

All rights reserved. Except for brief quotations in a review, this book, or parts thereof, must not be reproduced in any form without permission in writing from the publisher. For information, address Cornell University Press, Sage House, 512 East State Street, Ithaca, New York 14850.

First published 2012 by Cornell University Press
Printed in the United States of America

Library of Congress Cataloging-in-Publication Data

Ong, Lynette.
Prosper or perish : credit and fiscal systems in rural China / Lynette Ong.
p. cm.
Includes bibliographical references and index.
ISBN 978-0-8014-5062-4 (alk. paper)
1. Rural credit—China. 2. Rural development—China. 3. Banks and banking, Cooperative—China. 4. Local finance—China. 5. Central-local government relations—China. I. Title.

HG2051.C6O54 2012
332.7′10951—dc23 2012018812

Cornell University Press strives to use environmentally responsible suppliers and materials to the fullest extent possible in the publishing of its books. Such materials include vegetable-based, low-VOC inks and acid-free papers that are recycled, totally chlorine-free, or partly composed of nonwood fibers. For further information, visit our website at www.cornellpress.cornell.edu.

Cloth printing 10 9 8 7 6 5 4 3 2 1

For my papa and mama, Roger Ong and Philomena Lau

Contents

Figures

Tables

Abbreviations

ABC	Agricultural Bank of China
ADBC	Agricultural Development Bank of China
BoD	Board of directors
BoS	Board of supervisors
BRI	Bank Rakyat Indonesia
CBE	Commune and brigade enterprise
CBRC	China Banking Regulatory Commission
CCP	Chinese Communist Party
GDP	Gross domestic product
ICBC	Industrial and Commercial Bank of China
LGFV	Local government financing vehicles
MPF	Market preserving federalism
NGO	Nongovernmental organization
NPL	Nonperforming loan
OEM	Original equipment manufacturer
PBoC	People's Bank of China
RCC	Rural credit cooperative
RCF	Rural cooperative foundation
SBC	Soft budget constraint
SME	Small or medium-sized enterprise
SOE	State-owned enterprise
TBTF	Too big to fail
TVE	Township and village enterprise
UNDP	United Nations Development Programme
VAT	Value-added tax

Acknowledgments

I have accumulated numerous intellectual debts in the writing of this book. The idea for this project was first conceptualized while I was at the Contemporary China Centre at the Australian National University (ANU). I benefited tremendously from the expertise and guidance of Jon Unger, who was a co-editor of the *China Journal* at that time. The center's excellent resources in China studies and its collegial atmosphere provided a most fertile environment for conceptualization and deliberation of ideas. I also extend my utmost gratitude to Andrew MacIntyre at the ANU, whose intellectual guidance and encouragement has been monumental to the fruition of this project. I am most grateful to Andrew and Jon for their enthusiasm and unrelenting support for my project and generously giving of their time. They are simply the best advisors a student could ever have. Just as importantly, they are now among my dearest friends. I also benefited from the intellectual resources and advice given by various people at the Crawford School of Economics and Government and the ANU at large, including Christopher Findlay, Yusaku Horiuchi, Ben Kerkvliet, Ben Reilly, Luigi Tomba, and Andy Kipnis.

I have various people and institutions to thank for making my fieldwork in rural China possible—the CASS in Sichuan province, Shen Minggao and his friends at the Nanjing Agricultural University, Andy Kipnis of ANU, Li Shanfeng of Shandong CASS, Zhao Shukai and his friends in Hebei, the external affairs bureau of Zouping county, and He Baogang and his friends in Zhejiang.

The hot summer months of 2004 I spent in poor villages in Sichuan gave me one of the most unforgettable experiences: the many farmers and children I interviewed—their faces and their stories—have made this journey worthwhile. I promised not to name any of them, for obvious reasons, but by completing this research I hope I am doing my small part to support their cause.

In between those intense field studies, I enjoyed taking time off in Shanghai, particularly in the company of Ed Gwinn and his wife, Debbie. Ed, an extraordinarily kind soul, my friend and ex-boss, died in December 2009. He would be happy to learn that my back-breaking research on rural credit, one of his favorite subjects, is finally coming to fruition. Ed, you are badly missed.

I am also enormously indebted to my editor at Cornell University Press, Roger Haydon, for his enthusiasm for the project, and his generosity and guidance throughout the process. A postdoctoral fellowship at the Fairbank Center for

China Studies at Harvard University afforded me the time to revise the manuscript. I am particularly grateful to various people who took time to talk, read earlier versions of the manuscript, and provide constructive comments: Greg Chin, Bruce Dickson (who brilliantly suggested the title for the book), Kent Eaton, Joe Fewsmith, He Guangwen, Steph Haggard, Arthur Kroeber, Barry Naughton, Jean Oi, Liang Qinxing, Ren Changqing, Jonathan Rodden, Scott Rozelle, Victor Shih, Peter Timmer, Kellee Tsai, Wing Thye Woo, Dali Yang, and Zhou Feizhou.

More important, I thank various people at the University of Toronto, the place I have called home these past few years, who have provided much inspiration, intellectual guidance, and support—Harald Bathelt, Richard Bird, Loren Brandt, Christian Breunig, David Cameron, Joe Carens, Grace Skogstad, Joe Wong, and many others. The Department of Political Science affords junior scholars an extremely encouraging environment to develop and cultivate their research. The two anonymous reviewers at Cornell provided many constructive criticisms and helpful comments. I also acknowledge Reuven Shlozberg and Shi Jin for their excellent research assistance and copyediting. I also thank the Chiang Ching-kuo Foundation and the Association of Asian Studies for generously subsidizing the publication of this book, and my home department for a grant that covered the indexing cost.

Last but not least, I owe much to my family—my mum and dad, Philomena and Roger; and my brother and sister, Kelvin and Jean—without whose relentless encouragement and support, in both good and bad times, many things in my life would not have been possible. I thank them, particularly my parents, for their love.

Part I

OVERVIEW AND RESEARCH QUESTIONS

1

LOCAL GOVERNMENTS, RURAL CREDIT, AND REGIONAL DEVELOPMENT IN CHINA

In September 2008 a riot broke out in Jishou, a rather undeveloped city in rural Hunan province. More than ten thousand peasants who had lost their savings in an underground financing scheme took to the streets. By promising high rates of return, real-estate developers and other local companies in need of working capital had lured thousands of farmers to take out bank loans, using their savings and homes as collateral, in order to invest in these companies. When the scheme collapsed, the uproar persisted for several days and was finally quelled once the provincial government intervened to require the borrowing companies to repay all loans to the individual lenders.[1]

The Jishou incident was not the first instance of social unrest in rural China over unrecovered savings. In late 1998, several riots broke out in various rural locales, most notably in Sichuan and Hubei provinces, when local rural cooperative foundations (RCFs) proved unable to return the savings they held. RCFs were semi-official credit-and-saving institutions established by township governments outside the centrally regulated official banking system, though with tacit approval from the central government. By the mid-1990s, there were more than twenty-one-thousand township-based RCFs spread throughout rural China. They held deposits totaling almost one-eighth of those held by the official banking institutions servicing China's rural sector, the rural credit cooperatives (RCCs). Widespread misuse of funds by RCF managers, and mountains of nonperforming loans, mostly to local governments, brought about the eventual collapse of the RCFs. As in the later Jishou case, these riots were pacified only when the central government intervened to require local governments to pay off RCF debts to individual rural debtors.

On a hot summer afternoon in 2004 I joined a group of local Communist Party cadres for a spicy and sumptuous traditional feast in the only air-conditioned restaurant of a rural township in Sichuan. Toward the end of the meal, the township's party secretary sighed and lamented the dismal state of his government's finances. Knowing that local-government finance is a sensitive subject and that I was in the company of many of his subordinates, I did not press him, although I hoped he would elaborate on the source of his unhappiness. To my surprise, he did. The township, he said, was a few million yuan[2] in debt, with only a few thousand yuan in annual income. His subordinates interjected to provide more accurate figures regarding the township's income and expenses, but neither was willing to say who the creditors were. All they said was that the township owed money to "many people in this town."

As this conversation illustrates, the fact and scope of local-government debt is an open secret in China, but its specifics remain a sensitive subject. Only after spending time with numerous people in the township, including bank managers, shopkeepers, teachers, and farmers, was I able to piece together a more complete picture of the township's debt. The major creditors were (and probably still are) the local RCC, a construction company, and some private individuals. Because the RCC is the only government-recognized credit institution in the township (as in 90 percent of all rural towns in China), it absorbs the bulk of community savings. Loans from the RCC had been used to finance the now-collapsed rural enterprises that were owned and run by the township. The township had engaged a construction company to refurbish a run-down primary school, but it had failed to pay the company in full. Having exhausted its RCC lifelines, the township was then forced to take out loans from private individuals in order to pay wages for ordinary township cadres. Because a large amount of its loans to the local government were not repaid, the local RCC itself had a very high nonperforming loan ratio (close to 50 percent). This made it extremely difficult for the RCC to do what a bank is supposed to do: generate profits by lending.

To be sure, this is not the reality of every township in rural China. In the townships of rural Zhejiang where I have conducted fieldwork, for instance, most grassroots governments had either very modest or no debt. Most of Zhejiang's township governments were able to provide basic education and health care to the citizenry. Compared to the townships of Sichuan, the rural banks in Zhejiang had healthier balance sheets and fewer nonperforming loans. As a result, the Zhejiang banks were able to make better use of funds by lending to thriving private businesses. The people I spoke to in rural Zhejiang, as well as in Jiangsu and Shandong, were relatively content with what they had, far from the misery and bitterness exhibited by the citizens in the economically deprived Sichuan township described earlier.

These anecdotes provide a flavor of the issues addressed in this book. I seek to explain the bias in lending toward local government–related enterprises. I also explain why the mobilization of rural savings has contributed to successful industrial development in some locales but not in others. This is not a volume devoted to the functioning of rural credit institutions—a subject best left to development economists. Nor is it a study solely of local-government finance, an important subject about which many practitioners in the World Bank and other development agencies have already written. Rather, this book tells the story of the nexus between these fascinating issues.

Rural Savings, Uneven Regional Development, and the Implications for China's Political Economy

RCCs are China's main official banking institutions servicing the rural sector. Lack of alternative savings institutions and investment channels has made RCCs very popular savings options in rural China, where they are often the only option besides keeping household savings under the mattress. Their official mandate is to support agricultural development among farm households. Nonetheless, nationwide statistics on RCC loan portfolios show that rural households receive a much smaller proportion of loans compared to township and village enterprises (TVEs) (figure 1.1). Throughout the 1980s and 1990s, about half of all RCC loans

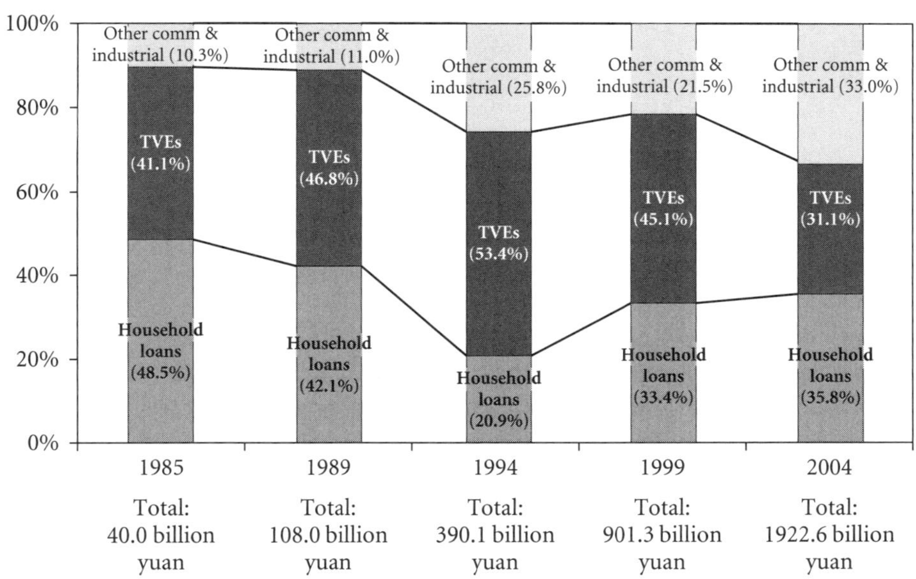

FIGURE 1.1 Composition of RCCs' loans nationwide (1985–2004)

went to TVEs, which are small or medium-sized enterprises (SMEs) located in, and managed by, townships and villages. Although many household-run businesses and private firms in rural China are also classified as TVEs, until the late 1990s the overwhelming majority of TVEs were collective firms owned and run by local authorities.[3] This despite the fact that rural households contributed over 85 percent of RCCs' total nationwide deposits during this period (figure 1.2).

Loan allocations by rural banking institutions to large rather than small borrowers are not uncommon in developing countries. But there are unique political-economic reasons for this phenomenon in China. At the end of the 1990s, RCCs' official nonperforming loan (NPL) rate was estimated to be 50 percent of total loans.[4] Indeed, before RCCs were restructured in 2003, about half of China's forty thousand RCCs were technically bankrupt or had negative net worth. Though no nationwide statistics indicate the proportion of loans to TVEs that have gone bad, my own field research and that of others suggest loans to farmers generally perform much better than those to TVEs.[5] My own estimate suggests the NPL rate of loans to TVEs was as high as 80 percent in the late 1990s.[6] Given that Chinese credit institutions often used accounting tricks to avoid registering loans as nonperforming, the actual magnitude of RCCs' bad assets was likely significantly higher than even official estimates.

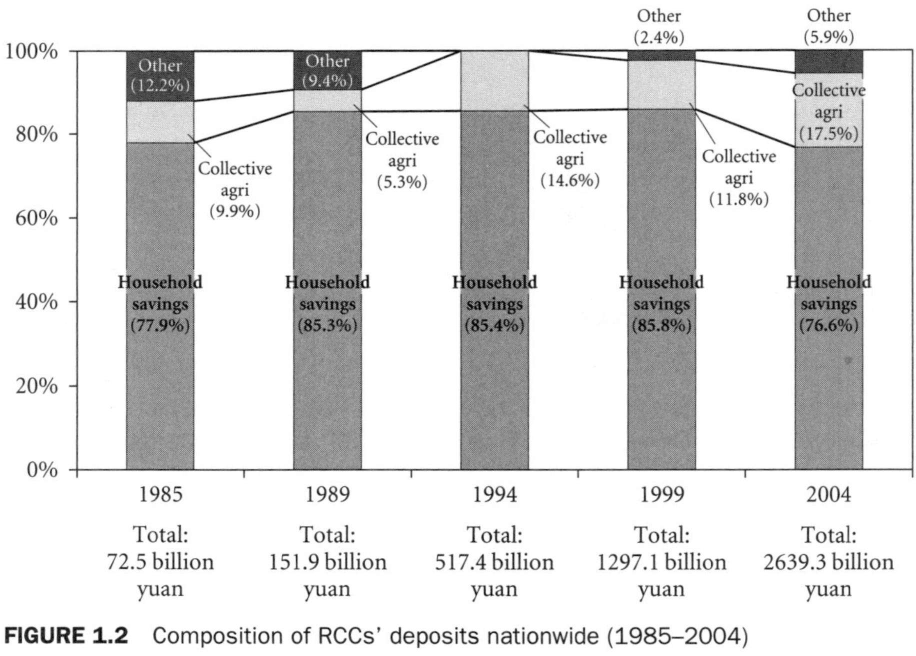

FIGURE 1.2 Composition of RCCs' deposits nationwide (1985–2004)

Source: *Zhongguo jinrong nianjian* [Almanac of China's finance and banking].

Subnational data on collective TVEs also show significant regional variations in terms of size, output, performance, and efficiency. At the peak of their development in 1994, TVEs in the eastern region accounted for about three-quarters of national industrial production, operating revenue, and fixed assets (figure 1.3). Nonetheless, eastern enterprises accounted for only half of the national total of workers and of enterprises. Although western enterprises obtained twice the amount of bank finance per sales unit as those in the east, eastern enterprises exported three times as much as those in the central and western regions (figure 1.4). In addition, workers in the east were 1.5 times and twice as productive as those in the central and western regions, respectively. These data clearly suggest that eastern TVEs operated more efficiently than those in central and western China.

China is characterized by starkly uneven regional development, manifested not only in a yawning urban-rural gap but also in significant variations within rural areas. In 2006 the income level of an average urban resident was 3.3 times higher than that of his rural counterpart, 11,759 yuan per capita versus 3,587 yuan per capita.[7] According to the UNDP, China had higher income inequality than 80 of 177 countries worldwide.[8] Uneven regional development is more startling in terms of funds available for essential social services. The gap in health expenditures per capita for urban and rural residents stood at 3.5 in 2005, though it had fallen from 4.1 in 1990 (figure 1.5). The top-spending province typically

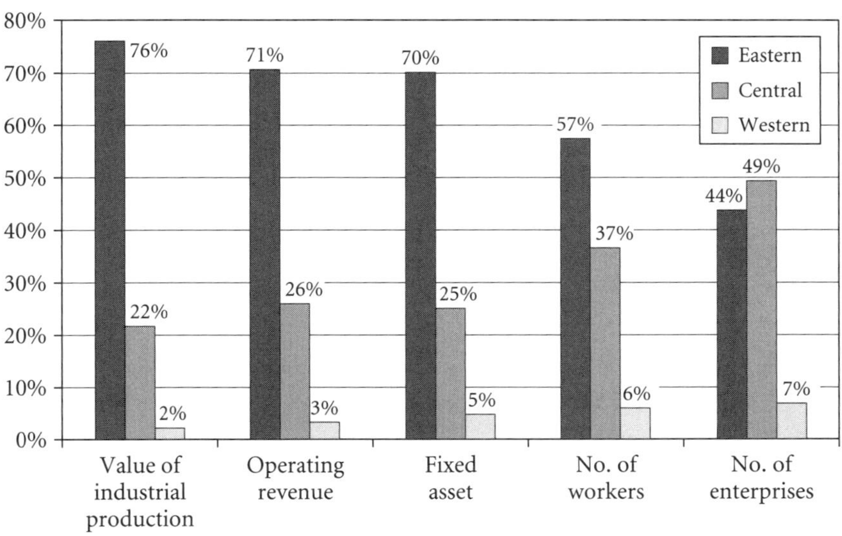

FIGURE 1.3 Share of collective enterprises measured by various indicators by region (1994)

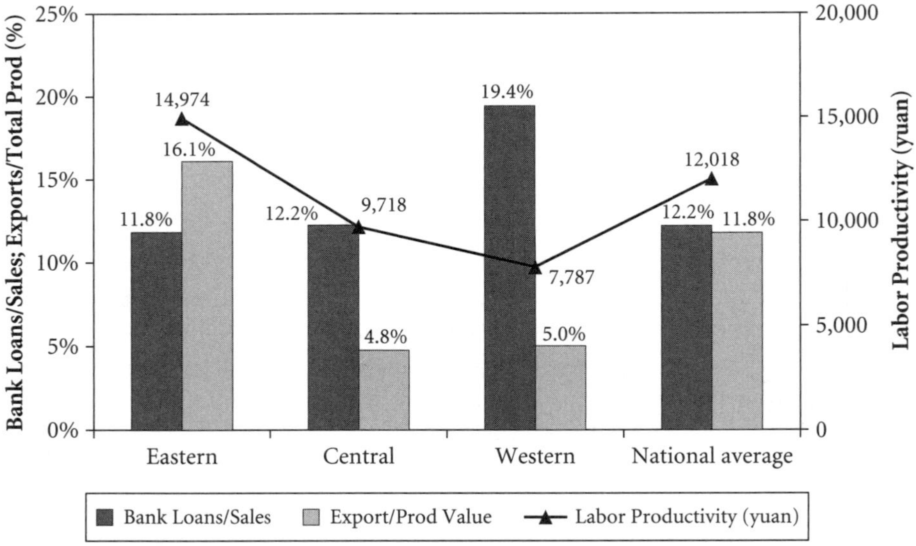

FIGURE 1.4 Performance of collective enterprises by region (1994)

Source: *1994 nian quanguo xiangzhen qiye jiben qingkuang ji jingji yunxing fenxi* [An analysis of the basic situation and operations township and village enterprises] (Ministry of Agriculture, TVE Planning Bureau, 1994).

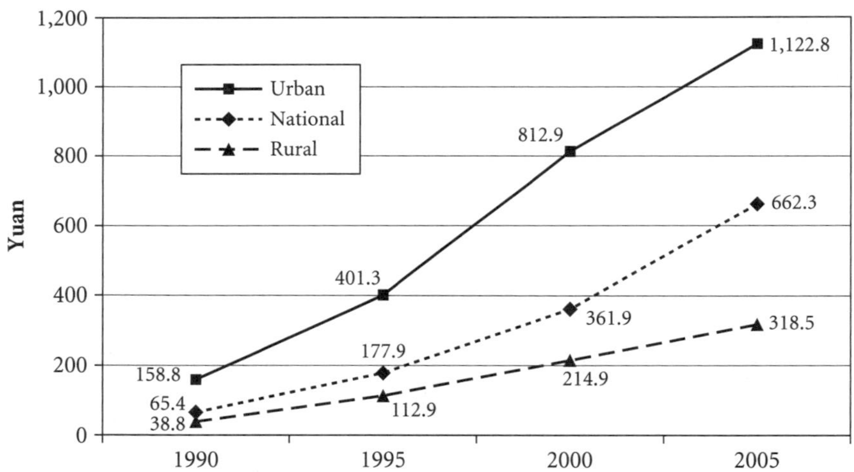

FIGURE 1.5 Health expenditures per capita for urban vs. rural residents (1990–2005)

spends ten times more than the lowest-spending one on health and basic nine-year education (primary and junior middle school).[9]

The World Bank has labeled China the most fiscally decentralized country in the world (figure 1.6). Local governments in China are responsible for financing

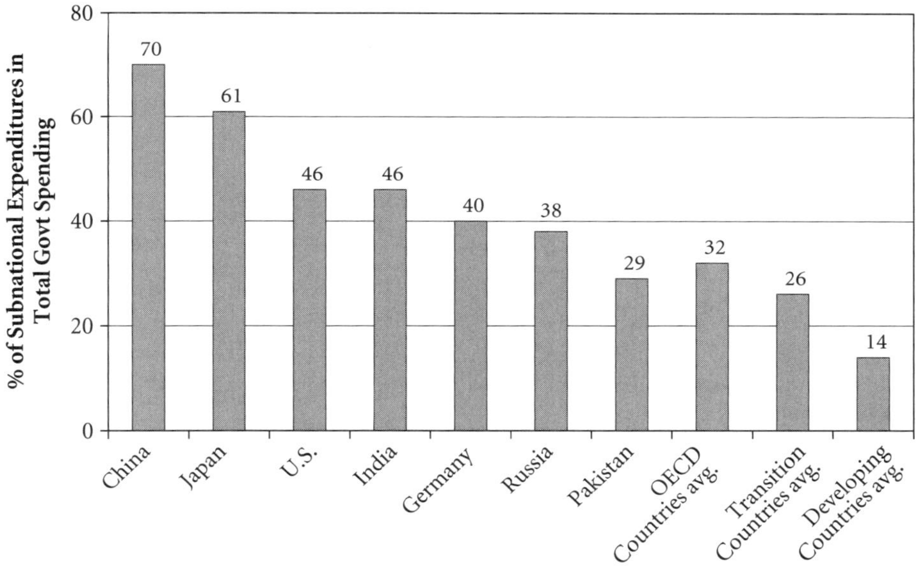

FIGURE 1.6 China's fiscal decentralization in comparative perspective

Source: C. Wong, "Can China Change Development Paradigm for the 21st Century? Fiscal Policy Options for Hu Jintao and Wen Jiabao after Two Decades of Muddling Through," a paper for the Stiftung Wissenschaft und Politik, Berlin, Germany, January 2005.

70 percent of government expenditures, significantly more than is common in other countries. These include the bulk of government social services. As a result of this highly decentralized fiscal structure, the disparate fiscal capacity of subnational governments largely accounts for the huge variations in social spending and, by extension, uneven regional development.

This book addresses important scholarly debates that go beyond rural credit and the fiscal system in China. Two of the major issues confronting China are social unrest and its growth model. I address each in turn.

Social unrest, which has been rising exponentially, poses a challenge to the authoritarian government. The number of "mass incidents" or "incidents of public disorder" has climbed from 30,000 annually, in the early 2000s, to 90,000 in 2006 and 180,000 in 2010.[10] This volume addresses several issues helpful in understanding the causes of social unrest in China. During the 1990s, peasant tax burdens were among the most common causes of rural unrest. After the elimination of rural taxes in the early 2000s, disputes and grievances over land requisitions by local governments became increasingly important in triggering social unrest. Other important causes of social unrest include cadre corruption and environmental-related disputes between residents and local factories or authorities, most if not all of which are related to local government schemes to augment income. The cadre evaluation system and fiscal imperatives, analyzed in chapter 4, shed light on the efforts of local officials to maximize revenue collection and to promote industrialization and urbanization, which contribute to their coffers. Imposition and collection of arbitrary taxes and fees supplement government revenue, and land requisitions are in turn motivated by the need for land for industrial-zone development or infrastructure building.[11] In fact, as the Conclusion will point out, land-collateralized bank loans, which have led to escalating local-government debt levels, are prerequisites of the country's much-touted grand infrastructure projects.

The political economy of the banking sector illuminate why China's effort to shift its economy from investment and export-led to consumption-driven growth, essential in sustaining its long-term development, has been largely unsuccessful. In the last three decades, China's economic growth has relied disproportionately on government-directed investment and expanding trade surpluses. Household consumption accounts for only about 35 percent of GDP, a figure lower than in most other countries. Investments in state-preferred enterprises and projects have been funded by loans with repressed interest rates. The implication of this repression is that while low lending rates help provide cheap capital to state-preferred businesses, savers or households receive lower returns on their capital, thereby depressing their consumption level. This is in effect a transfer of income from the household to the corporate sector.

Just like the four main state-owned banks in the late 1990s were, RCCs have been recapitalized in a government bailout.[12] The central bank has been keeping interest rates low in order to reduce the costs of borrowing. Hence, both government policies—keeping interest rates low to subsidize the cost of capital and bailing out insolvent banking institutions—represent a transfer of income from households to state-preferred businesses and have a dampening effect on household consumption.

Arguments in Brief

This book addresses two critical questions at the nexus of China's politics, finance, and development. First, *why have RCC loans been allocated consistently to local government enterprises and projects?* Second, *what is the local variation in industrialization outcome from savings mobilizations?* (See table 1.1.)

I seek to explain the pattern of RCC loan allocations through the design of political and economic institutions. Like all subnational agencies in China, RCCs are simultaneously accountable to their functional superiors and to local party leadership. Between 1979 and 1996, the period during which TVEs grew most rapidly, RCCs reported to the state-owned Agricultural Bank of China (ABC) on

TABLE 1.1 Dependent and independent variables

DEPENDENT VARIABLES	INDEPENDENT VARIABLES
I. Bias in lending pattern toward local government–related firms and projects across all locales	Institutional design • Dual accountability system • Fiscal imperatives • Cadre evaluation system
II. Local variation in industrialization outcome (prosper or perish) from savings mobilization	Local government/privately led industrialization

professional matters, but personnel decisions were made by local party committees. As a result, local party committees were able to exert great influence over credit officers.

Between 1996 and 2003, RCCs were loosely managed by China's central bank, the People's Bank of China (PBoC). It wrested decisions on RCCs' senior personnel appointments away from local party committees to newly established county-level unions largely under the influence of the PBoC. The PBoC, however, was caught between the often conflicting policy objectives of supporting the agricultural sector and making the RCCs commercially sustainable. Furthermore, the PBoC's institutional design itself weakened its capacity to supervise the financial activity of local RCCs, which remained largely grassroots institutions. As a result of both factors, the RCCs remained predisposed to pervasive local government influence even after they were placed under the professional control of the PBoC.[13]

Existing work on the political economy of credit in China is largely silent on the significant role of local governments in China's credit system. In *China's Unfinished Economic Revolution*, Nicholas Lardy argues that owing to a weak fiscal system, the central government was unable to finance many of its social obligations, such as pension and unemployment benefits.[14] Instead the central government forced state-owned banks to provide soft loans to prop up ailing state-owned enterprises (SOEs), which in turn provided pensions and other social benefits to workers. As important as Lardy's arguments are, they fail to capture the political-economic dynamics of China's rural credit system. As I shall show, local governments face a systemic imbalance between revenues and expenditures. To meet the central government's demands to augment revenue, local officials siphon resources from formal credit institutions to finance local industrial development for the purpose of generating income.

China's fiscal and banking systems serve inherently different economic and social objectives. The fiscal system plays a redistributive role: it collects taxes from the "haves" and redistributes the revenue in the form of social services to the "have-nots," at least in theory. In contrast, the banking system has an intermediary purpose: banking institutions pool capital from savers and allocate it to borrowers, with the price of loans reflecting the risk profiles of the borrowers. The intermediary role of banking institutions improves the efficiency of capital allocations by channeling funds from areas with excess supply to areas with excess demand. Accordingly, the use of savings to serve a fiscal role carries a cost: huge inefficiencies in capital allocations. Moreover, when capital is allocated according to political considerations rather than hard-nosed economic assessments, loans often end up in the hands of politically well-connected borrowers who have little incentive to repay them.[15]

Local interference in credit allocations becomes an unintended consequence of the systemic demands embedded in Chinese political institutions. The behavior of those in local government is largely motivated by the Communist Party cadre evaluation system and by the fiscal system. Both provide strong incentives to local officials to pursue industrialization at all costs for the purpose of maximizing revenue. The RCCs, due to their lack of institutional hierarchy and weak corporate structure, become easy targets for local officials ravenous for financial resources.

Next, I address the implications of savings mobilizations for rural industrialization in China. In *Back-Alley Banking*, a comprehensive study of informal finance across various localities, Kellee Tsai contends that informal finance is diverse in its institutional forms. She explains this as an outcome of differing orientations of local governments toward the private sector.[16] The present study, however, will demonstrate that diverse economic outcomes occur even when local incentive structures and credit institution designs are similar.[17] Such differences occur, as we will see, when local economic and geographical circumstances differ. China's strikingly uneven levels of development prima facie suggest that savings have been deployed in different locales for different ends. The case studies in this book, drawn both from the developed provinces of Zhejiang and Shandong and from the impoverished provinces of Sichuan and Hebei, will confirm this situation. These case studies reveal that rural savings have contributed to successful rural industrial development in some but not all locales.

One critical difference between the cases is whether local authorities actively promote industrial activities by channeling cheap credit to their preferred enterprises (local government–led industrialization) or whether bank credit is channeled by market forces to best-deserving (private) enterprises (privately led industrialization). As chapter 5 will illustrate, the latter occurs *not* because local government officials in those specific localities do not care about industrialization. Rather, all officials face the same set of political and economic incentives that motivates them to develop an industrial sector and to maximize revenue collection. The distinction is that in those locales where the tradition of local-government entrepreneurship is palpably and relatively nonexistent—such as the famous case of Wenzhou in Zhejiang province—local governments let the private sector take the lead. After all, all enterprises—public and private alike—contribute taxes to local coffers. The other critical distinction is proximity to urban markets and transportation linkages, which is determined by the township's geographical location.

Two of my eight township case studies have achieved successful development. In one of these success stories, in Taizhou (in southeastern Zhejiang province), enterprise development was not carried out by the local government at all. Rather, it was private enterprises, established from personal savings and financing from profit-oriented credit institutions, that took the lead. These private entrepreneurs were forced to use financial resources efficiently or risk going out of business and losing their life's savings. Taizhou's tax revenues from these private enterprises allowed it to provide social services (figure 1.7).

The other success story is a township in Zouping (in Shandong province).[18] Enterprise development in this township was local government–led. This case was also exceptional in a telling way. Proximity to urban centers and transportation linkages gave businesses in the Zouping township access to markets and a shortened time-to-market that are notably missing in most parts of rural China. Such geographical factors enabled local collective enterprises in the township to survive the collapse of China's collective sector in the mid- to late 1990s, even though the township utilized capital from local credit institutions to develop the collective sector. The township enterprises were subsequently bought out by individuals, who continued to expand the businesses. These industrial enterprises contribute taxes to the local government that enable it to finance the provision of public goods and services to residents (figure 1.7).

The case of Taizhou exemplifies successful rural development spearheaded by the private sector—the so-called Wenzhou model—whereas that of Zouping resembles local government-led industrialization, nicknamed the Sunan model.

Granted, not all localities succeeded in their efforts at industrialization. The cases in Sichuan and Hebei unveil a lesser known—but far more widespread—phenomenon of failed local government–led attempts at industrialization. Faced with revenue-maximizing pressures from fiscal decentralization and from the cadre evaluation system, local governments borrowed heavily from RCCs to finance collective enterprises throughout the 1980s and early 1990s.

Many collective enterprises were sustainable only for as long as the government had allowed them to continue operating. The fact that many of them were located in remote and mountainous regions meant that these firms had

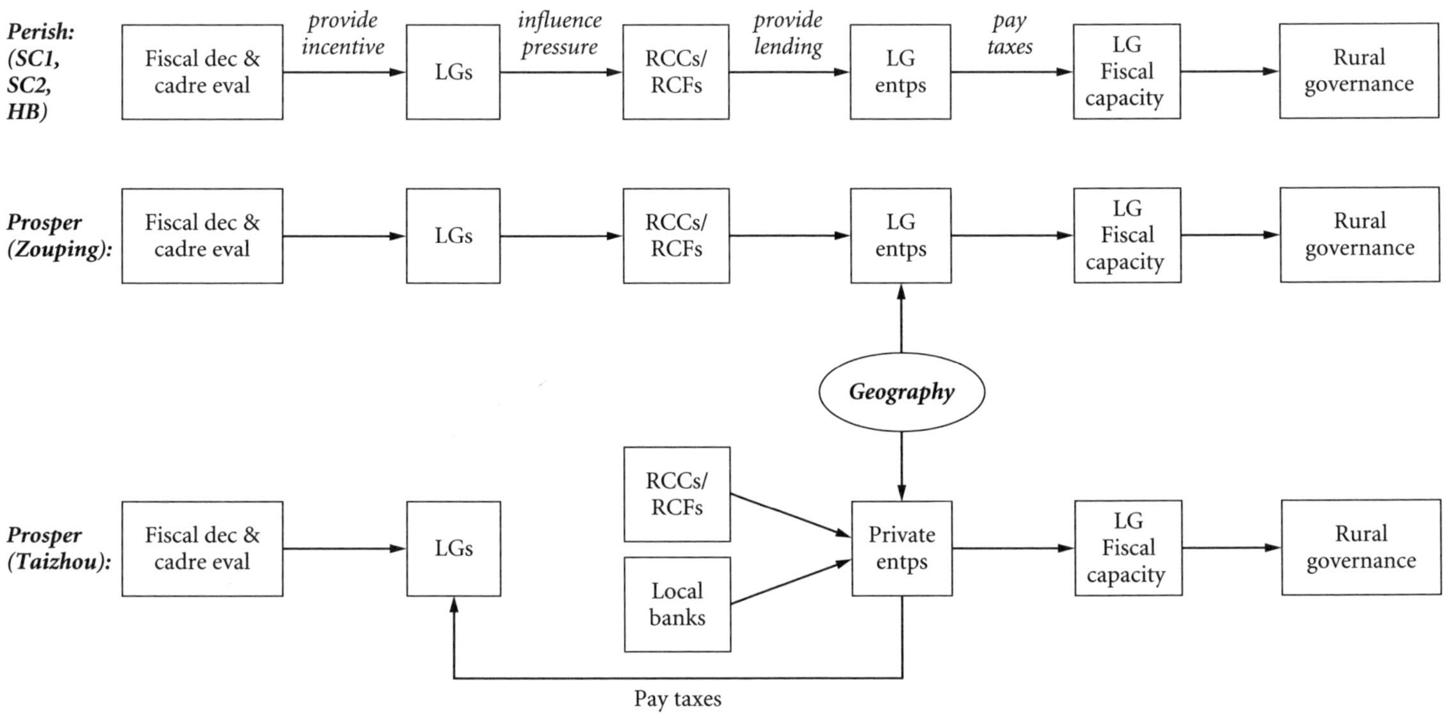

FIGURE 1.7 Causal chains of development

LG = local government; Fiscal dec = fiscal decentralization; Cadre eval = cadre evaluation; entps = enterprises.

enormous difficulties gaining access to technical know-how or large consumer markets. There was little business rationale for these local government–owned enterprises that relied on cheap credit and government subsidies to exist, and indeed many of them crumbled once competition stiffened. Beginning in the second half of the 1990s, a significant number of the collective enterprises experienced losses, and the problem worsened to such an extent that the enterprises became financial liabilities, instead of cash cows, to local governments. The central government began pushing for TVE privatization by the mid-1990s.

Lack of industrial development from that point onward triggered a series of local fiscal crises and, consequently, challenges for rural governance. In China's highly decentralized environment, where local authorities finance public goods and services, local governments that were mired in debt were incapable of delivering even basic social services, such as basic education and health care. Farmers in these locales bore substantial financial burdens as local officials arbitrarily imposed heavy fees and fines to supplement local government's revenues. Though the abolition of rural fees and taxes in the early first decade of the twenty-first century helped reduce peasant burdens, it exacerbated the dire straits of local government finances. In such locales, basic government services are largely paralyzed, and local governments survive thanks only to fiscal transfers from higher levels. The chain of causation is depicted in figure 1.7.

My eight township case studies and their outcomes lead me to discover three identifiable paths of rural industrialization:

I. **Prosper:** Locales that have embraced privately led industrialization and have successfully industrialized (Zen)
II. **Prosper:** Locales that have embraced local government-led industrialization and have successfully industrialized (Han)
III. **Perish:** Locales that have embraced local government-led industrialization and have failed to industrialize (Xiao, Zhang, Zhou, Cheng, Fan, Sun)

This has profound implications for our understanding of the role of local government in China. Traditionally, local governments in China have been described as "corporatist,"[19] "entrepreneurial,"[20] and "developmental,"[21] denoting an interventionist and instrumental role in rural industrialization and development. The best-known term is Jean Oi's "local state corporatism," used to depict local government's business-like behavior in running enterprises and managing local economies. Both Andrew Walder and Yingyi Qian similarly see local intervention in shaping the development of TVEs and in rural industrialization as positive.[22] This belief, which influenced a generation of China scholars,[23] may have been valid at the height of the TVE sector's growth in the early 1990s, but it now requires fundamental reevaluation. Not only were successful TVEs concentrated in certain geographical regions, these enterprises were later privatized. The varieties of rural industrialization paths delineated in this book imply that the "corporatist" or "developmental" local state is a time/region-specific phenomenon.

I also address an age-old debate in Chinese politics regarding the strength of the central government versus local authorities. On the one hand, Shaoguang Wang and Angang Hu argue that the center has lost much of its authority through fiscal decentralization. According to this argument, fiscal decentralization has enriched and empowered some coastal provinces to such an extent that they have become too dominant for the center to rein in.[24] On the other hand, in his studies of inflation and investment control in China, Yasheng Huang contends that despite economic decentralization, political power still rests firmly with Beijing. Through the Communist Party's appointment system, central leadership is able to exercise control over provincial and regional leaders, who otherwise have no incentive to keep inflation under control.[25] More recently, Pierre Landry argues that China is still a centralized authoritarian state despite having a highly decentralized fiscal system, which defies the high correlation between democracy and fiscal decentralization around the world.[26]

I contend that the center's power is often overestimated. The central government may be able to bring about desired outcomes, such as a certain rate of economic growth, by using the Communist Party's cadre evaluation system to set strict goals for local officials to attain. Nevertheless, it has no control over *how* the outcome is attained. The evaluation system effectuates top-down control but does not allow for feedback from the masses. In the past, local governments imposed arbitrary taxes and fees on farmers in order to meet centrally prescribed tax revenue targets, which led to massive "peasant burdens." As I will illustrate, local officials mobilize resources from banking institutions to fund tax-generating industrial activities that are often unjustifiable on economic grounds. Consequently, money that might otherwise be loaned to rural households is reallocated and local government racks up huge debts, paid for ultimately by the taxpayers.

What are the ramifications of channeling a huge proportion of savings to finance a largely unsuccessful government-enterprise sector? In the early first decade of the twenty-first century, half of the forty-thousand RCCs nationwide were technically insolvent. At the same time, all evidence pointed to unsustainable levels of debt by county, township, and village authorities. A large proportion of this debt was owed to the credit institutions. In this respect, my study also exposes the perils of fiscal decentralization when subnational governments face soft budget constraints. Montinola, Qian, and Weingast assert that "federalism, Chinese style" has contributed to China's growth by limiting the center's predatory power to encroach on local governments' economic autonomy, which provides political protection for economic reforms.[27] They therefore perceive "market-preserving federalism" as a substitute for the typical political institutions constraining predatory states that are currently politically infeasible in China, such as popular elections and a separation of powers.[28]

But what if the key assumption of Montinola, Qian, and Weingast that "all governments face hard budget constraints" is relaxed? As János Kornai has noted of the socialist Hungarian economy in the 1970s, chronic loss-making state-owned enterprises were always bailed out by the central government. This created an *expectation* of bailouts, which affected state-owned enterprises' behavior. This was the phenomenon Kornai labeled "soft budget constraint."[29] Local governments can face similar soft budget constraints when they are not allowed to fail despite massive indebtedness.

Existing studies on the sources of local soft budget constraints in China focus on the fiscal system.[30] But the fiscal system has fewer negative implications than does China's banking system. When local governments collect hefty and arbitrary taxes and fees from citizens and enterprises to supplement their income, resources are transferred from the taxpayers to local authorities. When local officials fail to use this tax revenue to provide goods and services to the citizenry, this is (merely) a problem of inefficient use of resources. Taxpayers *do not* expect the government to pay back their taxes. But when local governments borrow from credit institutions to finance their budgets, these loans will have to be repaid. Savers—unlike taxpayers—expect their savings to be honored, sooner or later. Failure to honor the hard-earned savings of hundreds of millions of rural households would pose significant risks to social stability. When unrepaid loans to local governments constitute a large proportion of the assets in the banking system, the central government is forced to step in. Therefore, in a decentralized environment where subnational governments lack fiscal discipline or face soft budget constraints, the center is often forced to absorb their debt and bail them out. The center cannot credibly refuse to intervene when a financial collapse would have widespread negative economic and political ramifications.[31]

From the central government's perspective, in other words, the RCCs are "too big to fail." Because they collectively hold more than 80 percent of total rural savings, their widespread collapse would be immensely destabilizing. Indeed, this was already illustrated on a smaller scale in the aforementioned rural riots in Jishou. China's central government has evidently recognized this potential danger. Between 2004 and 2006 the central bank injected about 300 billion yuan to bail out insolvent RCCs, also rescuing local governments, RCCs' largest debtors, as a consequence.[32] In this respect, my study also warns of the negative implications of fiscal decentralization, particularly in the absence of institutional checks and balances on subnational government finance. Fiscal federalism, Chinese style, does not induce economic growth, nor is it a substitute for the typical political institutions constraining predatory states.

Research Design and Methodology

Case Selection: A Few Blind Men and the Elephant

China is characterized by widely differing levels of development. Scholarship on the role of local government in development in China has reached conflicting conclusions, largely depending on the location of field studies and the subject under investigation. Tony Saich describes these efforts as "a few blind men and the elephant"—what we "see" is often a direct result of where we stand.[33] Of course, the methodological concern that case selection will bias analyses is not exclusive to studies of a vast country like China, but is endemic to social science analyses, especially small-*N* qualitative research.[34]

The most common cause of selection bias is researchers' selection of cases based on the dependent variable. Geddes' criticism of the much-publicized World Bank study *The East Asian Miracle*[35] is particularly illuminating in this respect. As she notes, the sample of East Asian countries represented in the study includes only those with high growth rates, countries with dismal economic performance were simply excluded.[36] As a result, Geddes correctly observes, it is questionable whether there was indeed a miracle in the region, as the World Bank argued.

While my first dependent variable is the bias in lending across all locales, the second dependent variable focuses on local variation in industrialization outcome—that is, whether the rural locales have financially prospered or "perished." A key independent variable is the nature of the industrialization effort—that is, whether it was led by local government or the private sector. Although fiscal decentralization provided the impetus for local authorities to undertake industrialization, not all took a leadership role in this arena. In regions where there was no tradition of local-government enterprise, local authorities took a back seat, putting the private sector in the driver's seat. I have selected cases that maximize variations in the independent variable. Had I considered only either the cases in which local government–led industrialization prospered or the cases in which it failed, I would have undermined the validity of my analysis: I would be likely to conclude either that an activist local state is a panacea for all poverty-stricken areas or that industrialization is an unwise development strategy.

I used several criteria in selecting the cases, which matters more for the second dependent variable, since the first deals with a nationwide pattern. My first consideration was to ensure that I included cases of both local government– and privately-led industrialization. (I had visited some counties in southern Jiangsu province, the cradle of the local government–led Sunan model; however, the data I collected were insufficient to make it a studied case. Fortunately, the local government–led model was found not only in Jiangsu but also in Shandong and other provinces.) The second criterion was to include cases from both coastal and inland or western provinces, cognizant of the fact that the former have usually more successfully industrialized than the latter. The third was to make sure that the townships selected were not either all next to the county seats or all located in remote areas. (In fact, I asked my Chinese hosts to pick the townships at random.) Next, I made sure that the townships were not all either rich or poor in natural resources, in view of the fact that natural resources may either provide localities an advantage or may be a burden for governance in light of the "resource curse" debate.[37]

The case studies in chapters 5 and 6 trace the development trajectory of eight townships located in four provinces: Zhejiang and Shandong provinces on the east coast, Hebei province in the central region, and Sichuan province in the west. Table 1.2 details the diverse socioeconomic indicators of the five counties where these townships are located. The level of industrialization differs markedly among the counties. Industry's share of total output ranges from 76 percent in Shandong's Zouping to 54 percent in Zhejiang's Wenling (in Taizhou prefecture) and to 25 percent in Sichuan's SC2 county.[38] They also differ in patterns of sectoral employment: whereas Zouping and Wenling are industry-oriented, the counties in Hebei and Sichuan are predominantly agricultural. The geographical locations of the cases are shown in figure 1.8. In addition, control variables that could potentially account for the variation in outcome are introduced to help isolate the effects of industrialization. These variables are provincial location, proximity to urban center, and natural resource endowment.[39] As the case studies will illustrate, these control variables allow me to differentiate a few cases that fall into the same outcome category.

Methodology

I conducted more than 120 in-depth semi-structured interviews with officers and managers of credit institutions and local officials. I also carried out a survey of about 280 rural household respondents. The household survey was extremely useful to systematically quantify rural households' perceptions of how RCCs work and how they are managed, the range of savings and loan options available to these households, and the ways in which these households have used financial resources. Nonetheless, there are many nuances in the political economy of the credit sector in China that a quantitative survey is unable to capture. In-depth interviews played a very useful role here. Furthermore, I utilized a range of secondary sources, including county annals (*xianzhi*) and various statistical yearbooks, to supplement the first-hand information obtained. The appendix to this chapter

TABLE 1.2 County-level socioeconomic indicators for the studied cases (2006)

	WENLING (ZHEJIANG)	ZOUPING (SHANDONG)	HB (HEBEI)	SC1 (SICHUAN)	SC2 (SICHUAN)
Basic indicators					
Administrative land area (sq. mi.)	836	1,250	2,802	2,469	1,770
Total population	1,160,000	720,000	330,000	150,000	1,080,000
Pop. density (per sq. mi.)	1,388	576	118	61	610
No. of townships	11	16	17	15	58
Value added of output					
2006 total (in million yuan)	35,131.1	27,803.0	2,682.1	1,549.4	3,703.3
Agriculture share of total	8%	6%	32%	23%	43%
Industry share	54%	76%	33%	49%	25%
Services share	38%	18%	35%	27%	32%
Employment by sector					
Agriculture	26%	39%	74%	51%	60%
Industry	35%	40%	14%	22%	14%
Services	40%	21%	12%	28%	26%
Other economic indicators (in million yuan)					
Total urban & rural household savings	21,627.6	5,841.4	2,072.9	906.8	3,605.2
Local govt budgetary revenue	1,580.1	1,401.9	54.1	44.4	58.0
Local govt budgetary expenditures	1,713.5	1,703.1	319.6	214.7	843.6
Expenditures/revenue ratio	1.1	1.2	5.9	4.8	14.6

Source: *China County Statistical Yearbook 2007*.

provides a fuller description of the methodology employed in this inquiry and the appendix to this book gives the full list of interviewees and their affiliations.

The rest of the book will take you from the mountainous southwest, to the cotton fields of the northeast, down to the boisterous coastal areas. The only constant among these diverse regions and locales is the desire of people to improve their livelihood—government officials with the ambitions of climbing the career ladder and ordinary people yearning for better lives. The strategies they employ and their success vary greatly.

I conducted my field research largely before the rural subsidy program was being rolled out by the central government in the mid- to late 2000s. While this program has evidently benefited some rural populations,[40] studies suggest that it has not been effective in assisting the poor and the disadvantaged. Subsidy

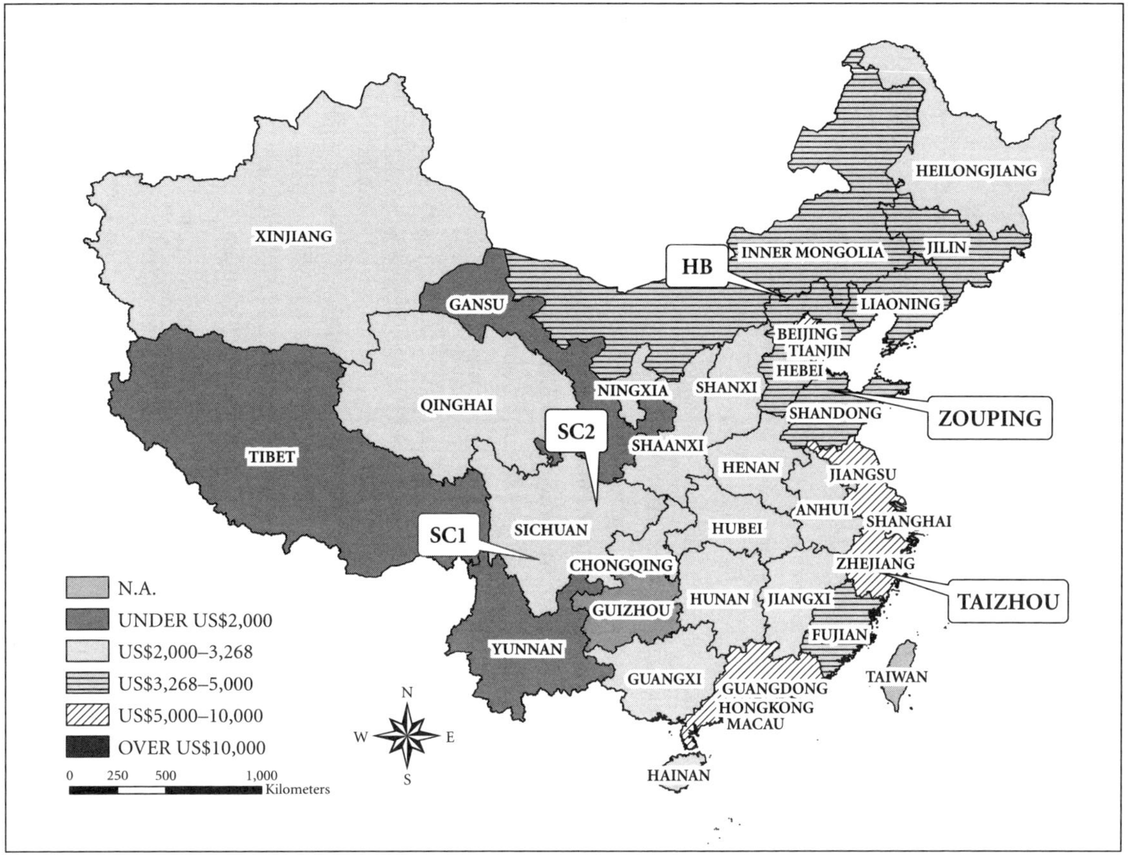

FIGURE 1.8 Locations of the case studies by provincial GDP per capita

implementation usually requires matching funds from provincial and local governments. Hence its success often depends on the fiscal capacities of local governments, reinforcing a trend in which rich locales get more public service provision and poor locales get less.[41] This exacerbates regional disparities in spending on public services.

While this book was being readied for publication, China, like the rest of the world, was hit by an unexpected economic downturn. Enterprises that were profitable at the time of my field studies were undergoing an extraordinarily trying time. Some were forced to close shop, while others were bracing for a sudden downswing in export sales. The decline in profitability was also affecting the fiscal health of local governments, which rely on business taxes and revenue from business-related activities.

Though it may be too early to draw firm conclusions, there are already several contending explanations for the downturn of the manufacturing sector in China. Macroeconomic factors such as the appreciation of the Chinese yuan since the mid-2000s, and rising labor costs have eroded manufacturers' profit margins. The global economic downturn in 2008 triggered by the subprime loan crisis in the United States further dented external demand for Chinese-made goods.

These factors have hit export-oriented firms harder than those primarily oriented toward the domestic market. China's traditional export powerhouse, the Yangtze River Delta (encompassing the municipality of Shanghai, northeastern Zhejiang, and southern Jiangsu), has borne the brunt of falling external demand.[42] This, in turn, has hurt the rest of the region's manufacturing economy, a large proportion of which comprised small and medium-sized suppliers of parts and raw materials to the bigger export-oriented manufacturers. My fieldwork sites in Zhejiang have not been spared by the global financial tsunami.[43] These external factors may also be mere triggers for a host of latent problems that have been plaguing China's manufacturing companies.[44]

However the recent recession may alter the manufacturing landscape in China, it has not fundamentally changed the ways China's credit institutions conduct business. Some enterprises have not survived the recent crisis. The survivors will offer valuable lessons for scholarly works in the future. Meanwhile, this book deals with the political economy of development in China up until the recent global financial crisis. The analyses in this volume remain valid irrespective of the current economic upheaval.

A Road Map: Structure of the Book

We start with a primer on the rural banking sector in China. Chapter 2 shows that the savings of rural households have been channeled to finance urban development, reflecting an inherent urban bias in China's development strategy. Part II (chapters 3 and 4) analyzes bias in RCC lending patterns across all locales (dependent variable I) from the perspective of institutional design. Chapter 3 draws on the literature on dual accountability systems—a fundamental feature of Chinese political institutions—to explain the RCC organizational design. I argue that RCCs were accountable to two principals: (a) local party leaders and the state-owned Agricultural Bank of China (1978–96) and (b) local party leaders and central bank officials (1996–2003). However, the influence of local authorities, who are single-mindedly committed to promoting economic growth and to maximizing revenue, is more pervasive. By contrast, the central bank vacillates between two often conflicting goals: making RCCs commercially sustainable and wanting them to support the agricultural sector. Chapter 4 argues that design of political and economic institutions—the Communist Party cadre evaluation system and China's fiscal system—have created strong incentives for local governments to promote industrial development and to generate income. Local government interference in credit allocations is thereby revealed to be a consequence of the systemic demands created by the configuration of institutional incentives.

We then assay the varieties of rural industrialization in China (dependent variable II), even where they have been similarly financed through rural savings. Chapter 5 examines the cases of two townships that successfully industrialized in spite of their diverse pathways. One followed a local government–led model, and its enterprises depended heavily on financing from formal banking institutions. The other, which relied primarily on private savings and loans from nongovernment banking institutions, was a privately led industrialization. The predominance of local government or private enterprise in the pre-reform era determined the paths these townships took. Proximity to urban centers and transportation linkages allowed both places access to outside markets and technical know-how. Chapter 6 analyzes six cases of failed local government–led industrialization, a far more widespread phenomenon than the successful cases. Despite massive investment of savings in local government–led enterprises, the collective TVE sector largely disappeared after the mid-1990s as competition stiffened. Industrial enterprises in these remote locales had few reasons to exist other than government coddling. The downfall of the collective industrial sector left local authorities deprived of revenue and incapable of financing public goods and services.

The Conclusion updates the RCC reform by analyzing the cost of its bailout by the central government. I argue that the bailout took place because the RCCs were "too big to fail," and that created a "moral hazard." I situate my findings in broader theoretical contexts before drawing normative implications for China's policies and its growth model.

Appendix

Case Study Indicators, Household Survey, and Sources

Indicators Used in Case Studies to Measure Success of Industrialization Strategy

There is no single indicator that can unequivocally represent whether a locale has prospered or "perished." Although income or gross domestic product (GDP) per capita is commonly employed to measure standard of living, reliance on a single indicator distorts the reality because many facets of rural livelihood are not captured by a quantitative income indicator.[45] Therefore, I have employed a range of indicators, broadly divided into two categories:

Local Government–Related

- **Local revenue per capita:** measures the financial capacity of local governments to provide public goods and services on a per capita basis
- **Percentage of intergovernmental transfers in total revenue:** measures the reliance of local revenue on transfers from higher-level authorities (The higher the percentage, the less independent local fiscal capacity is.)
- **Debt-to-revenue ratio:** measures the indebtedness of local governments, particularly the extent to which they can repay their debts using taxes generated locally
- **Debt per capita:** measures the degree of local government debt on a per capita basis

Farmer-Related

- Income per capita
- Taxes and fees paid per person—an indicator of the peasant (financial) burdens
- Affordability of nine-year basic education
- Incidence of wage arrears
- Incidence of land-related conflicts

The government-related indicators measure the financial capacity of local authorities to provide essential public services, such as basic education and health care. This is particularly significant in the context of China because, due to its decentralized structure, the bulk of the financing of public goods and services has fallen on the shoulders of grassroots governments. Local authorities that are rich can provide highly subsidized services to their citizenry, whereas those deprived of revenue are simply unable to do so.

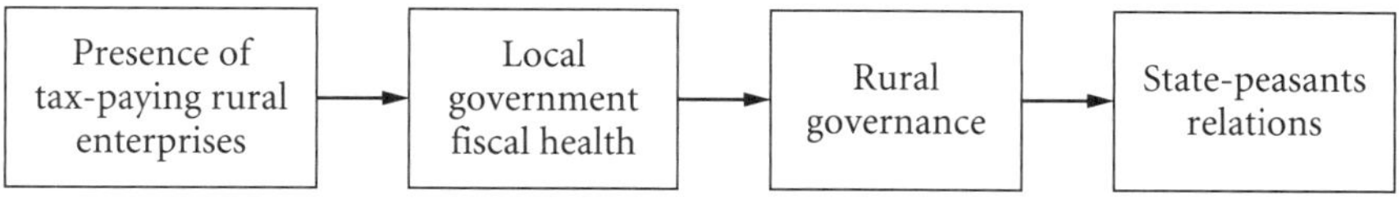

FIGURE 1A.1 Chain of causation from rural industrialization to state–peasant relations

Meanwhile, the farmer-side indicators provide clues about the degree of rural contentment or discontent. High financial burdens of peasants, wage arrears, and lack of affordability of basic education are often associated with a high degree of rural discontent. Similarly, high incidences of land-related conflicts between local authorities and farmers, such as the confiscation of farmland, are likely to lead to rural unrest.

How do these indicators relate to rural industrialization? As the case studies will illustrate, the fiscal health of local authorities is highly dependent on the existence of profitable enterprises or successful industrialization. The existence of taxpaying enterprises directly impacts the capacity of local governments to provide public goods and services to the citizenry. Moreover, given the many "unfunded mandates,"[46] local authorities are hard-pressed for revenue. Consequently, they resort to extracting arbitrary taxes and fees from farmers and taking farmers' lands to resell is at significantly higher prices.

By the same token, where local authorities are deprived of revenue, the nine-year compulsory education is most likely an investment financed by the farmer. In a nutshell, the availability of profitable industrial enterprises in a locale influences the local government's capacity to provide public goods and services, which in turn affects the dynamics of state-peasant relations. The chain of causation is depicted in figure 1A.1.

Household Survey

The respondents of the semi-structured interviews consist of two major groups: (a) officers and managers of the RCCs and state-owned banks from Jiangsu, Zhejiang, Shandong, Hebei, Sichuan, Shanghai, and Beijing; and (b) local officials from these provinces and municipalities. They come from various administrative levels: provincial capitals, prefectures, counties, and townships and villages. In total, I conducted studies in thirteen townships, five county-level cities, three district-level cities, one prefecture-level city, three provincial capitals, and two municipalities (Beijing and Shanghai). I had lengthy discussions with bankers from the Rural Commercial Banks in Jiangsu and the Shanghai City Commercial Bank

TABLE 1A.1 Basic information and wealth levels of household survey respondents

COUNTY	RCC MODEL	NUMBER	%	MEAN OF TOTAL WEALTH* (YUAN)	MEDIAN OF TOTAL WEALTH* (YUAN)	SD
Zouping	RCB	11	4	142,838	128,080	48,286
		9	3.2	110,428	97,200	33,746
SC1	RCC	43	15.5	76,583	61,840	50,922
		98	35.4	60,369	59,330	18,736
HB		51	18.4	60,173	60,930	18,748
SC2	RCC	8	2.9	49,079	34,835	25,625
		57	20.6	35,781	25,370	27,462
Total		277	100	62,365	58,700	37,244

*Total wealth level is the sum of household's annual cash income and value of their noncash assets.

to understand how these banks conduct businesses. Nonetheless, data on local fiscal health and peasants' livelihood are limited from these places; hence only cases for which detailed data are available are presented here, though investigations in other sites have no doubt enhanced my general understanding of the issues. See the back of the book for the full list of interviewees and their affiliations.

The household survey respondents were drawn from seven townships in four counties (Zouping, HB, SC1, SC2) across three provinces (Shandong, Sichuan, and Hebei). The respondents have varying levels of wealth, ranging from 35,000 yuan in SC2 to 140,000 yuan in Zouping (see table 1A.1). At the time of the survey, these locales also differed in terms of RCC shareholding models—Shandong was in the midst of establishing rural cooperative banks, while Sichuan and Hebei still had pre-reform rural credit cooperatives.

These primary sources aside, I have utilized a range of secondary sources, including county annals and various statistical yearbooks. The county annals (*xianzhi*) are particularly useful in providing a historical overview of the counties, supplementing first-hand information obtained from the interviews and the household survey. Among the various statistical yearbooks I have consulted, two of them are critical to the data presented in this study: the Township and Village Enterprise Yearbook (*xiangzhen qiye nianjian*) published by the Ministry of Agriculture contains the best available time-series data on rural enterprises, and China's Almanac of Banking and Finance (*zhongguo jinrong nianjian*) is the best available source for data on the RCCs.

2

THE RURAL FINANCIAL SYSTEM AND RURAL DEVELOPMENT IN CHINA

Drawing on secondary and some primary data, this chapter situates rural credit cooperatives (RCCs) in the context of China's rural financial landscape in order to highlight their significance to the rural economy and households. China's rural financial system serves roughly 800 million people, constituting 70 percent of the population. These people live in large swaths of hinterland in the central and western provinces and in rural and peri-urban locales in the eastern coastal provinces. Despite a diverse range of credit demands, the official rural financial sector has been largely monopolized by RCCs and, until the late 1990s, the state-owned Agricultural Bank of China (ABC). Rural savings were behind the spectacular rural industrialization of the 1980s and early 1990s. However, this feat was achieved primarily through funding collective township and village enterprises (TVEs) rather than private enterprises (as a recent study has claimed).[1] Hence, understanding how RCCs work is essential to understanding industrialization in China's countryside.

The Rural Financial Sector

Rural credit cooperatives (RCCs) are the backbone of official finance in rural China. They collectively account for over 80 percent of rural deposits and loans (figure 2.1). With respect to agricultural loans, the Agricultural Bank of China (ABC), one of the four big state-owned banks, has only one-tenth of the total, compared to over 80 percent for RCCs (figure 2.1).

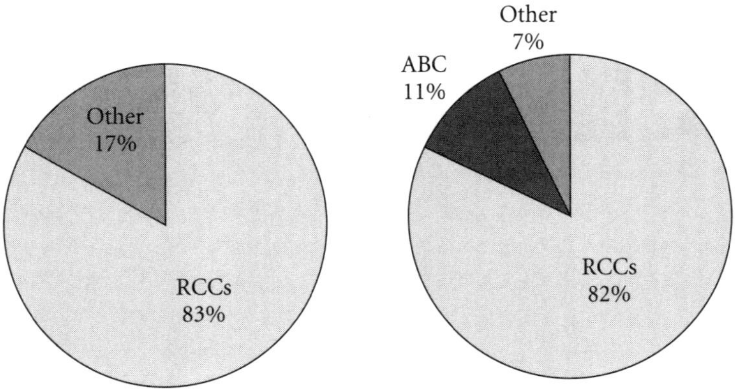

FIGURE 2.1 (left) Share of rural households' deposits by financial institution (2006). Total size: 2.88 trillion yuan. (right) Share of agricultural loans by financial institution (2006). Total Size: 1.32 trillion yuan.
Source: Almanac of China's Banking and Finance (2007).

As table 2.1 indicates, there were about 24,600 credit cooperatives scattered around rural areas as of 2005, covering about 60 percent of townships in the country.[2] RCCs' networks have been shrinking since the late 1990s due to ongoing efforts by the central government to save costs incurred in the RCC system. As part of this effort, the central government abolished village RCCs in the 1990s, reducing the number of RCCs from over forty thousand in the late 1990s (about one RCC in every township) to thirty-three thousand in 2003. Institutional reforms between 2003 and 2005 further reduced the number of RCCs to 24,600 in 2005. Some of the state-owned commercial banks and commercial shareholding banks have branches in the peri-urban areas, but not in remote rural areas, since such presence is costly to maintain. For savings accounts, RCCs' only real competition is the Postal Savings Bank, which has networks throughout both urban and rural areas.

TABLE 2.1 Rural credit cooperatives system by type (2005)

	NO. OF UNITS	NO. OF WORKERS
Township RCCs	24,596	
County unions	2,415	627,141
Provincial unions	25	
Rural commercial banks	12	19,278
Rural cooperative banks	58	29,294
Total	27,106	675,713

Source: *Almanac of China's Banking and Finance* (2006).

TABLE 2.2 Financial institutions by size of loans and deposits (2006)

	LOANS	%	DEPOSITS[1]	%
State-owned commercial banks	17,999	51.8%	17,547	56.0%
Shareholding commercial banks	5,830	16.8%	5,147	16.4%
Rural credit co-ops and rural banks	3,382	9.7%	3,886	12.4%
State-owned policy banks	3,244	9.3%	213	0.7%
City comm. banks and urban credit co-ops	2,247	6.5%	2,254	7.2%
Postal Savings Bank	870	2.5%	1,602	5.1%
Others[2]	1,191	3.4%	667	2.1%
Total	**34,764**	**100.0%**	**31,316**	**100.0%**

Source: Author's own calculation from the *Almanac of China's Banking and Finance* (2006).
All figures in billions yuan, 2006 year-end.
[1]Deposits are from households and firms.
[2]Others consist of overseas banks and finance companies.

To put this in a national perspective, the financial sector is still dominated by the four state-owned commercial banks, which have about 60 percent of total deposits and loans nationwide (table 2.2). The shareholding commercial banks, such as the China Merchant Bank and the Shanghai Pudong Development Bank, collectively have about 16 percent of total loans and deposits. Smaller in scale, RCCs have 10 percent of total loans and 12 percent of total deposits nationwide. Despite its rural reach, the Postal Savings Bank's total loans and deposits nationwide are less than half of those of RCCs (table 2.2).

The Agricultural Bank of China (ABC)

Despite its name, the ABC is relatively detached from agricultural households. The ABC was established by the central government in the 1950s to support agricultural production and to manage the RCCs that pre-dated it.[3] It took over the People's Bank of China (PBoC)'s rural branches in 1979 and assumed a range of policy and commercial functions, including lending to rural industries, financing state procurement of agricultural products, and managing the RCC system.[4] During the 1980s, it served mainly to finance the central government's projects in the agricultural sector. Before the Agricultural Development Bank of China was set up in 1994, the ABC was also responsible for financing all of the state's agricultural purchases.

In the late 1990s the ABC shifted its focus away from rural areas. In an effort to save costs and to improve profitability, the ABC closed down its branches in rural townships and villages in 1999. Currently, branches of the agricultural bank can be found only in county-level cities and some industrialized townships. In 2005 nearly all of the bank's funds came from household savings and deposits by enterprises. The bulk of its lending, however, went to large industrial and commercial enterprises at the county level and above (25.1 percent of total loans) and to local governments' infrastructure projects (16.7 percent). When the ABC withdrew its rural networks in the late 1990s, it also recentralized loan-making decisions to the county and higher administrative levels. This has meant fewer loans to borrowers in rural townships and villages. Collectively, lending to agriculture, rural enterprises, private enterprises, and individuals accounted for less than 15 percent of the ABC's total loans in 2005, as indicated in table 2.3.

The ABC and Poverty Alleviation Loans

Since 1998 the ABC has been responsible for administering China's poverty loan program (*fupin daikuan*). The poverty loan program provides loans at a subsi-

TABLE 2.3 Agricultural Bank of China's deposits and loans (2005)

DEPOSITS	AMOUNT (BILLION YUAN)	%	LOANS	AMOUNT (BILLION YUAN)	%
Deposits by households	2,435.8	61.3%	Loans to industry and commerce	632.6	25.1%
Deposits by enterprises	1,207.8	30.4%	Loans to construction firms	11.3	0.4%
Deposits by organizations	144.9	3.6%	Loans to agriculture	133.9	5.3%
Agricultural deposits	38.4	1.0%	Loans to rural enterprises	172.7	6.9%
Other deposits	143.5	3.6%	Loans to private enterprises and micro-enterprises (getihu)	61.7	2.5%
			Other short-term loans	256.0	10.2%
			Medium-term working capital loans	92.2	3.7%
			Loans to infrastructural projects	419.6	16.7%
			Loans to technical projects	27.8	1.1%
			Other long-term loans	709.3	28.2%
Total deposits	3,970.3	100.0%	**Total loans**	2,517.2	100.0%

Source: ABC Statistical Yearbook 2003–06, p. 6.

dized interest rate to rural households in poor counties. Loans under this program totaled about 10 billion yuan in 2005. However, the program is widely known to have extremely low repayment rates and to be fraught with administrative problems. The official repayment rate stands at 50 percent, but some sources estimate it to be as low as 20–30 percent.[5] As a result, not only has this program achieved little in alleviating rural poverty, it has compromised the ABC's commercial orientation.

The influence of local government is pervasive in the allocation of poverty loans. The loans are officially approved by local poverty alleviation offices (*fupinban*), which are under the direction of local governments, with the ABC merely doling out the money. Borrowers pay the subsidized annual interest rate of 2.88 percent, and the central treasury compensates the bank for the difference between market and subsidized rates. Because the poverty alleviation offices, like all other local administrative units, are led by local party leaders (though they also report vertically to higher levels in the ABC), loans are often directed to local government projects, such as infrastructure development.

Further, owing to the ABC's increased commercial orientation, it is not in favor of lending to poor households—the intended recipients—as such loans are comparatively costly to service. For instance, one Sichuan county in which I conducted research in 2005 is officially designated "poor by national standard" (*guojiaji pinkunxian*). Yet, the local ABC branch has been handing over all the county's poverty loans, totaling 100 million yuan annually, to a power plant in which the county government has a stake. The power plant may stimulate the development of local industrial enterprises and augment local tax revenues. But it brings little direct benefit to poor households, which is the intention of the poverty alleviation program.[6]

The Agricultural Development Bank of China (ADBC)

The ADBC was established in 1994 to take over the ABC's policy functions of providing subsidized loans for state procurement of grain, cotton, and wool and administering poverty alleviation loans. The central government's intention was to separate the ABC's policy responsibility from its commercial function in order to make it commercially sustainable. However, the function of administering poverty alleviation loans was transferred back to the ABC in 1998. The ADBC is a specialized policy bank not involved in rural retail banking. In contrast to the ABC and RCCs, which secure capital from household savings, the capital for the policy bank comes from the central government's budget.[7]

The China Postal Savings Bank

Postal Savings, a subsidiary of China Post until 2007, has approximately thirty-six thousand branches nationwide, including an extensive network in the countryside rivaling that of RCCs. However, Postal Savings could not give loans until it became the China Postal Savings Bank in 2007. As a result, RCCs were left to effectively monopolize the rural loan market until then. Nonetheless, thanks to its nationwide networks, the remittance service of Postal Savings has been a key channel for migrant workers in the cities to remit funds back home to their villages.[8] Until 2007, the China Postal Savings Bank's main sources of income were interest-rate differentials for deposits parked at the Central Bank and the modest fees collected from its remittance service.[9]

The Importance of Rural Savings

Savings provide the only means of financing major household consumption and retirement for rural residents. Moreover, rural residents—unlike their urban counterparts—have no entitlement to health-care benefits, pensions, or other social welfare. Household savings are therefore the only means of financing for old-age, health care, and even education expenses.[10] As a result, rural savings remain robust even during times of economic decline. The growth rates of rural savings have stayed above those of rural income, except for a big dip in 1992 (figure 2.2).

Capital Flows from Rural to Urban Areas and from Agriculture to Industry

The rural financial system exemplifies the urban bias in resource flows in China. Like most developing countries and communist economies, China has been extracting resources from rural areas and from the agricultural sector to support the growth of urban areas and of the industrial sector. The magnitude of the capital that flowed from rural to urban areas was almost double that from agriculture to industry. Jikun Huang and Scott Rozelle estimate that between 1978 and 2000 a total of 1.55 trillion yuan (in constant prices) flowed from the agricultural to the industrial sector, and a total of 2.73 trillion yuan (in constant prices) flowed from rural to urban areas.[11] (See figure 2.3.) To put these figures in perspective, the cash flows from agriculture to industry accounted for 3.2 percent of the gross value of agricultural production in 2000. The rural-urban flows (averaging about 129 billion yuan a year) are equivalent to 5.2 percent of agricultural production value.[12] Even though urban-biased policies are com-

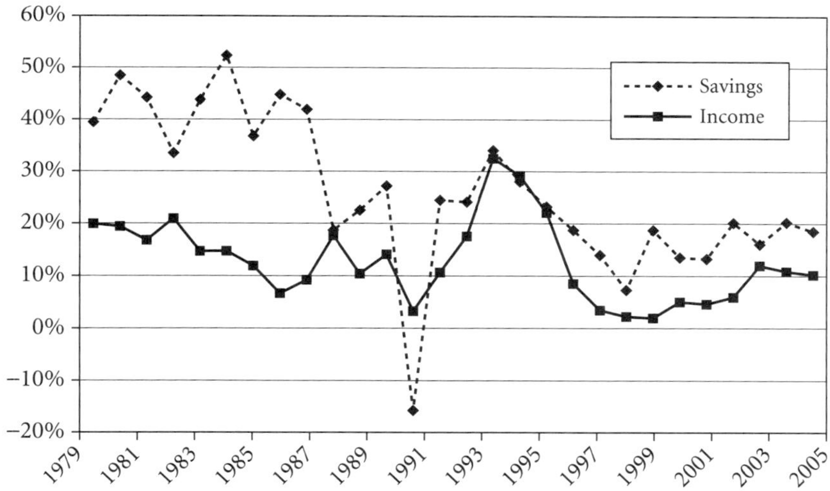

FIGURE 2.2 Rural savings and income growth rate (year-over-year)
Source: China Statistical Yearbook 2007.

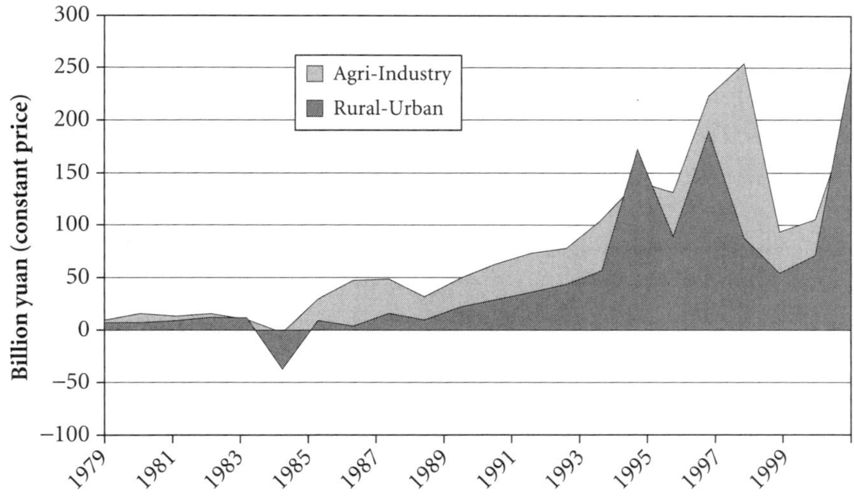

FIGURE 2.3 Capital outflows through the financial system (1978–2000)
Source: Jikun Huang, Scott Rozelle, and Honglin Wang, "Fostering or Stripping Rural China: Modernizing Agriculture and Rural to Urban Capital Flows," *Developing Economies* 44, no. 1 (2006): 1–26.

mon in developing countries as a means to jump-start industries, Huang and Rozelle conclude that the magnitude of this outflow has seriously stunted rural development in China. Rural financial institutions, namely RCCs and the ABC, have been the major conduits for these outflows. Of the three major arteries of capital outflow—the financial system, the fiscal system, and the implicit tax on farmers from compulsory grain procurement—the largest outflows, especially during the 1990s, have occurred through the financial system.

Rural Industrialization Financed by Rural Savings

The dependency of rural industrialization on rural savings is further borne out in the statistics on the destinations of rural loans. With the rise of rural savings over time, the amount of loans to the rural sector grew steadily from 4.5 billion yuan in 1978 to 523 billion yuan in 1995. An overwhelming proportion of rural savings had been directed to finance the development of collective township and village enterprises (TVEs). According to a statistical series compiled by the Ministry of Agriculture, which ended in the peak of enterprise development in 1995, TVEs had soaked up the bulk of rural loans (figure 2.4). The percentage of rural loans allocated to TVEs rose steadily from 38 percent in 1984 to 64 percent in 1993, while the proportion that went to agricultural households fell from 51 percent to 26 percent over the same period.

What Are Township and Village Enterprises (TVEs), Really?

The definition of TVEs has been a source of contention among China scholars. Until the mid-1990s, TVEs were largely local government–owned or collective enterprises. Since then, many TVEs have collapsed, and those that survived have been privatized. As a result, most TVEs still in existence are, as Yasheng Huang has argued, private firms—not, as conventional wisdom would have it, collective enterprises.[13]

I contend, however, that Huang's claim is misleading with regard to the period prior to the collapse of the TVE system in the late 1990s. As shown by the data in table 2.4 and further on in table 2.5 (collected from the Ministry of Agriculture, the same source cited by Huang), collective enterprises (*jiti qiye*) were fewer in number but employed more workers, and produced more, than did private (*siying qiye*) and household firms (*geti hu*). In fact, prior to 1985, there were no private or household TVEs at all.[14] Though there were fewer collective enterprises than privately owned ones, prior to 1993 collective firms employed more workers than did private and household firms combined.[15]

More important, prior to the restructuring of the collective TVE sector in the mid-1990s, collective firms consistently produced more than private and

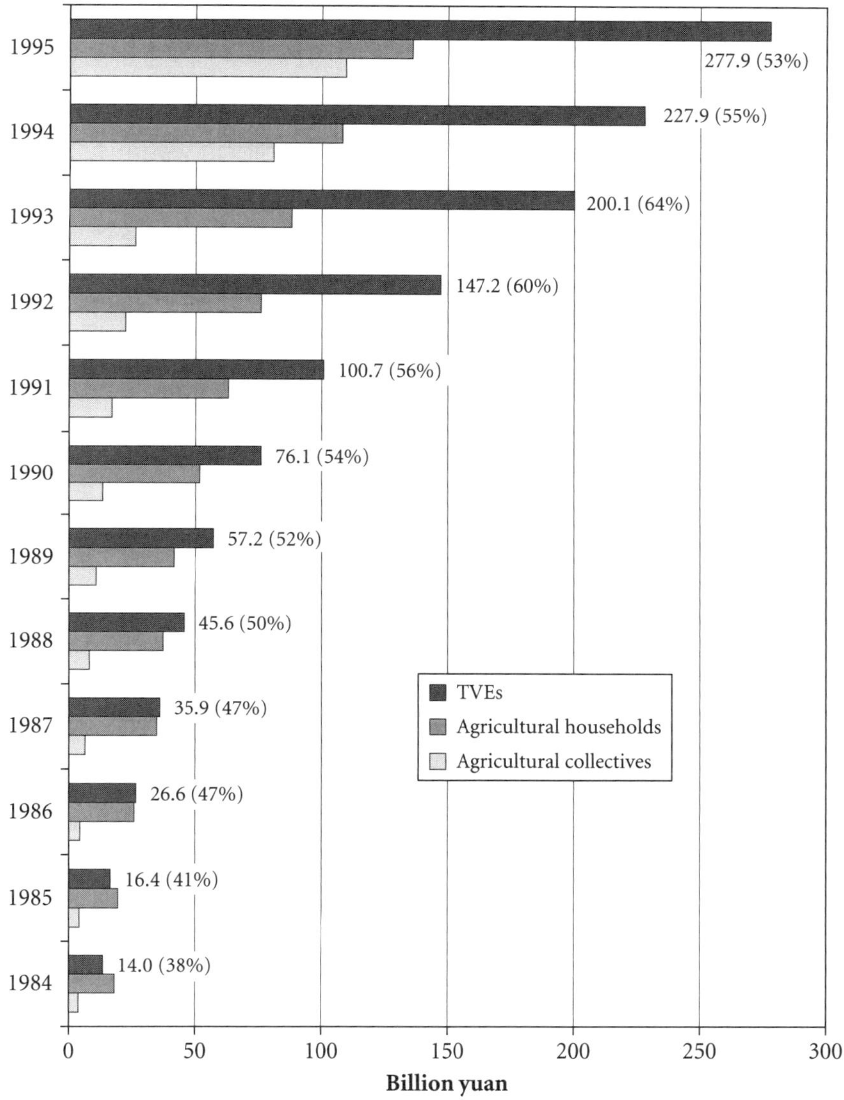

FIGURE 2.4 Destination of rural loans (1978–95)

Source: China's Rural Economy Statistics (Zhongguo Nongcun Tongji Ziliao) (1997).

household firms combined, accounting for about 60–70 percent of the total production value from 1985 to 2006, as indicated in table 2.4 (see also figure 2.5). This reaffirms the conventional wisdom that the TVE phenomenon during the 1980s and the mid-1990s was largely one of collective enterprises owned and managed by township and village authorities.

TABLE 2.4 Indicators of township and village enterprises (1985–2006)

	NO. OF ENTERPRISES (THOUSANDS); OF WHICH (%)				NO. OF EMPLOYEES (THOUSANDS); OF WHICH (%)				TOTAL PRODUCTION VALUE (MILLION YUAN); OF WHICH (%)				BANK LOANS (MILLION YUAN); OF WHICH (%)		
	TOTAL	COLLECTIVE-OWNED	PRIVATE-OWNED	HOUSEHOLD-OWNED	TOTAL	COLLECTIVE-OWNED	PRIVATE-OWNED	HOUSEHOLD-OWNED	TOTAL	COLLECTIVE-OWNED	PRIVATE-OWNED	HOUSEHOLD-OWNED	TOTAL	COLLECTIVE-OWNED	OTHER
1985	12,225	*13%*	*4%*	*83%*	69,790	*59%*	*7%*	*34%*	222,881	*89%*	*8%*	*2%*	28,800	*96%*	*4%*
1986	15,153	*11%*	*7%*	*81%*	79,374	*57%*	*11%*	*32%*	371,705	*70%*	*9%*	*21%*	53,834	*97%*	*3%*
1987	17,503	*9%*	*7%*	*84%*	88,052	*54%*	*10%*	*36%*	505,498	*68%*	*9%*	*23%*	59,756	*97%*	*3%*
1988	18,882	*8%*	*6%*	*85%*	95,455	*51%*	*10%*	*38%*	750,244	*67%*	*10%*	*23%*	78,503	*93%*	*7%*
1989	18,686	*8%*	*6%*	*86%*	93,668	*50%*	*9%*	*40%*	840,182	*66%*	*8%*	*25%*	96,013	*90%*	*10%*
1990	18,734	*8%*	*5%*	*87%*	92,618	*50%*	*9%*	*42%*	978,035	*67%*	*8%*	*25%*	112,827	*94%*	*6%*
1991	19,087	*8%*	*4%*	*88%*	96,136	*50%*	*8%*	*43%*	1,181,058	*68%*	*7%*	*25%*	144,409	*94%*	*6%*
1992	20,920	*7%*	*4%*	*88%*	106,247	*49%*	*7%*	*44%*	1,787,996	*67%*	*7%*	*26%*	207,092	*89%*	*11%*
1993	24,529	*7%*	*4%*	*89%*	123,453	*47%*	*7%*	*46%*	3,213,232	*64%*	*7%*	*29%*	310,721	*90%*	*10%*
1994	24,945	*7%*	*3%*	*90%*	120,175	*49%*	*6%*	*45%*	4,612,404	*54%*	*14%*	*32%*	305,840	*87%*	*13%*

1995	22,027	7%	4%	88%	128,621	47%	7%	46%	6,956,867	54%	16%	31%	444,102	85%	15%
1996	23,363	7%	10%	84%	135,083	44%	18%	38%	7,677,764	54%	17%	30%	531,651	84%	16%
1997	20,149	6%	12%	82%	130,504	41%	20%	39%	8,990,060	49%	21%	30%	551,074	83%	17%
1998	20,039	5%	11%	84%	125,365	39%	21%	41%	9,669,366	45%	22%	33%	579,608	79%	21%
1999	20,709	5%	10%	85%	127,041	34%	22%	43%	10,842,607	39%	24%	36%	628,850	72%	28%
2000	20,847	4%	10%	86%	128,196	30%	25%	45%	11,615,027	35%	28%	37%	628,207	65%	35%
2001	21,155	3%	9%	87%	130,856	26%	28%	46%	12,604,688	30%	31%	38%	650,257	58%	42%
2002	21,327	2%	12%	86%	132,877	13%	42%	45%	14,043,450	14%	50%	36%	690,533	47%	53%
2003	21,851	1%	13%	85%	135,729	9%	46%	45%	15,236,072	10%	55%	34%			
2004	22,132	1%	15%	84%	138,662	7%	48%	45%	17,251,673	7%	58%	35%			
2005	22,496	1%	23%	76%	142,724	5%	54%	41%	21,781,860	5%	65%	30%			
2006	23,145	1%	24%	75%	152,081	3%	59%	37%	24,980,796	4%	67%	28%			

Source: *China's Township and Village Enterprise Statistics*, Ministry of Agriculture, various years.
Note: The bank loan series was discontinued in 2003.

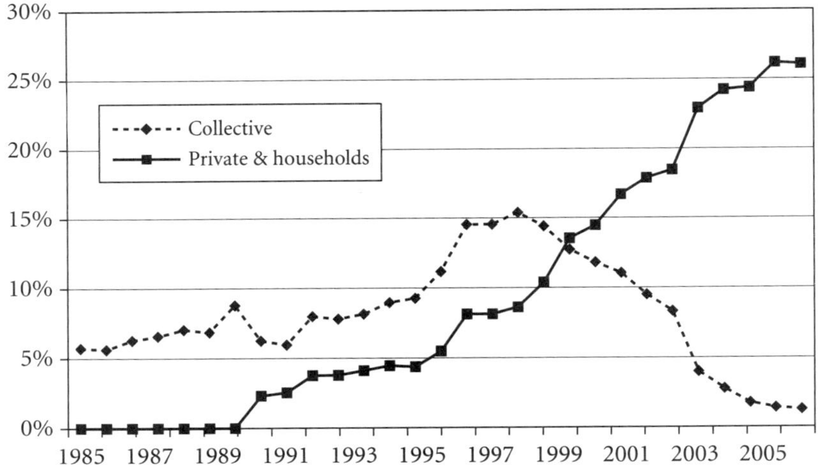

FIGURE 2.5 Collective and private enterprise value added as a percentage of GDP

Source: China's Township and Village Enterprise Statistics, Ministry of Agriculture, various years.

The History of Rural Credit Cooperatives (RCCs)

A brief history of RCCs demonstrates how they have metamorphosed from peasant-organized cooperatives into the grassroots branches of a state bank and subsequently into quasi-state credit institutions under strong influence from local authorities. Throughout their transformations, RCCs have been caught between local authorities, the central government, and their member households, each of which has distinct goals and priorities with regard to RCCs.

Peasant-Organized Cooperatives (1949–57)

Between 1949 and 1957, before the Communist Party established the people's communes, RCCs were largely grassroots cooperatives organized by peasants (*minban*)—instead of by the state—and serving peasants' credit demands. This was the fastest growth phase in the history of the credit cooperatives. The initial aim of establishing the cooperatives was to protect the peasantry against widespread usury. Peasants' demand for agricultural credit rose after the land reform in 1952, which redistributed rural lands from the landlords to the peasants. Reflecting the peasants' rising confidence in the system, from 1953 to 1955 the number of credit cooperatives grew nearly eight times—from twenty thousand to one hundred fifty-nine thousand (covering 85 percent of townships). Their membership expanded during the same period to 100 million (accounting for 86 percent of total rural households), and the total loans disbursed reached 1 trillion yuan.[16] In sum, between 1949 and 1957, the RCC system became a major conduit in pooling excess capital and channeling it to peasants needing loans. These RCCs exhibited the basic characteristics of a "cooperative" (as opposed to a state-controlled) system: member households contributed to the capital base, elected the personnel who ran the organizations, and had access to loans as a service provided by the organizations.[17]

The Financing Arm of the People's Communes (1958–78)

With the collectivization movement of the late 1950s, the communes (which later became the townships of today) gained control over the rural credit cooperatives. In 1958, China's Communist Party Chairman Mao Zedong collectivized agriculture and established the people's communes (*renmin gongshe*) to manage production in the countryside. This meant that the credit cooperatives became government-run (*guanban*) rather than peasant-organized (*minban*).[18] Peasants effectively lost control over the cooperatives, as credit decisions were made by the communes. RCCs had thereby effectively become the financing arm of the communes. However, the communes misallocated RCC savings, which disrupted the RCCs' ability to provide credit services to their members. Members' confidence in the credit institutions was greatly diminished, as reflected in falling savings, from two billion yuan in 1958 to 970 million yuan in 1962.[19]

The credit cooperatives went through a tumultuous time during the "Cultural Revolution" (1966–76).[20] The central government transferred official control of RCCs to the People's Bank of China, the country's only bank at the time. RCC loan approvals and human resources decisions were centralized to the PBoC. The credit cooperatives essentially became an apparatus of the state bank at the grassroots level, further divorcing them from their earlier "cooperative" (*minban*) nature.

Grassroots Branches of a State Bank (1979–96)

With the restoration of the state-owned ABC in 1979, the central government put RCCs under the auspices of the ABC. For one and a half decades, the credit cooperatives functioned as grassroots branches of the ABC and their employees were managed as part of the bank's bureaucracy.[21] Management by the state-owned bank compromised some key interests of the credit cooperatives. First, the RCCs were required to place 20–30 percent of their deposits with the ABC as reserve. These became the single largest source of capital for the state-owned bank, accounting for nearly half of its total deposits in the early 1980s.[22] Further, while

RCCs were paid about 4 percent interest for the reserve they left at the ABC, they had to pay around 9 percent interest on farmers' deposits. The negative interest margins were a major source of structural losses for RCCs.[23] Subordination to the ABC also meant the credit cooperatives had limited control over their capital, as the state bank directed their loans to designated borrowers, such as township and village enterprises.[24]

Remotely Managed by the Central Bank (1996–2003)

RCCs' relationship with the ABC was formally severed in 1996, as part of the central government's move to restructure the rural financial system. This restructuring divided the sector up among three institutions with distinct tasks. The ABC was left in charge of commercial loans, the ADBC was put in charge of agricultural policy loans, and RCCs were put in charge of household credit.

RCCs were managed—albeit indirectly—by the central bank between 1996 and 2003. The central government set up more credit unions at the county level to manage the grassroots credit cooperatives. The county credit unions in turn were managed by the central bank's RCC management offices, which were part of the bank's bureaus at the provincial and prefecture levels.[25] During this period, the PBoC took on a dual role: managing (through the control of the county credit unions) *and* supervising the RCCs (as part of its role as the supervisor of the banking sector).[26]

Capital Injection and Subsidized Loans

In the late 1990s it became abundantly clear to central policymakers that without a capital injection the RCC system was simply unsustainable. According to the central bank's statistics, the overall nonperforming loan rate reached a peak of 50 percent in 1999, though falling to 37 percent in 2002. The RCCs were not only bleeding financially, their collective liabilities exceeded assets by 330 billion yuan. As table 2.5 shows, both capital adequacy ratio and net equity was negative, which meant RCCs' liabilities were so enormous that they were eating into shareholders' equity. Further, official estimates indicate that more than half of RCCs nationwide (55 percent, or 19,542 credit cooperatives) were technically bankrupt.[27] By "technically bankrupt," I mean their asset value was smaller than the sum of their liabilities and equity, which implies that they would have closed for business if they had operated under market conditions.

The problem was that for the central government, shutting down RCCs was very much out of the question. As a prominent former central banker and a chief architect of RCC reform has explained, this is because RCCs are both the primary

TABLE 2.5 Financial indicators of RCCs nationwide (2002)

	BILLION YUAN
Financial losses	5.8
Nonperforming loans	514.7
Net equity	–330.0
Financial loss coverage*	33.5%
Nonperforming loan rate	37.0%
Capital adequacy ratio	–8.5%

*Number of RCCs suffering financial losses divided by total number of RCCs.
Source: CBRC; available at www.cbrc.gov.cn.

holders of rural households' savings and the primary providers of rural households' credit.[28] As a result, closing down RCCs would deprive rural residents of their only formal credit service and expose many of them to abject poverty.

More important, because RCCs hold the bulk of rural savings (totaling about 1.6 trillion yuan at 2002 year-end), any sign of financial instability would trigger panic and social unrest in the countryside. As I argue in the Conclusion, this risk of social instability is buttressed by peasants' perception that their savings at the credit cooperatives are being guaranteed by the central government. Granted, the central government is under no formal obligation to do anything should RCCs fail. However, as I show in chapter 4, the government has strong incentives to keep the RCC system from collapsing. Indeed, while the central government got rid of many unstable financial institutions after the Asian Financial Crisis in the late 1990s, RCCs have remained in business, despite having negative net assets.[29]

The PBoC introduced the micro-loan (*xiaoe daikuan*) scheme in 1999 to simultaneously improve rural households' access to loans and enhance RCCs' profitability. Under this scheme, the central bank provides wholesale loans with subsidized interest rates to RCCs in poor areas in order to alleviate fund shortages that negatively affect their lending capacity. The subsidy in turn allows RCCs to raise lending rates to farmers up to two to three times the subsidized rate, thereby helping improve RCCs' profitability. Though actual lending rates differ according to loan terms, with higher rates attaching to longer-term loans, they are still below the prevailing rates due to the subsidized nature of the loans.[30] Between 1999 and 2006, the central bank provided a total of 128.8 billion yuan in highly subsidized loans to RCCs, more than 90 percent of which went to recipients in the western and central regions.[31] An essential feature of the micro-loan scheme is that household borrowers need not have collateral or any guarantor once they are awarded "credit passes" with good ratings by RCCs. This has worked to farmers' advantage because a primary impediment to their credit access is lack of collateral, as the collectively owned land on which farmers' houses (their most valuable assets) are built is not legally admissible as collateral.[32]

My household survey results indicate that the micro-loans to rural households, the size of which differ from county to county, account for a large proportion of loans allocated by RCCs.[33] The size of the micro-loan differs from one county to another: while Zouping county—the richest of the four counties surveyed—classifies all loans under 10,000 yuan as micro-loans, all other surveyed locales classify all loans under 5,000 yuan under the micro-loan scheme.[34] Figure 2.6 indicates that the median loan size for SC1, SC2, and HB was about 2,000 yuan while that for Zouping was considerably higher at 19,000 yuan. This indicates that while a majority of borrowers in the three poorer counties took advantage of the no-collateral micro-loan scheme; this was not the case in Zouping. Loan sizes for Zouping were a lot more widely dispersed than those in the other three counties, though the latter had quite a few outliers. Overall, it appears that loan size—and the proportion of borrowers who took up micro-loans—differs according to the borrower's income level.

Despite the high proportion of loans to rural households, repayment is still a serious issue, because the way micro-loans work in practice differs from theory. Credit ratings are supposed to be given on the basis of borrowers' creditworthiness, the consideration of which includes their age, asset value, income level, and job type. Nevertheless, because a few loan officers in a township RCC typically have to deal with a few thousand borrowers, they lack the resource capacity to

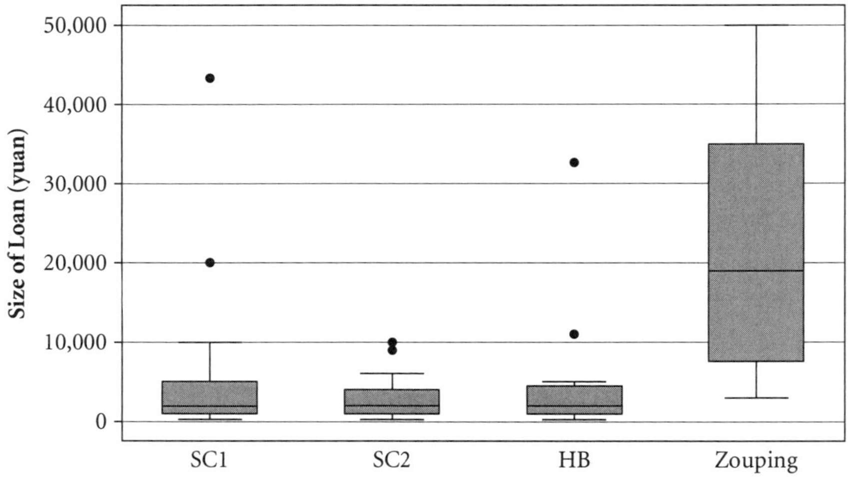

FIGURE 2.6 RCC loan sizes by surveyed county

Source: Author's Survey.

accurately assess the creditworthiness of all potential borrowers. As a result, one universal credit rating is typically given to all borrowers in a village, giving rise to the title of "a creditworthy village" (*xinyongcun*). Obviously, such a sweeping classification often fails to capture villagers' diverse risk profiles.

Further, owing to the fact that RCC officers lack intimate knowledge of the repayment capacity of individual villagers, they often have to rely on information given by township and village heads or cadres. This provides opportunities for rent-seeking behavior (e.g., corruption or providing special favors to friends and relatives) or consideration of factors unrelated to a borrower's ability to repay. For instance, local leaders can talk up their relatives or cronies so as to get loan officers to lend to them.[35] While nearly 70 percent of respondents in my household survey thought "ability to repay" was one of the RCC loan conditions, 40 percent thought *guanxi* (relationships) were important too (see figure 2.7).

In no small part, the enormous expansion in loan size from subsidized agricultural loans has contributed to a recent reduction in nonperforming loan rates and therefore to an increase in the profitability of RCCs.[36] RCCs' official nonperforming loan rates fell from 29.7 percent in 2003 to 17.5 percent in 2005. Two other forms of financial assistance from the central bank—the 168 billion yuan debt-for-bonds swaps and 830 million yuan earmarked for loans—further assisted RCCs in disposing with bad assets and writing off historical losses.

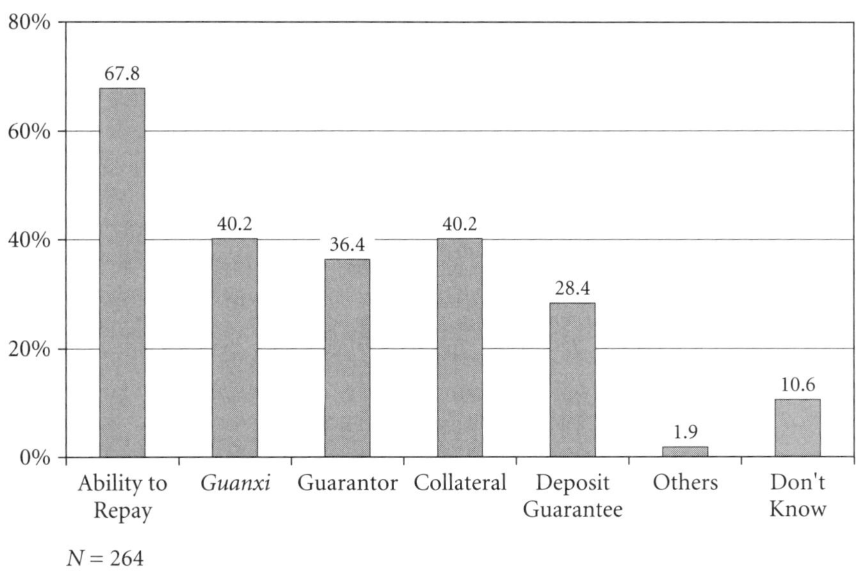

FIGURE 2.7 Survey: What do you think are RCC loan conditions?
Source: Author's Survey.

However, as I argue in the Conclusion, although the subsidies are contingent on improvement in RCCs' corporate governance, actual change in RCCs' governance structure has been rather cosmetic.

Provincial Credit Unions and Multiple RCC Models (2003–)

In 2003 central policymakers agreed that there should not be a "one-size-fits-all" model (*yidaoqie*) of RCCs. They therefore introduced two major changes to the RCC system.[37] Starting with a pilot reform in seven provinces and one municipality in 2003,[38] changes were rolled out to the rest of the country over the following three years.

One change was the removal of RCCs from the professional and supervisory oversight of the PBoC. RCC management rights were transferred from the PBoC to the provincial governments, with the intention of making regional governments financially responsible for the credit cooperatives in their jurisdictions.[39] The provincial RCC unions are administrative organizations (*xingzheng jiguan*) that do not take deposits or give loans. They represent the respective provincial governments in managing the credit cooperatives in their territories. Their functions are similar to those of the pre-reform county credit unions, except that their control over local credit cooperatives is stronger. The prerogatives of the provincial RCC unions range from personnel appointments, appraisals and dismissals, the setting of province-wide remuneration systems, veto rights on large loans, and approval rights of major expenditures to auditing and service provisions, such as province-wide management and support of IT systems and personnel training.[40] In addition, the PBoC's supervisory function (over all banking institutions nationwide, not only RCCs) was transferred in 2003 to the newly set up China Banking Regulatory Commission (CBRC).

Additionally, subject to certain conditions, RCCs could choose to adopt one of three institutional models: the rural commercial banking model, the rural cooperative banking model, or the existing rural credit cooperative model. RCCs in highly industrialized locales with better financial performance could become rural commercial banks. These are allowed to conduct business like any urban commercial bank and are similarly bound by few policy requirements. Rural cooperative banks are a hybrid of rural commercial banks and credit cooperatives. While they can raise equity by bringing in individual and enterprise investors, they are required to allocate a certain proportion of their loan portfolios to agricultural projects. A majority of RCCs nationwide, particularly those in the central and western regions, opted to become rural cooperative banks, with only a handful in the industrialized province of Jiangsu becoming rural commercial banks. Except for some RCCs in poor western areas that retained the original RCC model, independent legal entity status of township RCCs was abolished, to the effect that they are now part of the county union cost centers.

Recent Rural Financial Market Liberalization

Since its inception in 2003, the CBRC has been pushing for reform in the rural financial sector. Aside from the restructuring of RCCs, these reforms include the restructuring of the Postal Savings system and the establishment of township and village banks and new rural financial entities. This liberalization of the rural financial market is premised on the belief that existing financial institutions have limited coverage in rural areas and the sector suffers from a shortage of capital and limited competition.[41]

One promising reform was the establishment of the Postal Savings Bank in 2007. Since its inception, this bank has rolled out a micro-loan program intended to reach a vast number of small borrowers by allowing them to use time deposits as collateral. As of April 2007, the micro-loan program has been tested in thirteen provinces.[42] The bank's nationwide network makes it a potentially successful channel for improving credit access for poor households and small businesses.

The new types of rural financial institutions introduced in late 2006 are (a) township and village banks (*cunzhen yinhang*), (b) micro-credit companies (*xiaoer daikuan gongsi*), and (c) community-based cooperative credit organizations. Their introduction was a regulatory break from the long-standing pattern of government control of the rural financial sector that has allowed RCCs to maintain their dominance for such a long time.

Of the three, township and village banks have attracted the most enthusiasm from private domestic banks and foreign banks.[43] In December 2007 London-based HSBC became the first international investor to open a wholly owned subsidiary in a rural county in Hubei province, offering savings accounts to local residents and businesses and providing loans to agricultural companies.[44] Some domestic regional banks, such as the city commercial banks, have also acquired township-and-village-bank licenses that enable them to conduct business in rural areas otherwise beyond their territorial boundaries. The new micro-credit companies conduct lending, but unlike the rural banks, they are not allowed to accept deposits.[45] Nonetheless, equity participation in these companies is not exclusive to banks. Market deregulation opened up a possibility for informal lenders and underground money houses to operate legally by acquiring licenses to become formal credit companies. The reforms have also allowed for self-help organizations organized and managed by farmers, but enthusiasm for these new institutions has been lacking.

Overall, as of March 2008, twenty-five township and village banks and four micro-credit companies have reportedly been approved by the CBRC.[46] Even though the rural financial sector liberalization is encouraging, it is too early to assess whether it will make a substantial contribution to development.

Informal Credit Institutions

The heterogeneity in the levels of industrialization and income in rural China implies hugely diverse credit demands. Such demands can range from half a million yuan as working capital, to 10,000 yuan to start up a small neighborhood shop, to a few hundred yuan to pay for a funeral or a wedding. Therefore, it is beyond doubt that RCCs as a *single* set of financial institutions are *unable* to meet amazingly varied demands across rural China. Accordingly, the size of the informal rural credit sector differs from one locale to another depending on the extent to which the formal institutions are able to meet clients' needs.

Some informal lenders are more institutionalized than others. The degree of such institutionalization depends on the extent of information asymmetry between the two parties, and particularly on how well the lender knows the borrower's risk profile. It tends to be less institutionalized when credit transactions take place within communities sharing some common characteristics, such as living in the same village or sharing a lineage. The tightly knit nature of the relationships not only helps provide the lender with information about the borrower but also offers "peer pressure" and "peer monitoring" to ensure prompt repayments. Because peer pressure offers an alternative means of ensuring loan payments, it negates the need for collateral, which is the way formal institutions hedge against potential defaults.[47] Examples of this type of non-collateralized informal credit are interest-free (or low-interest-rate) interpersonal lending among relatives, friends, or neighbors, or trade credit given by wholesalers to vendors.

Another example of non-collateralized informal credit in China is credit associations (*hui*) consisting of a group of people involved in savings and lending. There are three major types of credit associations in rural China: rotating associations (*lunhui*), in which loans are given by rotations among group members; bidding associations (*biaohui*), in which loans are determined by a bidding process; and escalating associations (*taihui*) and pyramidal investment schemes, which are strictly illegal.[48]

When an informal lender does not know the likelihood of repayment, the lending tends to be more institutionalized and operate in ways similar to the formal institutions. Examples are money lenders or middlemen (*yinbei*), who broker savers and borrowers at high interest rates, and underground money houses (*dixia qianzhuang*) that operate like banks. Borrowers face varying degree of interest rates, some as high as four times the central bank's base lending rate.[49]

Additionally, there is microfinance, first launched in China in 1994, based on a variation of the Grameen Bank model popularized by Nobel laureate Mohammed Yunus. The essence of the Grameen model is to provide commercially sustainable financial services to the poor (or, sometimes, to women). Based on a set of innovative practices, microfinance utilizes various mechanisms, such as group guarantees, dynamic incentives, and regular repayment schedules, to reduce information asymmetry and to mitigate risk of default.

Some encouraging performance from the early NGO-run programs notwithstanding,[50] microfinance efforts in China hit a wall when it came to expansion and wider implementation. In no small part this was due to the political environment in China. All NGOs in China must be registered with the Ministry of Civil Affairs (*minzhengbu*) and must have a sponsoring government unit (*guakao danwei*) supervising activities.[51] Therefore, NGOs in China are *not*—strictly speaking—nongovernmental organizations, since they cannot set their own agendas. They also face the threat of being closed down due to their dubious legal status. Further, the Communist Party and government apparatus, which deeply penetrates rural society, plays a prominent role in the success or failure of any development initiative. Smooth implementation of these so-called nongovernmental grassroots programs, from loan disbursement to collection, requires cooperation from local officials.[52] The programs' lack of legal status as financial institutions means they cannot take deposits, which makes them dependent on external funding.

This chapter highlights the indispensable role of the RCC in rural industrialization, and sketches the rural credit outcome that will be analyzed in the rest of the book. Rural savings have been instrumental in financing the development of rural industries, which were largely local government–owned enterprises from the early 1980s to the mid-1990s and subsequently private enterprises. RCCs may be small players among financial institutions nationwide, but they are the dominant force in the rural financial sector, accounting for over 80 percent of rural loans and deposits. The ABC's withdrawal of its network from rural China in the late 1990s further strengthened RCCs' position in the rural financial sector. The

Grameen model of microfinance has failed to take off in China on a large scale, despite its international success. Various subsidized loan programs, such as poverty alleviation loans, have achieved little or have not met program objectives. The central government has recently opened up the sector by issuing licenses for new types of rural financial institutions. Nevertheless, it is too soon to assess meaningfully whether the liberalization will have a lasting impact on rural development.

Part II

THE DESIGN OF CHINA'S ECONOMIC AND POLITICAL INSTITUTIONS

3

THE DESIGN OF CHINA'S RURAL CREDIT INSTITUTIONS

Does the institutional design of rural credit cooperatives (RCCs) explain patterns in their lending? In this chapter I illuminate the factors that shape loan officers' behavior and affect the loan allocation process by analyzing the findings of my household survey. Though not part of the state bureaucracy, RCCs are subject to a dual accountability system similar to that of any subnational bureau in China. Comparison of RCCs' line of reporting and supervisory structure with that of state-owned banks further illustrates why credit cooperatives are more susceptible to local-government influence.

I begin by reviewing existing explanations for the rural credit sector outcome, particularly bias in lending toward local government-owned enterprises described in chapter 2, and explain why China's banking regulator cannot supervise RCCs effectively. The problem, I show, stems from the central government's dual and contradictory objectives with regard to RCCs. I also account for patterns of lending by rural cooperative foundations (RCFs), once the largest informal credit institutions in China. In particular, I account for the fact that, until the central government shut RCFs down in 1999, more than three-quarters of RCFs' loans went to projects related to local governments.

As shown in chapter 2, RCCs have undergone a great deal of institutional restructuring since 1979: from being part of the state-owned Agricultural Bank of China (ABC) between 1979 and 1996, through being managed and supervised by local offices of the central bank between 1996 and 2003, to coming under the management of the provincial unions after the 2003–5 restructuring. This chapter will focus on the earlier periods, for two reasons. First, these two periods are more pertinent to the development of the collective township and village enterprises (TVEs) during the 1980s and 1990s, which is the issue under examination. Second, when I conducted my fieldwork in 2005–6, many provincial unions were still being set up, so the implications of the 2003–5 restructuring were not yet clear.

Existing Explanations for the Rural Credit Sector Outcome

Though RCCs were intended as sources of credit for farmers and other small and medium-sized borrowers, they lend mostly to local government–related enterprises and other big borrowers. The most common explanations for this phenomenon point to two interrelated factors: (a) government regulation of interest rates and (b) long-standing institutional biases against small and/or non-government related borrowers.

Until the deregulation of banks' lending rates in 2005,[1] formal lenders had shied away from small and medium-sized enterprises and from rural households because these borrowers are more costly to service and are deemed to carry higher default risks. Since interest rate is the cost of capital, if lenders are unable to adjust rates to reflect their cost structure, they will refuse to lend to high-cost borrowers. (This is a common reason that small and rural borrowers fail to obtain formal financing in developing nations where interest rates are controlled.)[2]

Another impediment to private enterprises' ability to obtain formal credit prior to 2004 was the communist regime's ideological bias against private ownership. Until the official recognition of private property rights in 2004,[3] private enterprises operated in a gray economy and were forced to adopt various covert strategies to survive. Many private enterprises chose to register as "collectively owned" firms, commonly called "wearing a red hat," to avoid government harassment.[4] Many bank officers I interviewed told me that if a loan they had approved to a private enterprise went sour, it could cost them their jobs. By contrast, loans to state-owned enterprises or government-linked firms did not carry such personal risk since they came with a tacit local-government guarantee.[5]

Lack of legal recognition for collective lands as collateral also impedes farmers' and private rural enterprises' ability to obtain formal credit. Rural borrowers' most valuable assets are the lands on which farmers build their homes and private enterprises set up their factories. However, rural households or enterprises have only user-rights in such land because rural land is collectively owned.[6] As a result, farmers and private enterprises cannot use their most valuable assets as collateral for bank borrowing. The absence of a developed legal system in property-value assessment or guaranteeing a minimum livelihood for farmers also makes seizing collateral a cumbersome process for formal credit institutions.

The rural credit market is also beset by information asymmetry, since borrowers often have more information on the riskiness of the project the loan will finance and the likelihood of repayment than they are willing to share with the lender.[7] Each township RCC employs only a few loan officers to look after a few hundred to a few thousand households in the territory. As a result, it is extremely difficult for a local credit cooperative to obtain reliable information on the risk profile of every borrower and therefore to determine the repayment likelihood. This is compounded by rural financial institutions' lack of modern accounting techniques in assessing private property values. Lack of secondary markets for trading cattle and livestock also make assessment of the value of these assets an arduous task.

While these explanations may account for the bias in lending to some extent, there is a more compelling explanation for why RCCs are often forced to compromise their professional objectives. This explanation becomes apparent once we examine RCCs' institutional design.

RCCs' Corporate Governance Structure

Since the establishment of Communist China in 1949, RCCs have never been free of local-government influence. The corporate governance structure of credit cooperatives may have the façade of a cooperative organization, but is devoid of any cooperative elements in substance.[8] This may not come as a surprise, since no cooperative in China is genuinely organized or managed by its members. Nonetheless, examining how practice differs from theory reveals some interesting facts about RCCs.

In theory, the highest governing body of an RCC is the member representative meeting, the *huiyuan daibiao dahui* (figure 3.1). In the meeting, members are supposed to nominate and elect those who sit on the RCC's board of directors (BoD) and board of supervisors (BoS), the latter supervising the former. The head of the BoD becomes the key decision maker for the organization and monitors its management.[9] In reality, however, the member representative meeting consists of township and village leading cadres rather than farmers. My household survey shows that among the 111 RCC members in the sample, only 13 (11.7 percent) had ever participated in a member representative meeting, while the rest had never participated.

Who actually took part in these meetings? Only 13 of the 113 people (or 11.5 percent) had ever taken part in an RCC member representative meeting. Further, nearly 80 percent of those who had ever taken part in a meeting were themselves

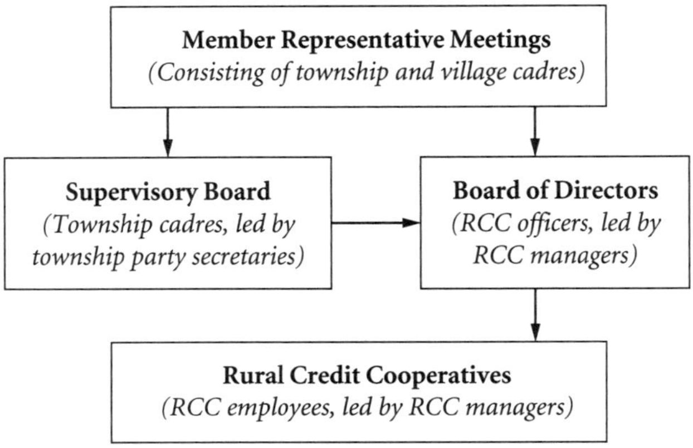

FIGURE 3.1 RCCs' corporate governance structure

TABLE 3.1 Number of participants and nonparticipants in RCC member representative meetings who are cadres or spouses of cadres

	ARE YOU OR IS YOUR SPOUSE A TOWNSHIP OR VILLAGE PARTY SECRETARY, OR TOWNSHIP OR VILLAGE HEAD?		
HAVE YOU EVER TAKEN PART IN A RCC MEMBER REPRESENTATIVE MEETING?	YES	NO	TOTAL
Yes (Number)	10	3	13
Yes (%)	*76.9*	*23.1*	*100.0*
No (Number)	3	97	113
No (%)	*2.7*	*85.8*	*100.0*
Total	13	100	113
Fisher's exact test (p-value)	**1-sided**	**2-sided**	
	0.000	0.000	

party secretaries or township or village heads, or their spouse was one (table 3.1). Put differently, if the household *head* was a township or village party secretary or a township or village leader, he or she was significantly more likely to take part in the member representative meeting.[10] However, those households with family members or extended family members who were party cadres were not significantly more likely to participate (table 3.2).

When asked who they thought owns credit cooperatives, one-third of people surveyed responded farmer cooperatives, while 18 percent responded township governments (figure 3.2). The high response of "farmer cooperatives" may reflect the oft-heard rhetoric in the countryside that "RCCs are here to serve farm-

TABLE 3.2 Number of participants and nonparticipants in RCC member representative meetings who are related to cadres

HAVE YOU EVER TAKEN PART IN A RCC MEMBER REPRESENTATIVE MEETING?	DO YOU HAVE ANY RELATIVE OR MEMBER OF EXTENDED FAMILY WHO IS A CADRE? YES	NO	TOTAL
Yes (Number)	3	10	13
Yes (%)	*23.1*	*76.9*	*100.0*
No (Number)	32	68	100
No (%)	*32.0*	*68.0*	*100.0*
Total	35	78	113
Fisher's exact test (p-value)	**1-sided**	**2-sided**	
	0.38	0.751	

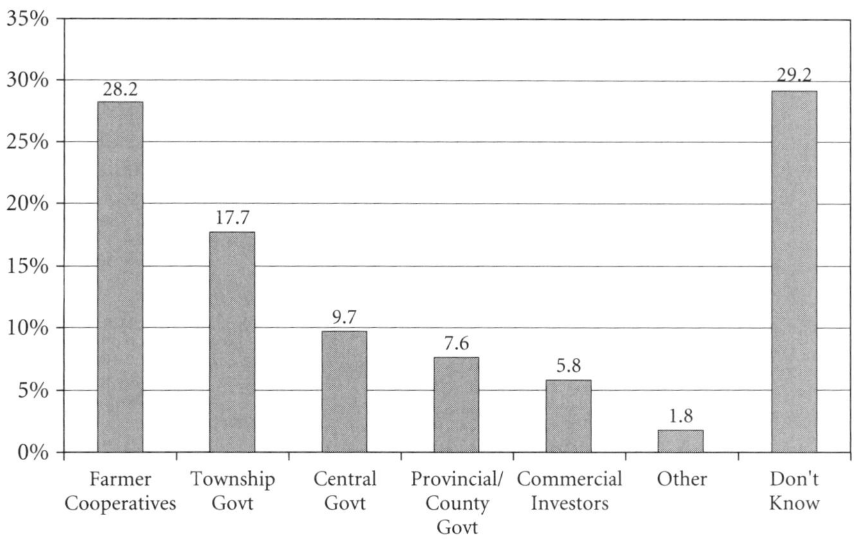

FIGURE 3.2 Survey: Who do you think owns RCCs? (*N* = 277)

Source: Author's survey.

ers" (*nongcun xinyongshe wei renmin fuwu*), rather than a true portrayal of the respondents' perceptions. When asked who they thought manages RCCs, only 40 percent of respondents answered correctly—a quarter choosing county credit unions and 15 percent choosing RCC managers (either answer is correct). Notably, 14.5 percent of the respondents thought the credit cooperatives were managed by township governments (figure 3.3).

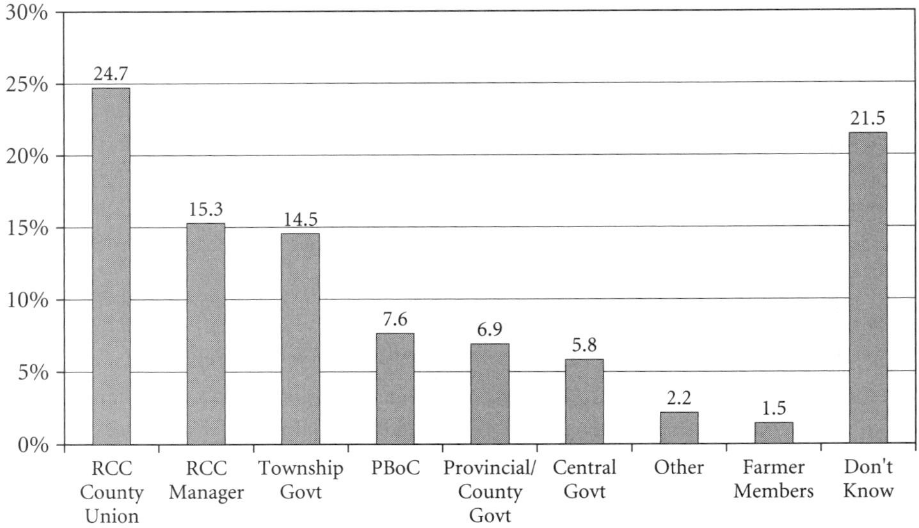

FIGURE 3.3 Survey: Who do you think manages RCCs? (*N* = 277)
Source: Author's survey.

Strong Influence by Local Governments

A significant factor affecting RCCs' loan allocation process and shaping the behavior of rural loan officers is the design of the RCCs and the accountability structure that it fosters. This accountability structure resembles most closely that of local agencies. Therefore, to fully appreciate the effects of RCCs' design on their decisions, it is helpful to first examine the accountability structure of local agencies.

Administrative power in China is divided between the center and four subnational levels: provinces (municipalities), prefectures, counties, and townships.[11] All government bureaucracies, for example the Ministry of Environmental Protection, have agencies at each administrative level. Each subnational bureau reports vertically to its counterpart at the level above it. For example, a township environmental agency reports to a county environmental bureau, which is in turn accountable to a prefecture bureau. The prefecture bureau answers to a provincial ministry, which in turn answers to the ministry in Beijing. This is the agency's functional accountability or "professional relationship" (*yewu guanxi*). In addition, the CCP has a committee at each administrative level that is intended to lead the government at each level and to which all bureaus at each level must also report. This is the agency's party accountability or "leadership relationship" (*lingdao guanxi*).

This design allows the CCP to penetrate deeply into the bureaucratic apparatus. But it inevitably creates a dual accountability system for all subnational bureaus, which becomes problematic when the two masters have vastly different sets of goals and priorities. This is what Kenneth Lieberthal terms the "matrix muddle" or *tiao-kuai guanxi*, a characteristic of China's political institutional design that gives rise to a problem of "fragmented authoritarianism."[12] For example, the fiscal decentralization policies implemented since the early 1980s have made maximizing revenue a central task for all subnational government institutions in China. When protecting the environment, for instance, requires compromising economic growth and fiscal revenue (for example, denying investment to a factory that causes pollution even if it pays handsome tax revenue), the local environmental protection agency has the challenging task of balancing the conflicting directives of its two superiors. Scholars who study environmental issues in China have long held this to be a major impediment to successful implementation of environmental policies there.[13]

The Principal-Agent Problem and Contested Control of Local Bureaus

To help illustrate the complexities and implications of China's bureaucratic accountability system, I propose to consider it through multiple principal-agent literature, used extensively in the study of U.S. congressional politics. The essence of a principal-agent relationship is the delegation of authority from the principal to the agent. The principal seeks to structure the relationship in such a way that the agent's actions produce the outcomes desired by the principal. However, the agent has an *informational advantage* over the principal, and this gives rise to the problems of "adverse selection" and "moral hazard."[14]

In the U.S. political system, any given federal bureau, as an agent, is accountable to more than one principal. A bureau is subject to direct oversight by both the president and Congress, and within Congress to both the House and the Senate.[15] The question of who has ultimate control depends on the type of control mechanisms the principal uses and the extent to which the mechanism can help alleviate the problems of "adverse selection" and "moral hazard." For instance, McCubbins and Schwartz argue that for Congress to secure bureaucratic compliance with legislative objectives, fire-alarm oversight (e.g., establishing rules and procedures to provide citizens and interest groups with information on administrative decision-making processes, so that feedback loops to Congress if something goes wrong) is more effective than police-patrol oversight (e.g., conducting field observations and commissioning scientific studies).[16]

In China, of the two principals that local bureaus face, local party committees usually have an upper hand. This is because party committees control personnel appointment and allocation of financial resources to agencies, through controlling *bianzhi* and *nomenklatura*.[17] *Bianzhi* are the authorized numbers of personnel or ordinary cadres in a government administrative organ. Control over *bianzhi* gives party committees the power to determine the level of budgetary appropriation for the bureau.[18] *Nomenklatura* is a list of positions of leading cadres over whose appointments the party exercises control.[19] Control over the *nomenklatura* gives party committees the prerogatives to nominate, appoint, promote, and dismiss leading party cadres.

These two powers enable local party committees (*kuai* authority) to dominate over professional superiors (*tiao* authority) when local officials (agents) are conflicted between them. Ministries can hand out various assignments and targets for local bureaucracies, but local officials are *incapable* of carrying them out without the necessary manpower or financial means. Agents are further held hostage by the principal who has the power to determine the agent's career prospects. As a result, whenever conflicts arise between orders given by the two principals, party accountability usually overrides functional accountability.

RCCs Report to the ABC (1979–96)

Between 1979 and 1996, RCCs reported to the state-owned Agricultural Bank of China (ABC) on professional banking matters. Formally, credit cooperatives functioned as grassroots branches of the state-owned bank during that time: township RCCs had to report to county ABC offices on all professional work, and RCCs were expected to support state industries. There was an implicit division of labor between the two credit institutions, the larger of the two (the ABC) providing state marketing departments with capital for agricultural procurements, mostly grain and cotton, while RCCs supported local government–owned township and village enterprises (TVEs).[20]

Nevertheless, key RCC personnel decisions, like those of the state-owned banks, were made by local party committees. The pivotal institution within the credit cooperative is not the member representative meeting or the BoD. Rather, it is the internal party committee (*dangwei*), which does not appear in the RCC's formal corporate governance structure. The internal party committee is headed by the credit cooperative director (*zhuren*), who is also the party secretary and is by far the pivotal decision maker (*yibashou*) in the RCC. The other party committee members usually include the assistant director (the second in charge), the head of the BoS (who is also the party disciplinary committee member, the *jilv jiancha weiyuan*, in charge of investigating and disciplining party members' misconduct), and the bookkeeper or accountant. Each of the party committee members has an administrative ranking indicative of his or her seniority in the *nomenklatura* system: a township credit cooperative director is usually a *keji*, the lowest rank, while a county union manager is usually one rank higher, a *chuji*.

An internal party committee answers to the corresponding local party committee, in accordance with the CCP's accountability system. Township party secretaries therefore have the power to appoint the internal party secretaries (and effective managers) of the township credit cooperatives, to evaluate their job performance, and to determine their career advancement. These veto rights over personnel matters in RCCs are similar to those that local party secretaries have over local bureaus—all party members answer to their territorial party secretaries. Township credit cooperatives, as agents, were therefore answerable to two principals: the state-owned ABC and township party committees. But because they appointed them and determined their career advancements, township party secretaries were far more powerful in dictating actions taken by RCC managers.

Furthermore, the state-owned bank was uninterested in turning the credit cooperatives into profitable entities. Not only were RCCs required to place one-third of their deposits with the ABC as reserve, they were also paid lower interest rates than those they paid rural depositors. While the mandatory reserve was a major source of RCCs' structural losses, it was the foremost contributor to the ABC's bottom line.[21] In other words, not only did RCCs' functional superiors have no control over personnel decisions but also they were lackluster in shaping RCCs into profitable and professional credit institutions. Moreover, the actions of ABC managers were themselves dictated by local party secretaries, given that the latter were the ones who appointed the former in the first place.

Therefore, during the period that RCCs were under the auspices of the state-owned bank, while township RCCs were subject to two reporting lines, their relationship with township party committees superseded that with their functional superiors (figure 3.4). Not coincidentally, this period was also the era during which collective TVEs grew most rapidly. Unequivocally, RCCs played a pivotal role in the development of collective TVEs, and this was in no small measure due to credit cooperatives' political accountability to local party committees.

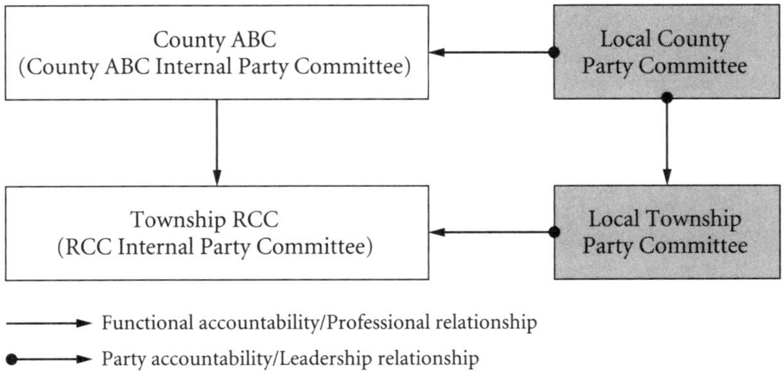

FIGURE 3.4 RCCs' accountability system (1979–96)

RCCs Report to the Central Bank (1996–2003)

The relationship between RCCs and the ABC was formally severed in 1996. Between 1996 and 2003, the central bank managed the RCC system by setting up county RCC unions that managed township RCCs directly. County unions in turn reported to central bank offices in the prefectures and provincial capitals.

In the mid- to late 1990s, the central government restructured the financial sector to weaken the power of local party committees over personnel matters. Specifically, the power to appoint the state-owned bank managers at all subnational levels was centralized, first in the hands of the Central Finance Work Commission (CFWC) between 1998 and 2002, and subsequently in the hands of the Leading Group on State Banking Reform, both institutions reporting directly to the CCP Central Committee.[22]

RCCs' personnel appointment system was centralized to a lesser degree than the state banks when the central bank took over management control from the ABC in 1996. Between 1996 and 2003, top officials of township credit cooperatives were appointed by county unions, and those of county unions by central bank offices at the prefectures and provincial capitals, rather than by top-ranking bureaucrats in Beijing (as was the case with the state-owned bank managers).[23] Local party committees' influence on RCCs, though attenuated, remained pervasive throughout this period. In addition, as the next section will illustrate, the central bank lacked organizational capacity and resources to effectively manage or supervise RCCs. Hence, RCCs remained largely grassroots credit institutions that lacked a strong vertical accountability system.

The Central Regulator's Dual Objectives for RCCs

The People's Bank of China (PBoC) was formally recognized as China's central bank with the enactment of the Central Bank Law in 1995. This law established the PBoC as the sole agency in charge of supervising and regulating the financial sector and of formulating monetary policies. In 2003 the central government transferred the supervisory function to the newly established China Banking Regulatory Commission (CBRC), leaving the PBoC to concentrate on formulation of monetary policies.[24]

Representing the interests of the central government, the PBoC and subsequently the CBRC has two major—and at times conflicting—goals in the RCCs:[25] improving farmers' living standards and ensuring RCCs' commercial sustainability. These objectives were imposed on RCCs when the central bank took on management and supervision of the RCC system in 1996. Although the 2003–5 restructuring placed RCCs under the management of provincial unions,

RCCs are still expected to meet these central government-imposed goals. The evaluation performance indicators described here were not changed by the 2003–5 restructuring.

GOAL ONE: IMPROVE LIVING STANDARDS IN RURAL AREAS

The central bank requires RCCs to service the credit demands of rural residents in order to meet the objective of improving rural living standards. Since the mid-1990s, central policymakers became increasingly aware that two decades of dizzying economic growth has widened the urban-rural income gap, to the detriment of farmers. The central government characterized the plight of the countryside as "the problem of the three agricultures" (*sannong wenti*): the agricultural sector (*nongye*), villages (*nongcun*), and peasants (*nongmin*). The Hu-Wen administration ratcheted up the rhetoric by professing a "new socialist countryside" (*shehui zhuyi xinnongcun*) as crucial for realizing a "harmonious society" (*hexie shehui*). In 2008 the CCP announced the goal of doubling rural income by 2020.

Though left unmentioned, what fueled these rhetorical pronouncements was the steady escalation in rural unrest since the mid-1990s. It has been estimated that during this period more than ninety thousand incidents of social unrest occurred annually, more than nine times as much as reported the decade before.[26] Such unrest, triggered by yawning gaps between the "haves" and the "have-nots" in rural areas and between farmers and their affluent urban counterparts, directly threatens the regime's legitimacy and the country's stability. Central policymakers believe RCCs, being the cornerstone of rural finance, are critical to solving such social and economic problems in rural areas.

In 1999, the central bank began providing wholesale loans with subsidized interest rates to credit cooperatives to encourage lending to agricultural borrowers. This loan scheme was intended as a subsidy to RCCs, as it allowed them to benefit from the wide interest margins. Between 1999 and 2006, the PBoC disbursed a total of 128.8 billion yuan of wholesale loans to credit cooperatives through the agricultural on-lending scheme (*zhinong zaidaikuan*). The wholesale loans were given at a subsidized interest rate of 2.25 percent per annum; and RCCs in turn charged agricultural borrowers at a rate of 8–12 percent, depending on the riskiness of the projects.[27] As we will see later in this section, expansion of this agricultural loan scheme has been made a criterion in loan officers' performance evaluations.

GOAL TWO: FINANCIAL SUSTAINABILITY OF RCCS

The second—and equally important—goal of the central bank with regard to RCCs is to ensure their self-sustainability. The central bank will have to come to RCCs' rescue if they collapse or if "bank runs" occur.[28] It is imperative that the central bank prevent this from happening, for several reasons. Until the late 2000s, RCCs were the only formal credit institutions with networks penetrating rural areas. If RCCs go out of business, hundreds of millions of rural households will be deprived of their only channel to formal credit services. Rural borrowers will then be forced to turn to informal lenders, such as money houses and pawn shops, which charge higher interest rates, and which the communist regime considers exploitative and keeps strictly outside the legal sphere.[29]

Furthermore, the RCC system nationwide collectively holds more than 80 percent of rural savings. As the 2008 events in the U.S. financial market attest, bank runs could rattle consumer confidence and cause major societal upheavals, despite protective mechanisms such as the Federal Deposit Insurance Corporation (FDIC), which provides protection for individual depositors. China does not have a comparable insurance system, which means farmers will lose their savings if the credit cooperatives go under. The central government can therefore ill afford to let credit cooperatives fail.

The possibility of a bank run is harrowing for the authoritarian regime. The largest bank run in recent Chinese history occurred in Sichuan and Hebei provinces in 1998 over the failure of local rural credit foundations (RCFs), to be discussed more fully later in this chapter. RCFs were informal credit institutions organized by township governments. By the mid-1990s, RCFs had amassed as much as 100 billion yuan in rural household savings, equivalent to roughly one-eighth of the nationwide savings of RCCs at that time. To pacify millions of rural savers and to prevent such bank runs from spreading nationwide, the central government instructed RCFs to close down immediately—and ordered township governments to honor savings of individual depositors. A majority of township governments raked up huge debts as they frantically borrowed from all sources to honor these individual savings.

RCCs' financial sustainability is also important to the central government because savings at credit cooperatives carry an implicit central government guarantee. When I asked my survey respondents why they kept their savings in RCCs (multiple responses were allowed), 48 percent responded that it was safer than keeping money at home; 41 percent said savings at the credit cooperatives carried a central government guarantee (figure 3.5). Since four out of ten depositors at RCCs think their savings are guaranteed by the central government, any financial crisis will have widespread negative implications for the regime's legitimacy.

CONFLICTS BETWEEN THE TWO GOALS

The potential for conflict between the central bank's objectives with regard to RCCs is best illustrated by the performance evaluation criteria for loan of-

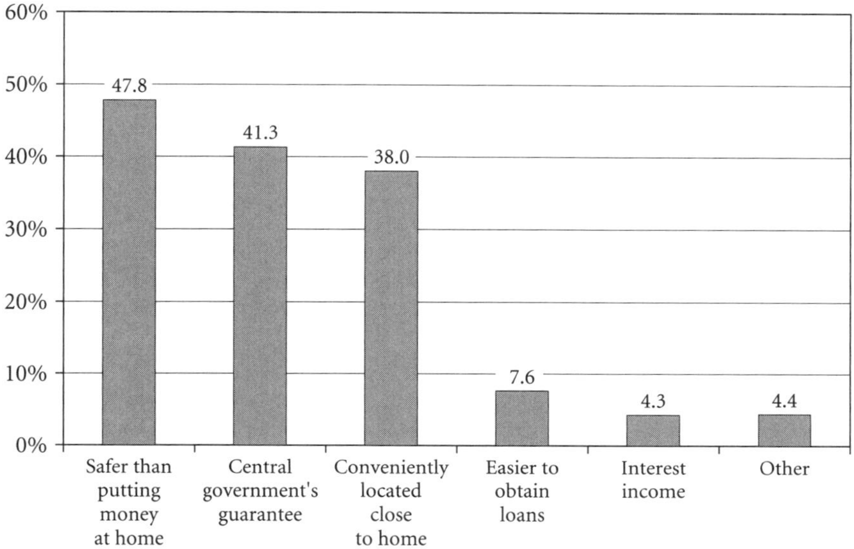

FIGURE 3.5 Survey: Why do you keep an RCC savings account? (N = 132); multiple responses allowed

Source: Author's survey.

ficers. Loan officers' remuneration consists of a base salary, which is nonvariable, plus performance-based components that vary according to set criteria. These variable components can account for as much as three-quarters of total compensation.[30] Performance evaluation by county unions is conducted according to two sets of criteria, applied quarterly and annually. The quarterly criteria are:

- Quality of assets, measured by the ratio of nonperforming loans to total loans
- Deposit-to-loan ratio per employee
- Average profit per employee
- Average expense (administrative and operational) per employee

At year's end, the credit cooperative is subject to another set of evaluation criteria, which in combination with the previous determine credit officers' variable wage components:

- Deposit growth
- Reduction of nonperforming loans
- Expansion of agricultural loans (at least 75 percent of newly disbursed loans annually must be allocated for agricultural purposes)

- Collection of interest income
- Overall management

These performance indicators suggest the central bank is more interested in profit maximization and asset quality than in serving the agricultural sector. Nonetheless, it is noteworthy that expansion of agricultural loans is one of the criteria for determining the magnitude of variable wage. As demonstrated in chapter 2, the principle of profit maximization directs credit institutions to lend to large businesses rather than to farmers. Since the fixed costs of disbursing a loan, such as administrative and human resource costs, are similar for big and small loans, a bigger loan will incur lower cost *per transaction*. Therefore, notwithstanding the fact that lending to the poor—if conducted with the right incentives—can be commercially viable (as international microfinance experience has amply demonstrated), there is a degree of tradeoff and therefore contradiction between increasing profitability and reaching out to poor agricultural households.

While credit cooperatives are expected to operate on the basis of profit maximization on the one hand, they have to shoulder the responsibility of supporting the agricultural sector and farmers' livelihoods on the other. RCC loan officers were given no clear signal what their priorities should be. This meant local party bosses were still able to influence lending, and loan officers could blame perennial losses on the policy of supporting the agricultural community.

In spite of that, in the absence of effective audit systems, loan officers often "cook the books" to inflate profitability or polish their performance to please their superiors. Such prohibited practices are more common in RCCs than in commercial banks, which are subject to stricter regulations.[31] A common tactic is the "rolling over" or "ever-greening" of loans if a borrower is unable to repay the loan when the term is due. This has two variants. Under one, called *jiexin huanjiu*, the lender issues the borrower a new loan, the principal of which is then used to repay the old loan. Under the other, called *zhuandai*, the lender demands only interest payments from the borrower while postponing the payment date.[32] When asked whether they conducted such practices, all of my RCC interviewees confirmed that they used to, and roughly half conceded that they still do. It is noteworthy that in China, unlike in industrialized countries, borrowers do not have to repay any principal until the end of the loan term, thus postponing the risk of delinquency. These are frequently referred to as "bullet" loans.[33]

The Central Bank's Supervision of the Banking Sector

Though established to regulate and supervise China's banking sector, the capacity of the PBoC or CBRC to carry out its task is weak, for several reasons. First, whereas elsewhere risk management is considered the cornerstone of financial supervision, in the Chinese context "banking supervision" traditionally denotes *regulatory compliance* and *points-of-entry assessment*. As a result, banking supervision in China consists primarily of official approval of new banking institutions or new business activities of existing banks, or of assessments of senior candidates' professional qualification prior to their appointments.[34] It therefore did not traditionally involve paying much attention to credit risk (the risk that borrowers will fail to fulfill the credit contract), operational risk (risk of losses due to poor corporate governance, inadequate internal controls, and operating procedures), or liquidity risk (arising from insufficient liquidity to meet contractual obligations).[35] As a result, bank officers, including the officers of RCCs, were subject to lax supervision, and credit managers were not systematically held accountable for unsound financial decisions.

The organizational structure of the banking sector regulator is also exceedingly inadequate for supervising RCCs. The organizational networks of the PBoC/CBRC are concentrated in provincial capitals and prefectures; they do not penetrate below the county level. County-level PBoC/CBRC offices are typically staffed by three to four people, who handle all bank branches (state-owned, commercial-shareholding banks, and RCCs) within the jurisdiction. However, the overwhelming majority of RCCs are at the township level, one level below the county. This makes on-site financial supervision, essential for ensuring banks' sound internal control and operating procedures, an almost impossible task.

The misuse of agricultural on-lending by some credit cooperatives provides a stark illustration of the central bank's lack of organizational capacity and resources for supervising RCCs. In principle, RCCs have to report regularly to the regulatory authority on the borrowers of the agricultural on-lending scheme, in order to ensure that the subsidized loans are used only for agricultural purposes. However, in many cases, agricultural loans were diverted to nonagricultural purposes. In many other cases, RCCs "rolled over" loan repayments in an attempt to reduce the nonperforming loan rates appearing on the books.[36] Such cases could be uncovered only by on-site supervision; they went unnoticed when supervision consisted primarily of an examination of the books.[37]

Most importantly, the PBoC or CBRC lacks disciplinary power in most cases of financial mismanagement. Because almost all senior bankers are party members, the substantial majority of financial fraud cases are handled by the Chinese Communist Party's (CCP) anticorruption watchdog—the party discipline inspection committees—within the banking institutions. Cases serious enough to be considered criminal are handed over to the police. As a result, despite the regulator's technical know-how and access to banks' accounts, it partakes in disciplinary action when its expertise is sought by the CCP, or in areas left in a vacuum by the political institutions. Obviously, this robs the industry watchdog of a strong deterrent.[38]

In addition, before the financial sector reform introduced by the former premier Zhu Rongji in the mid-1990s, appointments to central bank positions at the local level rested with local party secretaries. Local authorities were therefore often able to force the central bank offices at the local level to revise their credit ceilings upward, fueling inflationary pressure. This lack of independence from local governments has been blamed for eroding the PBoC's control over monetary policy and is therefore considered one of the causes of macroeconomic instability and inflation during the 1980s and early 1990s.[39]

The central government has made changes to the central bank's organizational structure meant to distance it from local administrative influence. Specifically, it replaced the provincial central bank bureaus with nine cross-provincial regional offices, which do not have corresponding regional administrative authorities. This change, however, has been criticized as no more than cosmetic. More importantly, this organizational restructuring did not augment the PBoC or CBRC's organizational capacity below the prefecture level. As a result, this organizational restructuring had little effect on the central bank's capacity to supervise RCCs.[40]

Provincial RCC Unions and Multiple RCC Models

The 2003–5 restructuring introduced a few improvements in RCCs' corporate governance structure that made them subject to less suasion by township party committees, but the CCP's weight on the credit institutions remains pervasive. The restructuring transformed RCCs into one of three models: rural commercial bank, rural cooperative bank, or the original RCC model. (For more information on these models, see chapter 2.) With the exception of a few in the poor central and western regions that have retained the original RCC model, the independent legal entity status of most township RCCs has been abolished. Instead, they became branches of county unions. Consequently, most township RCCs lost the power to make lending decisions (particularly those involving large sums), which became centralized at the county level.

Moreover, in the new models, there is more power sharing. In RCCs, the head of the BoD, formally in charge of the RCC, used to take care of both strategic decision making and day-to-day operations. In the new rural cooperative banks and rural commercial banks these functions have been split, with the newly established bank governor's office taking over daily operational decisions.

Furthermore, in the new system, the provincial unions have taken over supervisory and personnel management functions previously performed by local offices of the PBoC. Currently, RCC personnel are appointed by county and provincial unions, subject to assessments of professional qualifications by the CBRC and to approval by local party committees. Though township or county party secretaries no longer have veto power over personnel matters, they still need to be consulted before any appointment is made. Their influence may have waned, but it has by no means dissipated.

The most disturbing facet of the new system is the persistence of CCP institutions within the organizations. The internal party committee still reigns supreme in such areas of personnel (*yongren*) and finance (*yongqian*) as employees' remuneration and big expenditure items. The BoS and party disciplinary inspection committee (*jilv jiancha weiyuan hui*) that are supposed to supervise the head of the BoD are still rather ineffective. Because members of the BoS and party disciplinary inspection committee are inferior to the head of the BoD in party ranking, and because their career advancement is very much determined by the head of the BoD, these institutions cannot be expected to keep a check on abuse of power by the head of the BoD.[41]

RCCs' Institutional Structure as Compared with the State-Owned Banks

RCCs' institutional structure makes them more susceptible to local-government influence than are the state-owned banks, such as the Industrial and Commerical Bank of China (ICBC) or the ABC. As a result, local authorities' influence over local branches of the state-owned banks is relatively *weaker* as compared to their influence over RCCs.

As shown in figure 3.6, prior to the 2003–5 reform, each township credit cooperative was an independent cost center or a legal entity responsible for its own profit and loss (*zifu yingkui*). By contrast, the state-owned banks have a vertical institutional structure extending from the county, prefecture and province all the way up to the center. All state-owned bank offices are branches of the headquarters or the independent cost center in Beijing. Moreover, branch managers of the state-owned banks have to report to their superiors on asset quality and nonperforming loan ratios. By contrast, township credit cooperatives, being independent cost centers, did not need to answer to anyone about their financial performance.

In short, this lack of a vertical reporting line above the county level (prior to the establishment of the provincial unions in 2003–5) rendered RCCs more vulnerable to local-government influence. This by no means implies that the state-owned banks are immune from local-government interference in lending

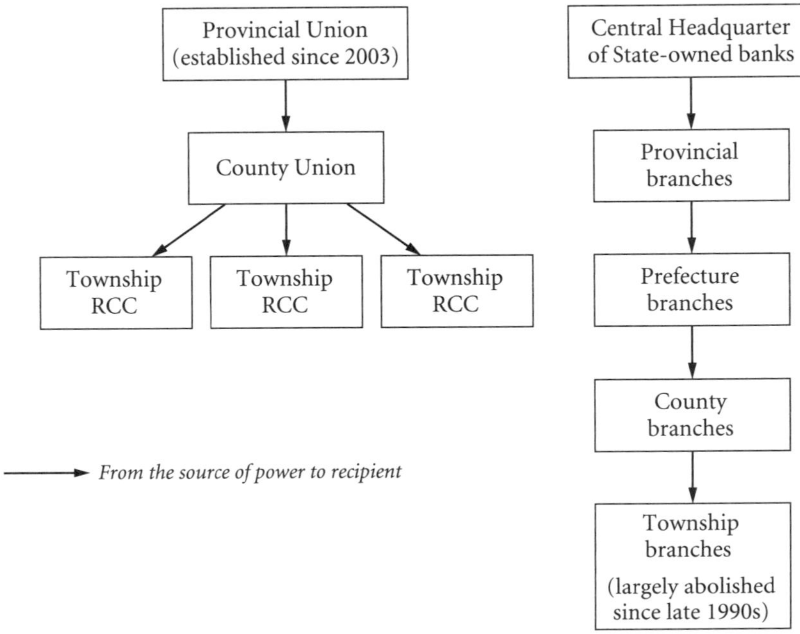

FIGURE 3.6 Institutional hierarchy of RCCs vs. state-owned banks

decisions. In fact, a number of existing studies have pointed to political meddling in lending within the state banking system.[42] But the credit cooperatives were and are still *more* susceptible to local-government influence *in comparison* to local branches of the state banks.

Another fundamental difference between RCCs and the state-owned banks has to do with loan approval rights. Township credit cooperatives had the exclusive power to approve loans. With the exception of big loans, which require approval from county unions, township credit cooperatives still have loan-approval power now. By contrast, township branches of the four state-owned banks were largely abolished in the late 1990s by the central government in an effort to save costs. For instance, the remaining ABC branches found in large and industrialized townships only take deposits.[43] Further, county branches of the state-owned banks have limited lending power; they have to refer large loans to the prefecture level or above. Additionally, grassroots credit cooperatives are subject to fewer restrictions compared to the state-owned banks in loan-approval thresholds.[44] Thresholds for loan approval rights differ from one locale to another and from one financial institution to another, though generally industrialized areas tend to see higher thresholds being granted to lower-level branch managers.

Rural Cooperative Foundations (RCFs)

The other major rural credit institutions in China were RCFs (*nongcun hezuo jijinghui*). RCFs were informal credit institutions established by local governments—largely townships—in the mid-1980s. They were informal because they were *not* officially regulated by the central bank.[45] RCFs were shut down by the central government in 1999.

RCFs were set up and managed by grassroots authorities. Most RCFs were established by township or village governments' economic organizations (*xiangcun jiti jingji zuzhi*), effectively under the control of township governments and village cadres. Initially, they were set up for the purpose of amassing collective funds and household savings in order to stem the outflow of rural savings to urban state-owned enterprises and to channel capital into income-generating agricultural activities.[46] After fiscal recentralization in 1994, some county governments set up RCFs to finance local economic development given their declining shares of fiscal revenue.[47] During the 1980s and 1990s there were massive outflows of financial savings from rural to urban areas within the mainstream banking system, most of which were used to finance inefficient state-owned industrial enterprises as described in chapter 2. Though falling short of giving them an official blessing, the central government tacitly approved the formation of RCFs, believing they would be able to channel some farmers' savings into rural development.[48] However, not all RCF funds were invested in income-generating activities, and some had lined the pockets of township and village officials, which was a major reason for their eventual closure. Audits of RCF accounts show that the negative effects from the abuse of their funds far outweighed the positive impacts they had generated.

RCFs' start-up capital came mainly from collective funds (*jiti zijin*) of township and village governments. However, their subsequent growth and an overwhelming proportion of their capital came from the hard-earned savings of farm households. RCFs were able to attract savings because they were not regulated by the central bank and therefore were able to offer higher interest rates to depositors than the official credit institutions did. The credit foundations' ability to attract farmers' savings was further aided by the perception that they were backed by the central government and therefore deposits into them carried an implicit government guarantee.[49] The spread of RCFs was not uniform across the country; in locales where local governments were not satisfied with the ability of formal banking institutions in meeting credit demands, RCFs were likely to be set up, but the reverse was true when credit needs were met by formal institutions.[50] By the 1990s, RCFs had grown to become the single largest informal credit institutions ever established in China, rivaling the formal RCCs. In 1996 there were twenty-one thousand township-based credit foundations with total deposits surpassing 150 billion yuan, about one-eighth of the 800 billion yuan held by the official and more established forty thousand RCCs nationwide.[51]

The central government eventually shut down the credit foundations because their fund shortages were so serious they threatened social stability in the countryside. In the late 1990s, there were bank runs on some RCFs in Sichuan and Hebei provinces. In some locales these bank runs grew to such a massive scale that social and political stability were put at risk. In addition, since the credit foundations, not unlike RCCs, carried an implicit central government guarantee, the failure of these RCFs put the central government's credibility at stake. The central government's concern over the financial turmoil was also partly driven by the poignant lesson of the 1997 Asian Financial Crisis, which, aside from economic hardship, also brought down the authoritarian Suharto regime in Indonesia. As a result, the central government intervened to resolve this situation in 1999 by closing down all RCFs nationwide and ordering the honoring of all household deposits.[52] The closure was accompanied by audits of RCFs' accounts, which revealed serious problems with nonperforming assets and misuse of funds by local governments.[53]

Patterns of RCFs' Lending

Data on the credit foundations is inherently difficult to obtain, not only because the institutions no longer exist, but also because the official record keepers (namely, the provincial Ministry of Agriculture agencies) are not willing to share data that show pervasive abuse of funds. The data presented here were obtained from my study in Sichuan province, supplemented where appropriate by secondary statistics from published works. Owing to RCFs' local nature, no national data exists for the institutions as a whole.

In Sichuan, one of the provinces where the credit foundations were most widespread, direct loans to local governments and government-related departments accounted for nearly one-fifth of total RCFs' loans. More than half of the credit foundations' loans in Sichuan were directed to township authorities, most of which could not be recovered. Table 3.3 shows the consolidated accounts of the RCFs in Sichuan after deposit honoring. Township enterprises and governments were the top and third-highest recipients of loans, accounting for 35.6 percent and 13.1 percent of the total, respectively, while lending to rural households accounted for about a quarter of the total loans. All loans allocated *directly* and *indirectly* to local governments constituted *no less than half* of the credit foundations' loan portfolios, as shown in the table. Further, recovery rates for these loans were much lower compared to household loans. While loans to house-

TABLE 3.3 Sichuan province RCFs' consolidated accounts: After deposits honoring (as of December 31, 1999)

	MILLION YUAN	%
Net fixed assets	551	
Total credit/loans	**9,584.70**	
of which:		
Township enterprises' loans	3,416.80	*35.6*
Households' loans	2,611.00	*27.2*
Governments' loans	1,255.90	*13.1*
Other departments' loans	1,152.30	*12.0*
Education departments' loans	343.9	*3.6*
Village group collectives' loans	322.8	*3.4*
Agricultural organizations' loans	269.8	*2.8*
Transport departments' loans	99.1	*1.0*
Health departments' loans	18.3	*0.2*
Total government-related loans	6,878.90	*71.8*
Total debt/liabilities (million yuan)	**16,128.80**	
Members' shares (individual)	5,520.90	*34.2*
Borrowings from central government	5,500.00	*34.1*
Borrowings from provincial ministry of finance	1,652.50	*10.2*
Borrowings from work units and individuals	863.5	*5.4*
Borrowings from extrabudgetary funds (*yusuanwai zijin*)	848.8	*5.3*
Members' shares (collective)	780.0	*4.8*
Commissioned funds (collective)	506.2	*3.1*
Loans from financial organizations	286.3	*1.8*
Commissioned funds (*daiguan zijin*)(individual)	170.5	*1.1*
Total recovered loans	**1,191.10**	
Households	651.9	*54.7*
Township enterprises	233.8	*19.6*
Governments	137.2	*11.5*
Education departments	49.2	*4.1*
Agricultural organizations	43.6	*3.7*
Village group collectives	37.3	*3.1*
Transport departments	29.5	*2.5*
Cultural departments	5.2	*0.4*
Health departments	3.3	*0.3*

Source: Sichuan Ministry of Agriculture (the base of the former Sichuan Rural Cooperative Management Station).

holds accounted for 27.2 percent of the total loan portfolios, they constituted 54.7 percent of the total recovered loans (table 3.3). By contrast, while township enterprise loans took up more than one-third of total loans, they accounted for only one-fifth of total recovered loans.

Local authorities, the de facto owners and managers of RCFs, were clearly not in a position to honor all deposits, suggesting they had grossly mismanaged and misallocated funds. Table 3.4 indicates that total deposits, 30.7 billion yuan, were roughly the size of the total asset value, inclusive of loans. Two-thirds of the credit foundations' assets were loans; and half of the loans—amounting to 10.8 billion yuan—were officially classified as nonperforming. That meant that even in the best-case scenario—had RCFs been able to recover *all* performing loans (10.6 billion yuan), and *all* the non-loan assets could be liquidated (10.2 billion yuan)—the credit foundations would be able to honor only two-thirds of the deposits! This indicates that the central government's decision to honor *only* individual depositors, but not enterprises or collectives, was not solely a political decision for fear of rural unrest. It was also a decision borne out of necessity.

Evidence suggests Sichuan was not the only province where RCF funds had been siphoned off to local government–related borrowers. Audits of credit foundations in Hebei province in 1998 revealed that loans to township and village enterprises accounted for 40 percent of total equity. Over 90 percent of such loans were a result of township governments' directives. Unsurprisingly, most of the

TABLE 3.4 Sichuan province RCFs' consolidated accounts: Before deposits honoring (as of March 16, 1999)*

	MILLION YUAN	%
Total assets	31,620.00	
Total loans/credit	21,460.00	
of which:		
Households	7,960.00	37.1
Enterprise	6,760.00	31.5
Government and government-related units	3,850.00	17.9
Village collectives and agriculture service organizations *of which*:	2,890.00	13.5
Nonperforming loans	10,840.00	50.5
Performing loans	10,620.00	49.5
Total deposits/liabilities (million yuan)	30,680.00	
of which:		
Individuals	25,690.00	83.7
(members' share)	(21560.0)	(70.3)
Village collectives and agriculture service organizations	4,130.00	13.5

Source: Sichuan Ministry of Agriculture (the base of the former Sichuan Rural Cooperative Management Station).

*The consolidated accounts are as provided to the author by the source. Readers may notice that total loans are only two-thirds of total assets. The other one-third of assets is unaccounted for, which further illustrates the inadequate management and nontransparent nature of the organizations.

loans could not be recovered. A portion of the RCFs' funds was also siphoned off by township governments to finance public infrastructure, such as road-building and construction of schools and hospitals. Some local authorities even went to the extent of channeling funds to make up for their fiscal shortfalls (*dianshui*).[54] A separate audit conducted on RCFs in Hebei province revealed similar *dianshui* behavior of local officials for the purpose of meeting revenue targets set by higher-level governments.[55]

Notwithstanding the primary data presented here, it is worth mentioning that a study has found RCFs to have prevented fund outflows from rural areas and reduced demand for usurious loans.[56] Some economists' surveys, particularly those conducted in the early 1990s, tend to suggest that RCFs had relatively good financial performance and improved financial intermediation by raising the proportion of lending to rural households.[57] Considering the liquidity problem throughout the late 1990s that led eventually to the bank runs, however, these studies capture RCFs' performance only in their early stage.

Accountability

Local governments were able to manipulate RCFs' financial resources, for two reasons: First, the credit foundations were managed by agricultural economic management stations (*nongye jingji guanlizhan*), which local governments directly control. Second, the RCFs were *not* regulated or supervised by any third party.

RCFs' corporate governance structure was grossly inadequate for checking abuse of power by management. The credit foundations were managed by the Ministry of Agriculture (MoA) apparatus, from the provincial level to agricultural bureaus at prefectures and counties, and extending to agricultural economic management stations at townships. The MoA apparatus at each administrative level reports to the respective local governments. Township credit foundations were managed by heads of agricultural economic management stations (*zhanzhang*), who were part of township government bureaucracies. Payrolls of heads of agricultural stations were directly determined by township party secretaries.[58] In addition, the board of directors to whom RCF managers were accountable was headed by township heads or township finance bureau directors (both are leading cadres of township authorities).[59]

Being informal credit institutions unregulated by the central bank, RCFs gave local authorities better credit access than did formal credit institutions, such as RCCs. Because RCFs were not regulated or supervised by any third party, they were not subject to any interest rate, capital adequacy, or minimum reserve requirement. In addition, their informal status meant that local governments could borrow *directly* from RCFs, which they could not do with RCCs.

Other factors also contributed to RCFs' high nonperforming asset rates. Because managers were township cadres, they usually had no previous training in banking or experience in running a credit institution. Supervision by the Ministry of Agriculture apparatus also did little to provide RCFs with professional industry knowledge or experience.

The collapse of the collective township and village enterprises during the late 1990s also precipitated RCFs' downfall. The lion's share of the credit foundations' capital was lent to these collective enterprises. Therefore, the declining profitability of these enterprises during the late 1990s, and the collapse and privatization of some of them, all contributed to RCFs' deteriorating loan performance. When such enterprises closed shop, their loans became unrecoverable and their liquidated assets could barely cover the principal. When such enterprises were sold, usually at discounted prices and to insiders, the new owners usually refused to take responsibility for the loans. Additionally, given the change in their fiscal incentives during the late 1990s from revenue-based to profit-based, local governments were eager to quickly dispose of their financial responsibility over hemorrhaging enterprises. Even though the unpaid loans ended up decaying their equity bases, RCFs' financial losses did not become evident until they had difficulties fulfilling requests for withdrawals. Until bank runs began to occur, RCFs' financial sustainability was a less urgent concern for local authorities than was the selling of loss-making enterprises.

When central policymakers ordered RCFs to close in 1999, they put the blame for the financial fiasco squarely on township authorities and made them take ultimate responsibility for cleaning up the mess. The State Council's Document No. 3, issued in 1999, specified that "the local governments are responsible for taking the necessary actions to protect the legal rights of farmer depositors, and to maintain social stability in the countryside." Township authorities had to scrounge for funds in order to honor deposits, and these outstanding loans are financial liabilities for them to this day. Table 3.3 shows that, to honor deposits made to RCFs in Sichuan, local authorities had to borrow from various sources, including the central government (5.5 billion yuan), the provincial ministry of finance (1.6 billion yuan), various work units (864 million yuan), and extra-budgetary funds (849 million yuan).[60] In spite of that, 5.5 billion yuan of deposits by rural households remained outstanding and unhonored as of December 31, 1999. RCFs' remaining liabilities, inclusive of unhonored deposits and borrowings from various sources, in turn became the debts of township authorities. Case studies in chapter 6 provide finer details of the RCF fiasco.

While RCCs' dual accountability or *tiao-kuai* system entails their reporting to two masters with conflicting goals and objectives, the local party committee wields more influence than does RCCs' functional superiors or the central bank. Horizontal accountability to local party committees is an inherent feature of the Chinese political system, designed to enable the party to exert control over economy and society. When RCCs were organized under the ABC, the vertical line of accountability was particularly weak. It also did not help to ensure that RCCs' capital was used efficiently, because the state-owned bank was more interested in exploiting RCCs' resources to its own ends. When the central bank took over management control from the state bank in 1996, RCCs' operations became more professionalized, and local party committees' veto power on personnel matters was abrogated. Nevertheless, RCCs remained largely localized credit institutions that lacked a strong vertical responsibility system. Compounding the problem were the conflicting goals imposed on the credit cooperatives by the central government. Until today, RCCs are not given a clear and defined message as to whether their priority is to maximize profits or to support the agricultural community.

RCCs' vulnerability to influence and suasion by local government becomes even more pronounced when their institutional structure is compared to that of the state-owned banks' local branches. Throughout the 1980s and most of the 1990s, township credit cooperatives were independent cost centers that did not have to answer to anyone regarding their lack of profitability or perennial losses. By contrast, all local offices of the state-owned banks are merely branches of the independent cost center in Beijing. As a result, the state-owned banks have a vertical reporting system that extends from the county all the way to the center.

Given RCCs' institutional design, it is no wonder that the lion's share of their loans were allocated to local government–related projects, as shown in chapter 2. As for RCFs, local governments could gain direct access to their capital because they were directly managed by local cadres and were not subject to central regulation. The next chapter explores political and financial incentives of local political leaders to shed further light on why they interfere in lending.

4

THE IMPLICATIONS OF CADRE EVALUATION AND FISCAL SYSTEM FOR LOCAL-GOVERNMENT BEHAVIOR

Local-government interference in lending operations can be explained through an analysis of political institutional design. Specifically, the Chinese Communist Party (CCP)'s cadre evaluation system and the fiscal system combine to create overpowering individual and collective incentives for local government to pursue local industrialization and to maximize revenue *at all costs*. Rural credit cooperatives (RCCs), due to their weak corporate governance structure (as detailed in chapter 2), became easy targets for local officials ravenous for financial resources. The central government seeks to control lower-level officials by setting binding quantifiable performance targets for them. But this outcome-oriented oversight is undermined by the fact that the central government cannot control the process through which these hard targets are achieved. Local-government interference in credit operations thus becomes an unintended consequence of the systemic demands embedded in China's political institutions.

Cadre Evaluation and the Drive toward Local Industrialization and Revenue Maximization

After the launch of market-oriented reforms in the early 1980s, institutional incentives replaced Maoist ideology as the central government's key instrument for attaining compliance from local authorities. After embarking on liberal economic reforms, Deng Xiaoping could no longer rely on ideology to ensure the center's orders were carried out by local governments in far-flung regions. Institutional mechanisms and incentives were therefore needed. The *nomenklatura* system became the most significant of these mechanisms.

The *nomenklatura* system is an essential feature of the CCP's political institutional design. It allows the party to manage and control the appointment, promotion, transfer, and removal of all leading cadres (*lingdao ganbu*). Through the *nomenklatura* system, higher-level governments are able to create effective incentives for lower-level officials to align their interests with those of higher-level governments. Party organization departments maintain confidential dossiers (*dang'an*) on senior personnel at lower administrative levels.[1] Leading cadres at the township level, which include the party secretary, the government head, and all those who are ranked second-section (*fu keji*) and above,[2] are controlled and managed by a county party organization department. Ordinary cadres—officials who do not occupy leadership positions—are managed separately, by a county government personnel department (*renshibu*) under the civil service *bianzhi* system.[3]

Between 1980 and 1984, the party employed a "two-ranks-down" system of managing local officials. Under this system, the central organization department appointed leading cadres in the provinces (one rank down from the center) and prefectures (two ranks down from the center), the provinces appointed those in prefectures and counties, the prefectures appointed those at the county and township levels, and the counties appointed leading cadres in townships. This enabled central party officials to control leading officials in provinces and prefectures while leaving the prefectures to control the massive numbers of officials in rural counties and townships. The intention of this relative decentralization was to enable central party officials to retain control of party cadres while reducing the party's enormous costs in monitoring all cadres. However, the system also created overlaps in responsibilities between two party committees that had power over officials who were one level below.[4] It was also undercut by information asymmetries between party superiors and subordinates who are two ranks down.

As a result, the "two ranks down" system encountered difficulties in implementation and high transaction costs and was therefore replaced with a "one rank down" system in 1984, which operates to this day. Under this system, township leading cadres are controlled and managed by the county party organization department (*zuzhibu*), county leading cadres by the prefecture, those of the prefecture by the province, and those of the province by the central party organizational department.

Though the current system is more decentralized than its predecessor, it still allows the center to effectively acquire local compliance to its policies and priorities. In principal-agent terms, the current cadre management system constitutes a chain of principal-agent relationships. The central leadership is the principal and the provinces the agent in the first chain, with the provinces being the principal and the prefectures the agent in the second chain, and so forth. The Beijing-level principal appoints the provincial-level agent who is most likely to follow through with Beijing's goals and priorities, and the provincial-level principal in turn does the same with its prefecture-level agent. Thus, targets and objectives set by the center are eventually rolled down to, and therefore followed by, grassroots officials.[5]

The cadre responsibility system (*gangwei zerenzhi*) was instituted by the CCP in the late 1980s as an additional instrument for central leadership to exercise control over lower-level cadres. It is also still in force today. Under the cadre responsibility system, leading cadres sign performance contracts with their immediate superiors (for example, township leading cadres sign performance contracts with their counties) in which they pledge to attain certain quantified targets. These targets reflect three broad goals of the central government—economic growth, social stability, and party building. The cadre responsibility system thereby provides strong incentives for leading cadres to work toward these goals.

However, leading cadres' performance targets (*kaohe zhibiao*) are not all equal. Rather, these targets are divided into three types, representing their significance in the eyes of the central government. One type is "veto targets" (*yipiao foujue*), such as maintaining social order. Failure to achieve a "veto target" means an overall failing assessment for the official, even if a township scores high on other criteria. However, achieving "veto targets" does not guarantee bonus compensation or career advancement. The veto targets are thus a necessary but *not* a sufficient condition for a successful political career in the CCP.

The other two types of targets are "hard targets" (*ying zhibiao*) and "soft or ordinary targets" (*yiban zhibiao*). "Hard targets" are quantifiable binding targets, such as tax revenue. "Soft targets" are non-binding targets that are more difficult to measure and quantify, such as health-care provision, cultural development, and social development. The "hard targets" are the determining factors in leading cadres' career prospects: those who score high on these binding targets are politically and financially rewarded, while those with dismal performance are not. As a result, the "hard targets" command far more attention and effort from cadres than do "soft targets," even though the latter are pivotal to broader social development in the long run.

Faced with immense pressure to meet revenue targets, local leaders often pass these targets on to bureaus in their jurisdictions. If a township is required by the county to generate 500,000 yuan of extra income in the coming year, the township party committee may require each township bureau to meet a target of 50,000 yuan, even if most of these departments' primary function is to provide services, such as education or agriculture, rather than generate income. Like the local leaders themselves, the leading cadres in the bureaus will also be awarded a bonus if they meet the performance indicators.[6] In this way economic growth or revenue targets set by central leadership become concrete deliverables that officials in subordinate administrative levels have a personal incentive to meet.

Owing to the service orientation of most government agencies, local officials must often turn to end users to generate revenue. Before 2002, when such service fees and fines were abolished, local government agencies in rural areas tried to increase revenue through various agriculture and education surcharges, township and village levies, fees and fundraising for road or school construction or other projects, and other "peasant burdens" that fostered widespread rural discontent.[7]

In addition to performance evaluation by their superiors, local leaders are also officially subject to "democratic appraisals," intended as an institutional response to social demand for a more transparent and accountable civil service. However, this appraisal system falls short of fulfilling this intention. Lack of guidelines as to who should partake in these appraisals leaves the choice of respondents in the hands of the organization department or party superiors. As a result, those who are at odds with the candidates being appraised are usually excluded from appraisals.[8] Traditional respect toward authority also inhibits appraisers from giving frank and open comments about the candidates. It is therefore unsurprising that many local leaders with known corrupt behavior and illicit dealings still manage to pass the appraisals. This, of course, renders the peer-review process far less important than performance evaluation by superiors in determining the political advancement of leading cadres.

The Cadre Management System in the Studied Townships

Since cadre evaluation criteria reflect the three separate central-government priorities in rural China (economic growth, social stability, and party building), evaluations tend to be complex and tedious. For example, in a Zhejiang township where I conducted fieldwork, the thirty-page description of evaluation criteria received from the county party organization department was broken down into over a hundred pages detailing each evaluation target, the respective departments and cadres in charge, and different ways of improving the scores.[9] The criteria are broadly divided into three major categories: (a) economic growth indicators, namely, fiscal receipts, farmers' income growth, investment attraction, and size of the private economy; (b) social and cultural development indicators, including social stability indicated by the number of petitions and incidents of social unrest, development of the rule of law, and environmental protection; and (c) party development indicators, such as inculcation of party ideology and development of party organization (see the appendix to this chapter for the detailed evaluation targets).

Analyses of the evaluation criteria from a number of townships with different resources, settings, and characteristics underscore the criteria's blanket overemphasis of gross domestic product (GDP) and industrial growth.[10] As the social and economic indicators in table 4.1 suggest, the four townships in my fieldwork sample located across Zhejiang, Shandong, and Hebei provinces vastly differ in income per capita, proximity to an urban center, economic structure, and natural resources. And yet, the "hard targets" for revenue and industrial development are almost identical across the townships.[11]

TABLE 4.1 Basic economic indicators and cadre evaluation criteria of four townships

	ZEN	HAN	SUN	FAN
		BASIC ECONOMIC INDICATORS		
Population (thousands)	190	38.7	39.2	7
Income per capita (yuan)	8,255	5,000	3,900	2,800
Land area (sq. km)	63	—	98.5	—
Population density (per sq. km)	3,020	—	398.0	—
Revenue (million yuan)	90.3	32.1	12.8	2.4
Revenue per capita (yuan)	753	828	327	338
Distance from county seat (km)	31	6	20	15
Provincial location	Zhejiang	Shandong	Shandong	Hebei
Natural resources	—	—	—	Phosphorus, iron
Main industries	Shoe making, manufactures of air compressors, scrap iron factories	Commercial production of vegetable oils; machinery production	Animal husbandry (some commercial), household cotton and wheat growing	Small retail businesses; household cotton and wheat growing, small-scale almond processing
Number of township enterprises	1,146	500	40	3
GDP ratio				
Primary	*21.4%*	*11.0%*	*35.0%*	*40.5%*
Secondary	*50.6%*	*67.0%*	*48.0%*	*18.0%*
Tertiary	*28.0%*	*22.0%*	*17.0%*	*41.5%*

	ZEN	HAN	SUN	FAN
	CADRE EVALUATION CRITERIA			
Priority targets with veto power *(yipiao fojue)*	Population control Social stability Petition cases Revenue Industrial production Amount of investment attracted	Population control Workplace safety Revenue Industrial production Amount of investment attracted	Workplace safety Amount of investment attracted Revenue Industrial production	Population control Social stability Petition cases Revenue Industrial production
Hard targets *(ying zhibiao)*	Number of large industrial enterprises Number of industrial parks Farmers' income Education and health-care provisions	Size of private economy Farmers' income	Size of private economy Farmers' income	Amount of investment attracted Farmers' income Agricultural development
Soft targets *(yiban zhibiao)*	Grassroots organization development Cultural and social development	Education and health-care provisions Social stability Petition cases Grassroots organization development Cultural and social development	Education and health-care provisions Social stability Petition cases Grassroots organization development Cultural and social development	Forestry conservation Cultural and social development

Sources: Social and economic indicators are from the respective townships' websites, county yearbooks, and interviews with township finance bureaus; cadre evaluation criteria are from interviews with various township party secretaries, township heads, or organization departments.

The imposition of industrial production and amount of investment attracted as "hard targets" on Zen and Han townships may be justified given that they are largely industrial locales, as evidenced by industry's share of GDP in each. But, the same industrial targets are unrealistic for the largely agricultural Sun and Fan townships. Close to half of the population in the two agricultural locales are still wheat and cotton growers. Since they are distant from any urban center, it is difficult to imagine how they might acquire skilled labor or technical know-how, or how they might bring manufactured products to large consumer markets. Yet, the cold reality remains: unless leading cadres in these locales are able to add revenue, pump out ever more industrial products, and attract higher investments every year, their careers will stall and their financial rewards will be significantly less than those of their peers who meet the targets.

The "veto targets" common across all townships studied were upholding social stability, increasing workplace safety, minimizing petition cases, and observing the one-child policy. As previously mentioned, meeting these criteria constitutes a necessary but not a sufficient condition for local leaders' career advancement. A noteworthy exception is the fact that amount of investment attracted, commonly a "hard target," was a "veto target" in Sun township. The agricultural-based Sun was the shining star in Zouping county during the 1980s and 1990s, when other townships in the county were still destitute. However, in the last decade, when local industrialization began to spread elsewhere in the county, Sun was overtaken by neighboring townships, such as Han. Hence, the unusually strong emphasis placed on industrial investments in Sun can be seen as the township's playing catch-up.[12]

While economic growth factors are "hard targets" crucial to career advancement, such factors as farmers' income, provision of education and health care, and social and cultural developments are classified as non-binding "soft targets." This is despite the fact that these factors have direct and immediate impacts, as well as long-term implications, for rural living standards and rural development. This sends an unequivocal signal to local officials that these criteria are not their priorities and are undeserving of any major efforts.

The cadre evaluation system also creates enormous pressure for leading cadres to compete with their peers from other townships. In a Zhejiang county where I conducted studies, all sixteen townships in the county are ranked, from the best to the worst, in terms of their performance in increasing receipts, investment in industrial activities, actual amount of investment attracted, and other economic growth indicators. The ranking results are widely circulated by the county government to the townships as part of the cadre evaluation information. In the county meetings, the townships' leading cadres are seated according to their respective ranking, reflecting their hierarchy in "political achievements," as measured by these indicators.[13]

While local leaders are thereby pressured into competition with each other, there is little difference in the types of industrial companies they can promote or attract. Whether or not the industries are capital or labor-intensive, or high or low value-added, is of secondary concern as long as they are capable of bringing in investment.[14] This partly explains the rapid proliferation of factories from the same type of industry in neighboring townships, such as the cluster of shoe factories in Zen township, or coal and sulphur mining in SC1 county in Sichuan province to such an extent that these factories compete merely on cost terms. This "me too" industrial strategy seems particularly impractical for townships with no obvious geographical advantage. Attracting investment is inherently more difficult in remote locations when every single town is pursuing an undifferentiated "me too" strategy.

Short-Term Opportunistic Behavior and Outcome Orientation of the Evaluation System

These over-meticulous evaluation criteria resulted in leading cadres working for the sake of meeting the quantitative targets rather than to improve the lives of local residents.[15] When cadres come under intense evaluation pressure, they focus on short-term observable "political achievements" (*zhengji*), such as the construction of grand office buildings, industrial parks, roads, and bridges. This comes at the expense of devoting energy and resources to activities that bring long-term benefits to the community, such as investment in health care, education, and other less visible social services.[16]

Moreover, frequent rotations and promotions of leading cadres also fuel short-term opportunistic behavior. Higher-level governments have used the frequent turnover of lower-level cadres, who are usually rotated every two to three years, to help curb local factionalism.[17] While this may help align the preferences of lower-level authorities to those of higher-level authorities, it also encourages short-term opportunism by creating short-term horizons among cadres. The leading cadres are interested in the welfare of the constituents only for the short time they remain leaders of the locales.[18]

This short-term opportunism underlines a fundamental flaw with the outcome orientation of the cadre evaluation system. The evaluation system does *not* assess leading cadres according to the process by which they achieve the outcome. In other words, leading cadres are rewarded, politically and financially, as long as they have brought about x amount of increase in receipts and y amount of investment, even if they have achieved this by incurring *z* amount of debt—with *z* being greater than the sum of *x* and *y*. This was how a township party secretary described his predecessors:

> Since cadres are assessed only by their achieved targets at day-end, rather than how much resources have been deployed to bring about the outcome, some of us borrow money from banks and other available sources to build industrial parks, develop town squares in order to showcase our "political achievements." In the first two years as the township party secretary, I have been trying to resolve the debts my predecessors have accumulated and left behind after being promoted to county-level positions.[19]

In other words, there is for leading cadres an intertemporal dimension to enjoying the benefits and suffering the consequences of economic growth. As a result, the outcome orientation of the cadre evaluation system has contributed to mounting local-government indebtedness in rural China, an important issue examined further in the Conclusion. Had the amount of debt incurred during the cadre's tenure, or the costs of achieving the targets, been included in the evaluation criteria, leading cadres would have been more reluctant to spend at the expense of future generations.

In appearance, then, China has undergone considerable administrative decentralization, to the point of running the risk of runaway provinces, and in the worst-case scenario even of the disintegration of the Middle Kingdom.[20] Nonetheless, its system still stands in stark contrast to democratic polities.[21] The *nomenklatura* system still allows higher-level governments to appoint local leaders of their choice, and the cadre evaluation system in turn enables the center to align local leaders' priorities, goals, and interests with its own.[22] Beijing is therefore still able to exercise effective top-down control. By contrast, performance evaluation systems in democracies such as the United States, the United Kingdom, Australia, and Switzerland are mechanisms for improving government service delivery by incorporating information collected by the service users, or the public. It is therefore a bottom-up mechanism for realizing the ultimate goal of enhancing public accountability.[23]

Fiscal Incentives, Local Industrialization, and Revenue Maximization

While cadre evaluation provides *individual* motivation for leading cadres to promote industrialization and maximize revenue, fiscal reforms have made it an imperative for local authorities to do so at the *collective* level. In the last thirty years, there were a number of fundamental changes to the fiscal system. Nonetheless, the incentive for local governments to maximize revenue persists despite modification of fiscal policies. What has changed is only the manner in which they do it.

Prior to 1979 the central government set spending priorities for local governments and approved all local budgets. Local governments remitted most revenues to the center and received transfers for expenditures from the national budget. Consequently, there were few incentives for local officials to promote industrialization or to maximize tax collection. Intergovernmental transfers pre-1979 were highly distributive and were formulated to finance the gap between locally collected revenues and local expenditures sanctioned by the center. For instance, prosperous Shanghai forfeited 80–90 percent of its revenue collection while more than two-thirds of poor Guizhou's expenditures came from central subsidies.[24]

During the 1980s, the central government implemented a series of fiscal reforms to provide incentives for lower-level governments to increase tax collection and to garner their support for economic reforms.[25] Consisting of separation of local governments' revenue and expenditure responsibilities in 1980, the Proportional Sharing System of 1982, and the Fiscal Contracting of 1988, these reforms transformed the system from a unitary to a nested hierarchy. Since then, the central government sets revenue-sharing rules with the provinces. The provinces in turn set such rules with the prefectures; the prefectures with the counties; and the counties with the townships. Each level of government has an independent budget approved by the people's congress at its own respective level and has to balance its revenue against expenditure.[26]

The incentivizing effects of fiscal reforms on rural industrialization in the early reform period are well documented. Jean Oi and Susan Whiting provide ample evidence of local governments' fervent development of township and village enterprises (TVEs) during the 1980s and early 1990s. Profits and taxes from these enterprises constituted the bulk of local governments' revenue during that period. Oi famously labeled local governments' entrepreneurialism in promoting rural industrialization "local state corporatism."[27]

However, other scholars have cautioned that the fiscal situation of local government has been worsening since the mid-1990s, with negative implications for rural governance and development. In 1994, the central government introduced a fiscal recentralization policy, called the Tax Sharing System (*fenshuizhi*), which reversed some of the massive decentralization of the 1980s. This move was prompted by the fear that a declining share of tax revenue would inhibit the central government's ability to address the regional income gap on the one hand, while risking losing political control over rich provinces on the other.

To avert these dangers, revenue responsibility over major taxes was reassigned to the central government. As a result of the revenue reassignment, the central government's share of total budget revenue rose from 22 percent in 1993 to 56 percent in 1994. Nevertheless, local authorities were still responsible for providing the bulk of public services, such as basic education and health care.

This, of course, worsened the fiscal plight of local governments, whose share of tax revenue has declined drastically while they continue to bear the brunt of public expenditures. Since 1994, the central-local share of revenue hovers around 60:40 while the expenditure share remains lopsided at 30:70. In 2003, while the central government's shares of revenue and expenditures were 71.0 percent and 30.1 percent respectively, those for provincial governments were 5.7 percent and 18.5 percent respectively, and subprovincial governments were 23.3 percent and 52.4 percent, respectively. This leaves subprovincial governments with the largest deficit, 28.1 percent, while the center enjoyed a surplus of 40.9 percent.[28]

Such economists as Albert Park and Scott Rozelle and those at the World Bank[29] have highlighted the distributional consequences of this mismatch of revenue and expenditure responsibilities at the grassroots level. In poor regions, grassroots authorities that are hard-pressed for revenue to meet their basic obligations, such as paying wages, tend to under-provide basic public goods and services. Meanwhile, local authorities in prosperous regions with profitable industries are better equipped to fund the provision of public goods and services.[30] Notwithstanding widespread calls for reform, the central government has not taken any action to date to address this problem.

Implications of Fiscal Recentralization and Declining Revenue for Local-Government Behavior

The recentralization of various revenues since the mid-1990s has affected the ways local governments pursue income growth, from owning and running their own industrial firms to taxing the profitable ones.

Until 1994 the bulk of local revenue came from the value-added tax (VAT) or *zengzhishui*. The VAT is based on a percentage of the added value in the local economy, for example the differences between raw material and end product prices. As a result, the magnitude of the VAT is determined by the number, size, and revenue scale of enterprises. The greater the number of collectively owned enterprises or the larger their scale or revenue base was, the more VAT local governments would receive. This gave local governments and officials a strong incentive to increase the number and scale of industrial enterprises, regardless of their level of profitability.

The 1994 fiscal recentralization reform reassigned 75 percent of the VAT to the center, which left 25 percent to be shared among various levels of local governments. This had a substantial behavioral impact on the ways industrialization was being promoted by local governments. After the recentralization, the company income tax (*qiye shoudeshui*) became the major source of local tax revenue. What mattered was no longer the sheer size of enterprises, but their profitability or efficiency. This provides an explanation for the timing of the tidal wave of collective TVE privatization by local authorities, which commenced in the mid-1990s.[31] With the loss of the lion's share of the VAT, township and village officials no longer had incentive to manage unprofitable firms. So, they privatized them to concentrate on extracting taxes from profitable ones. They were still interested in promoting industrialization, even though the manner in which the firms were managed had changed.

Of course, it is difficult to turn an unprofitable firm into a profitable and efficient one. As the case studies in part III of this book show, locales that successfully engineered a makeover from a collectively owned economy to a vibrant private economy constitute a small minority. Moreover, other critical factors, namely location, can determine the success or otherwise of privately run firms competing under market conditions. Some townships in the coastal provinces of Zhejiang, Jiangsu, and Shandong have successfully transformed from an economy dominated by collectively owned enterprises to one of profitable private firms. At the same time, a large majority of townships in Hebei, Sichuan, Shaanxi, and Yunnan have not.

INTERGOVERNMENTAL TRANSFERS

The plight of poor local governments is exacerbated by the intergovernmental transfer system, which has fallen short of meeting its objective of attenuating the distributional effects of 1994 tax recentralization. The transfer system is supposed to achieve greater equality across regions and locales by providing lower-level governments with more financial resources and reducing the intergovernmental fiscal gap that resulted from the recentralization policy. However, this system is fraught with endemic problems that make it an unreliable source of income for revenue-starved local authorities.

Transfers from the central government are divided into two broad categories: general-purpose and specific-purpose transfers. The general-purpose transfers are made up of revenue-sharing transfers, tax rebates, and equalization transfers aimed at addressing widening regional disparities. Specific-purpose transfers consist of grants for wage increases, for the rural tax reform, for minority regions, and for pre-1994 subsidies and more than 200 ad hoc or earmarked grants.[32]

The specific-purpose transfers lack transparency and undermine the rules-based redistribution that the 1994 reform had aimed to introduce. Specific-purpose transfers accounted for 36 percent of total transfers from the center to the provinces and 46 percent of total transfers from the provinces to their prefectures in 2004. More than half of the specific-purpose grants consisted of ad hoc transfers.[33] These are a series of short-term palliative measures meant to address the systemic problems of yawning vertical fiscal gaps and highly decentralized expenditure assignments. The ad hoc transfers are approved by the center to resolve such growing contingencies as wage and pension arrears, fiscal stimulus packages, and bailouts for local-government social responsibilities. While the center recognizes local government's inadequacy for financing basic social services, it lacks the ability to monitor how the grants are spent owing to their ad hoc and discretionary nature.[34] This lack of a monitoring mechanism allows the diversion of fiscal resources by local governments to areas for which the grants are not intended.

Over the last decade, the central government attempted to convert some ad hoc transfers into equalization grants, a form of general-purpose transfers. Nonetheless, equalization grants remain a small component of central-provincial transfers, accounting for only 5 percent of the total sum of transfers in 2004.[35] Other general-purpose transfers, about half of which are revenue-sharing transfers, are also extremely limited in realizing redistributive objectives. Revenue-sharing transfers are based on the "revenue returned" principle, which is regressive, favoring the richest coastal provinces and largest cities at the expense of regions and locales most in need of resources.[36]

The substance and types of intergovernmental transfers aside, the institutional channel for transferring the resources from higher to lower-level governments is also problematic. Because governments in China are organized in a nested hierarchy, any central transfer, such as a subsidy to compensate township authorities for loss of agricultural taxes and fees, needs to go through several administrative levels before reaching its destination. The central government determines transfers to the provinces only and gives *no* direct grants to prefecture, county, or township authorities.[37] In other words, fiscal transfers go through many layers of government: the provinces determine transfers to the prefectures; the prefectures in turn deal with the counties and the counties with the townships.[38] Hence, resource hoarding by intermediate levels of government, especially the prefectures, is not uncommon. By the time a central transfer reaches the county or township governments of its destination, it could end up being only a fraction of the original amount.

The rules determining intergovernmental transfers are also complex and opaque. This lack of transparency means the actual transfers are often determined by bargaining between governments. In addition, all intergovernmental transfers are instituted by executive orders not subject to any regulatory oversight and are therefore subject to abuse of power by higher-level government officials as well.[39]

The Worsening Fiscal Plight of Grassroots Governments

All levels of local authorities were starved for revenue after the recentralization of various fiscal incomes in the mid-1990s. However, township authorities, being formally the most grassroots administrative level, are particularly hard-pressed for revenue.[40] They have fewer sources of income compared to higher-level governments. Additionally, transfers from the center are least likely to reach them due to a greater likelihood of being hoarded by higher administrative levels.

Closer examination of the sources of revenue for township authorities provides evidence for its scarcity. As table 4.2 shows, the sales tax is now effectively the only viable source of within-budgetary revenue. Personal income tax is not a major source of revenue because of the transition nature of the Chinese economy and the low income of rural residents. The agriculture tax (*nongyeshui*), and other agriculture-related taxes, such as the special product tax and slaughter tax, used to be the main sources of revenue for agricultural townships with no industry.[41] However, the Hu-Wen administration abolished these taxes in 2005, as part of its attempt to address the growing urban-rural inequality. Though the intention behind this move was to assist the rural and agricultural population, many agricultural townships with no industry-related tax revenue have since been deprived of their only source of income.[42]

In the past, local governments were also able to supplement their revenue at will through such means as agriculture and education surcharges, township and village levies, or fees and fundraising for local infrastructure projects. This was extra-budgetary revenue in the sense that it was not subject to sharing with higher-level governments. However, these fees and fines were a cause of rural discontent, which led to their abolition by the central government in 2002, which bankrupted many grassroots authorities. These local governments were consequently forced to rely for their survival on intergovernmental transfers, which as we have seen are an unreliable revenue source.[43] This left the lucrative land conversion income (*tudi churangjin*) as local governments' only remaining independent and unshared source of revenue, which has catalyzed real-estate and construction development throughout China.

The cadre evaluation and fiscal systems make it imperative for local governments to maximize revenue. Local officials put their political careers and the survival of their administrative units at risk if they fail to fulfill the requirements generated

TABLE 4.2 Sources of townships' revenue

WITHIN-BUDGETARY REVENUE	*(YUSUANNEI SHOURU)*	SOURCE OR BASIS	RATIO (CENTRAL GOVT.: LOCAL GOVT.)*	REMARKS
Value-added tax (VAT)	(*zengzhishui*)	Percentage of added value; that is, difference in value between raw materials and final products	75:25	Became a largely central government's tax since 1994.
Sales tax	(*yingye shui*)	Percentage of turnover or sales of service industries, such as construction, real estate, transport, restaurants, and supermarkets	20:80	Used to be a 100% local tax.
Company income tax	(*qiye shoudeshui*)	Percentage of company's profits	68:32	Used to be a local government tax. Shared with the central government since 2002.
Personal income tax	(*geren shuodeshui*)	Percentage of individual's income	50:50	
Agriculture tax and agri-related taxes	(*nongyeshui*)	Percentage of size of farmland	Local; split between county and township	Abolished in 2005.
Miscellaneous, including stamp duty, land use tax	(*yinghuashui, tudishiyongshui*)		Local	

INTERGOVERNMENTAL TRANSFER	***(ZHUANYI ZHIFU)***			
Tax revenue transfer from central government	(*shuishou fanhuan or jishu fanhuan*)	Using 1993 figures as the base, for every 1% increase in VAT and company income tax, fiscal transfer increases by 0.3%		
Fiscal remittance/subsidy	(*dinge shangjie or buzhu*)	Based on agreement between county and township governments; relatively rich township remit fiscal revenue while poorer ones receive subsidies		
Agricultural tax abolition subsidy	(*nongyeshui buzhu*)			For 5 years after abolition. One of the special-item transfers (zhuanxiang zhuanyi zhifu)
EXTRA-BUDGETARY REVENUE	***(YUSUANWAI SHOURU)***			
Administrative fees and fines	(*tongchou and tiliu*)	Often collected at township government's will	100% township	Abolished in 2002.
Collective enterprises' profits			100% township	Largely disappeared with collapse and privatization of collective enterprises since mid-1990s.
Land fees and land conversion income			Local; split between county and township governments	

Source: Author's interviews with various finance bureaus.

*These are the ratios in Shandong; they may differ slightly in other provinces. "Local governments" refers to county and township governments.

by both systems. The "hard targets" impose revenue and industrialization as the top priorities for local governments, regardless of their situation—their level of development, their resources, or their location. Farmers' income, education, and health-care provision, which are essential for long-term rural development, are rendered as "soft targets" relatively unworthy of cadres' efforts.

Sources of revenue for local governments diminished significantly as a result of the fiscal recentralization in 1994. This, however, did not reduce their penchant for industrial promotion because their appetite for revenue grew as expenditure responsibilities remained unchanged despite recentralization. This is where the existing literature on industrialization in rural China, such as Oi (2007) and Whiting (2001), has left off. What has evolved as a result of changing tax incentive is the way that industrialization is being promoted—from owning and running TVEs themselves to shedding unprofitable firms and extracting income tax from the remaining private profitable ones.

The recentralization of the company income tax in 2002 reassigned 68 percent of the tax to the central government, leaving 32 percent to be shared among the various local administrative levels (see table 4.2). As a result, the sales tax (*yingyeshui*) is now the major income source for local governments. This predisposes local authorities to devote energy to promoting service-type industries, such as construction and real estate, from which the sales tax is extracted.[44] Thus, the change in fiscal policy has inspired local authorities to engineer a real-estate and construction boom, hastening the pace of urbanization throughout peri-urban areas.[45]

Regardless of fiscal policy, local leaders are able to siphon resources from local credit institutions with weak corporate governance structures to their preferred firms and projects with the aim of promoting industrialization and growing their coffers. Local-government interference in lending thereby becomes an unintended consequence of the systemic demands created by the design of China's political institutions. Further, many loans given to local authorities and local government-related companies go unrepaid. In order to salvage the rural financial system, the center was forced to intervene and bail out RCCs in the late 2000s. By extension, the center's intervention was also a bailout of the indebted local authorities. This point is further analyzed in the Conclusion.

Appendix

TABLE 4A.1 Township Cadre Evaluation Criteria in Wenling County, Zhejiang Province (2005)

EVALUATION ITEMS			MAX SCORES	TARGETS	WAYS TO RAISE SCORES	RESPONSIBLE OFFICE (AT TOWNSHIP)	EVALUATED BY (AT COUNTY)
Economic development	Total revenue	National revenue (*guoshui shouru*)	10	51 million yuan	An additional point for every 10% or 6 million yuan increase	Finance office	National tax bureau
		Local revenue (*difang caizheng shouru*)	18	37.2 million yuan	An additional point for every 5% or 6 million yuan increase	Finance office	Local tax bureau
		Current-year fiscal balance	2			Finance office	Local tax bureau
		Industrial investments	10	280 million yuan	An additional point for every 10% increase	Industry office	Industrial economy bureau, statistical bureau
	Industrial development	Production value of large-scale industrial enterprises	5	Increment of 25%	An additional 0.3 point for every 2% increase above 25%	Industry office	Industrial economy bureau, statistical bureau
		Construction of factories	5	10,000 sq. mi.	An additional 0.2 point for every 10% increase	Industry office	Development and planning bureau
		Construction of industrial parks	4			Industry office	Development and planning bureau
	Agriculture and villages	Agricultural production	2	217 million yuan		Agricultural office	Statistical bureau
		Average farmer's income	3	7,510 yuan	An additional 0.5 point for every 10% increase	Agricultural office	Agricultural relocation team
		Training of agricultural laborers	3	2,600 people	An additional 0.2 point for every 10% increase	Agricultural office	Agricultural and forestry bureau

TABLE 4A.1—*cont.*

EVALUATION ITEMS			MAX SCORES	TARGETS	WAYS TO RAISE SCORES	RESPONSIBLE OFFICE (AT TOWNSHIP)	EVALUATED BY (AT COUNTY)
Economic development		Grain seeded areas	3	58,000 mu[a]		Agricultural office	Agricultural and forestry bureau
		Animal epidemic prevention	2			Agricultural office	Agricultural and forestry bureau
	Service industry	Increase in industry value	4	15%	An additional 0.1 point for every 1% increase	Industry office	Development and planning bureau, statistical bureau
		Number of newly developed service enterprises	2	1		Industry office	Development and planning bureau
	Actual investments		15	US$1.2 million	An additional 0.1 point for every US$50,000 increase; and 0.5 point for every US$3 million project	Industry office	Foreign trade bureau
	Quality work	Quality work responsibility system	4			Industry office	Quality inspection bureau
		Innovation of enterprise system	+1	no ceiling		Industry office	Quality inspection bureau, commerce bureau, foreign business bureau, industrial economy bureau
Social development	Technological work		12			Industry office	Technological skill bureau
	Talent work		5	473 people		Industry office	Organization department

		Development of grass-roots cultural clubs	7.5			Social development office	Communication department, culture and sports bureau
	Cultural and sports work		7.5			Social development office	Communication department, culture and sports bureau
		Sports work	1		An additional 0.5 point for every one fitness centre constructed	Social development office	Culture and sports bureau
		Sports market management	–1		For every major sport incident	Social development office	Culture and sports bureau
	Educational work	Use of special educational expenses	4			Social development office	Education bureau
		Development of standard schools	2.5	1	An additional 0.5 point for every one school constructed	Social development office	Education bureau
		School's hygiene faculties	1			Social development office	Education bureau
	Hygiene work	Public hygiene	4			Social development office	Hygiene bureau
Harmonious society	Democratic and legal rule	Coverage of compulsory basic education	1	Above 85%		Politics and law office	Legal bureau
		Coverage of democratic and legally ruled villages	2	100%		Politics and law office	Legal bureau
		Legal implementation and political openness	8			Party politics office	Legal system office

TABLE 4A.1—*cont.*

EVALUATION ITEMS			MAX SCORES	TARGETS	WAYS TO RAISE SCORES	RESPONSIBLE OFFICE (AT TOWNSHIP)	EVALUATED BY (AT COUNTY)
Harmonious society	Civilization	Civilized community (village) development	3		An additional 0.5 point for every civilized village developed	Party politics office	Communication department
		Reform of funeral cremations	3			Party politics office	Civil affairs bureau
	Stability	Social stability work responsibility system	8			Party politics office	Politics and law committee
		Workplace safety responsibility system	8			Industry office	Safety supervision bureau
		Petition work responsibility system	8			Party politics office	Petition bureau
		Direct telephone service management	2			Party politics office	Direct telephone management centre
		Resolution of *falungong* incidents	3			Party politics office	610 Office
Citizens' livelihood		Pension fund coverage and collection of foundations	12	Complete target	An additional 0.5 point for every 5% increase	Industry office	Labor safety protection bureau, finance bureau
		Unemployment insurance	2	Complete target	An additional 0.25 point for every 5% increase	Industry office	Labor safety protection bureau

	Social protection	Workplace injury insurance	2		An additional 0.1 point for every 10% increase	Industry office	Labor safety protection bureau
		Labor contracts and collective contracts	1			Industry office	Labor safety protection bureau
		Development of new rural cooperative health system	5	75% participation rate	An additional point for every 5% increase	Social development office	Hygiene bureau
		Social benefits for the poor and disabled	3.67			Party politics office	Civil affairs bureau
		Villagers' drinking water project	1	Cover 5,000 people		Social development office	Water bureau
	Life quality	Construction of *liutongwang*	3		An additional point for every one constructed	Industry office	Trade and grain bureau, commerce bureau
		Food safety	1			Industry office	Food and medication supervision bureau
Ecological city development		Ecological city development	10			Village township office	Environmental protection bureau
		Birth control	8			Population planning office	Population planning bureau
		Village reconstruction	7			Village township office	Modern office

TABLE 4A.1—*cont.*

EVALUATION ITEMS			MAX SCORES	TARGETS	WAYS TO RAISE SCORES	RESPONSIBLE OFFICE (AT TOWNSHIP)	EVALUATED BY (AT COUNTY)
Ecological city development		River and drainage management	2			Agricultural office	Water bureau
	Urban township development	Handling of garbage	3.5	85%	An additional 0.5 point for every 5% increase	Village township office	Development and planning bureau
		Basic infrastructure completion	3			Village township office	Development and planning bureau
	Land resource	Farmland construction	2.5	10,000 mu	An additional 0.25 point for every 10% increase	Agricultural office	Land resource bureau
		Construction land redevelopment	3	100 mu	An additional 0.5 point for every 10% increase	Agricultural office	Land resource bureau
		Illegal use of land	2			Agricultural office	Land resource bureau
		Prevention of land hazards	1			Village township office	Land resource bureau
Party development	Party development		26			Party politics office	County party committee office
	Information work		+1			Party politics office	County party and government offices
	Management of suggestion cases		+1			Party politics office	People's Congress Committee, political consultative committee
Recognitions and criticisms			+/–1			Party politics office	County target evaluation leadership small group

[a]1 mu is equivalent to one-sixth of an acre, or 6.5 percent of a hectare.

Source: Wenling Organization Department, Zhejiang.

Part III

CASE STUDIES: BLIND MEN AND THE ELEPHANT

5

DIVERGING PATHWAYS TO PROSPERITY: PRIVATELY LED VS. LOCAL GOVERNMENT–LED INDUSTRIALIZATION

On a bitterly cold winter day in 2006, I was riding a coach to Taizhou, Zhejiang province, for some fieldwork. When I reached the city, I was greeted by a giant poster captioned "the first shareholding cooperative (*gufen hezuozhi*) in China." The ad was for a company called *Baolite* (pronounced bao-li-te) priding itself as a national pioneer of private enterprise. It was established in 1982, more than a decade before the central government formally recognized and permitted private ownership. Things are different now: private entrepreneurship is a much-celebrated attribute of Taizhou these days.

This chapter describes the journeys to prosperity traversed by two rural townships. One of these townships is Zen, in Taizhou prefecture in the southeast corner of Zhejiang province, a cradle of private enterprise. Taizhou's path to development greatly resembles that of its better-known neighbor, Wenzhou. On the eve of economic reforms, both Taizhou and Wenzhou were on a very low economic base. But they quickly prospered once market forces were unleashed by the reforms. Homegrown credit institutions played a significant role in the growth of small and medium-sized private enterprises in Taizhou.

The other township is Han, in Zouping county in central Shandong. The first locale in rural China to open its doors to foreign scholars, Zouping has been hailed as "typical" of rural China by those who studied its early development. But Zouping is not so typical anymore. It is now home to a cluster of textile industries and to the world's largest cotton weaving company. In contrast to Taizhou, economic growth in Zouping was prominently fueled by formal and state-owned credit institutions rather than by homegrown ones. Zouping's developmental history approximates the local government–led Sunan model of rural development and industrialization, famously championed by the region in Jiangsu.

Taizhou and Zouping on the Eve of Economic Reform

Zen is located in Wenling county, in Taizhou prefecture, in Zhejiang province. It neighbors the oft-studied township of Wenzhou, the epitome of private entrepreneurship in the country. The story of Taizhou's success, though much less publicized, greatly resembles that of Wenzhou.

Located in the mountainous southeast of Zhejiang province, Wenzhou and Taizhou were densely populated and extremely poor on the eve of Deng Xiaoping's economic reforms.[1] Much as in Wenzhou, Taizhou's population had grown at double-digit rates during the 1950s and 1960s. In the early 1980s, Wenling county, including Zen, had a population of 1.16 million, or 1,388 people per square kilometer, making it one of the most densely populated counties in China.[2] This high population density resulted in low arable land per capita, which together with the vast mountainous terrain significantly reduced the degree to which farm income was sufficient to support peasants' livelihood. As a result, Taizhou peasants had seized the earliest opportunity to reinstate household farming, making Taizhou one of the first locales to decollectivize agriculture in 1979.[3] Taizhou's financial plight was also worsened by the fact that, like Wenzhou, Taizhou historically received little investment from the communist government due to its geographical proximity to noncommunist Taiwan (Republic of China) (figure 5.1).

Located in Shandong's Binzhou prefecture, Zouping county borders Zibo, a highly industrialized prefecture, on the east, and the provincial capital, Jinan, on the west. Though it is not a coastal county, Zouping's residents have easy access to railroads and road transport, connecting them with Jinan and with the port city of Qingdao (figure 5.2). In comparison to Taizhou, Zouping was relatively sparsely populated (551 people per square kilometer in 2005).

Unlike in Taizhou, farm income in Zouping was mostly sufficient to support farmers' livelihood. Indeed, agricultural decollectivization in Zouping began as late as 1987—some six to seven years after it was declared a national policy, and almost a decade after it was carried out in Taizhou.[4] Agricultural income per capita in Zouping in 1980 was 100 yuan, compared to 80 yuan in Taizhou.[5]

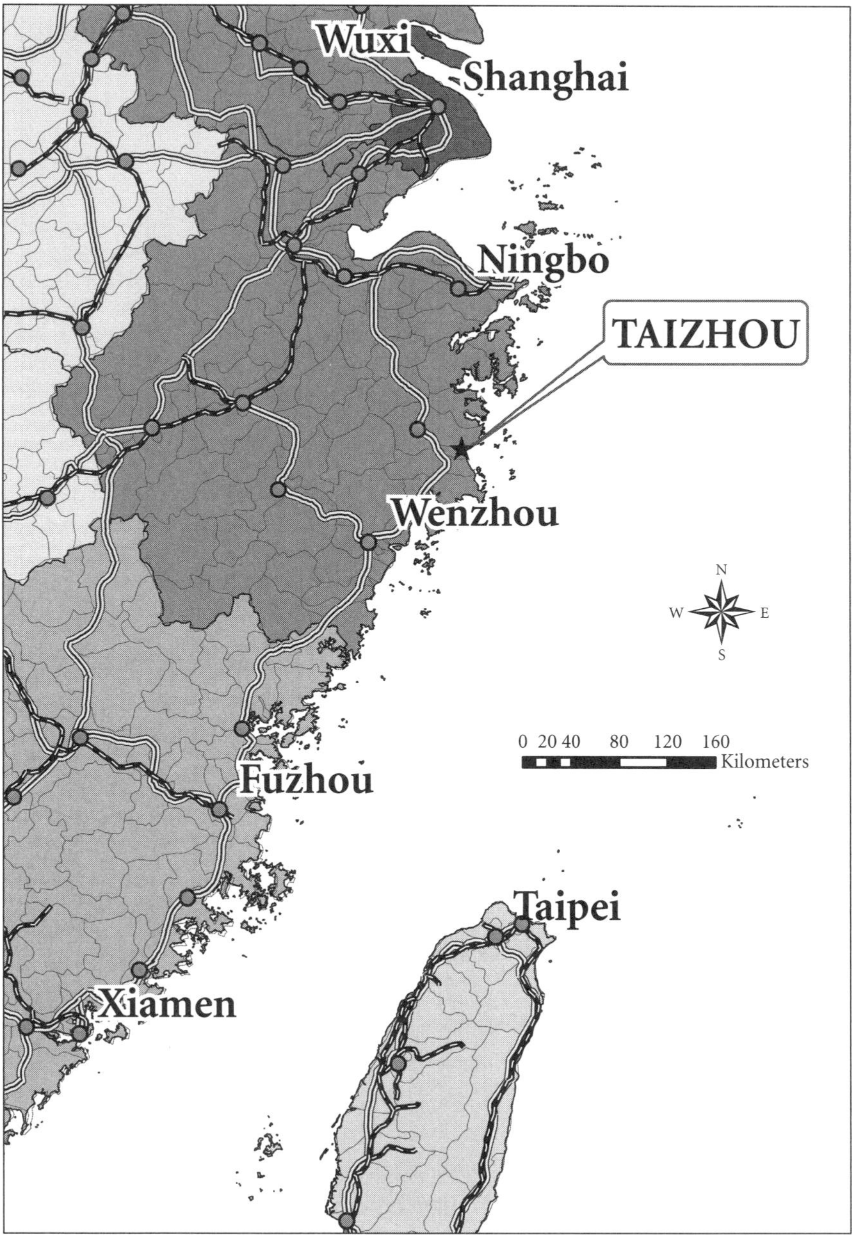

FIGURE 5.1 Map of Taizhou prefecture and surrounding area, Zhejiang province

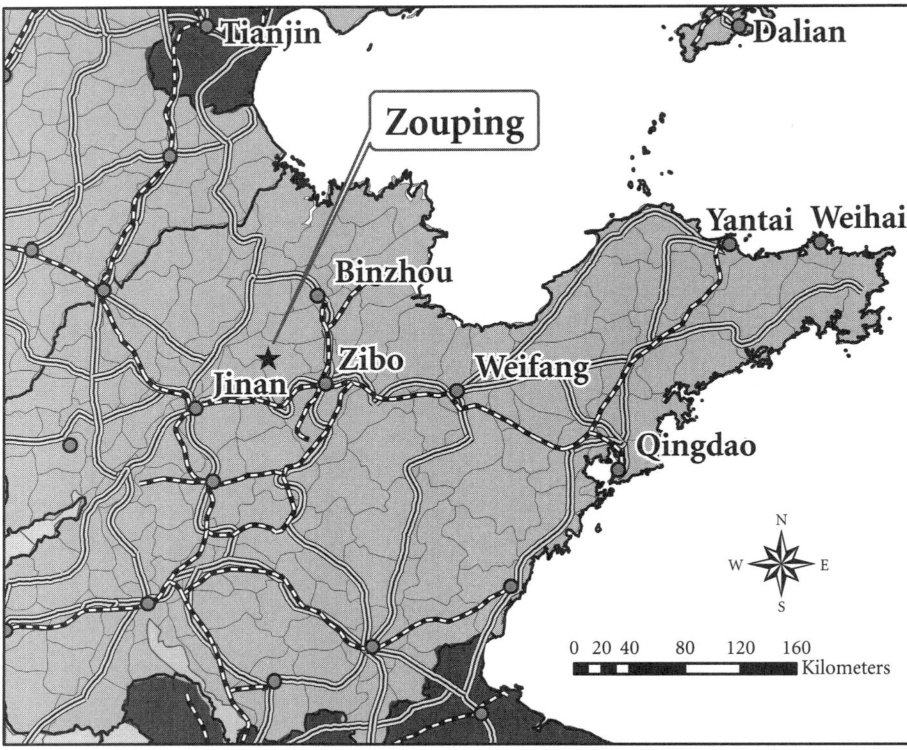

FIGURE 5.2 Map of Zouping county and surrounding area, Shandong province

Both Wenling county in Taizhou and Zouping county might have been poorer than the average county on the eve of economic reform, but the reverse is true now. In 1980 Zouping's income per capita was about half of the national average, and Wenling's was even lower (figure 5.3). Two and a half decades later, both have surged well beyond the national average. Wenling's income per capita is now 2.3 times and Zouping's is 1.5 times the national average. This strongly supports the proposition that their industrialization strategies have been hugely successful.

The nature of industrial development in rural China is path-dependent: whether or not local authorities chose to spearhead industrial development in the early 1980s depended to a large extent on the relative dominance of collective enterprises in the planned era. Collective township and village enterprises (TVEs) that emerged in the 1980s were the institutional remnants of the commune and brigade enterprises (CBEs) of the Maoist era.[6] During the Great Leap Forward (late 1950s and early 1960s), communes and brigades—now called townships and villages, respectively—were ordered to venture into industry in order to realize Mao's goal of "surpassing Great Britain in industrial supremacy."

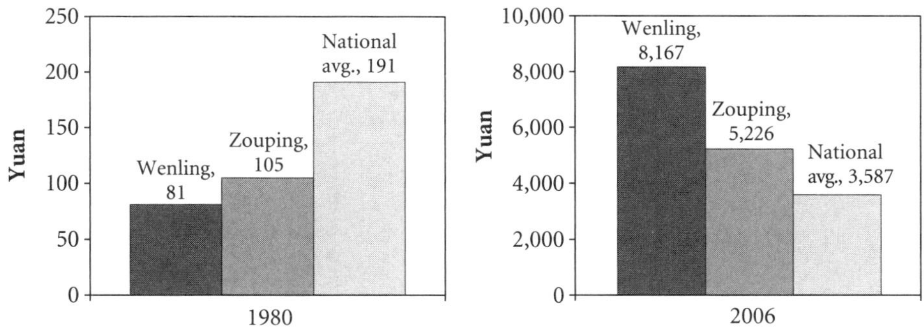

FIGURE 5.3 Wenling and Zouping counties' income per capita vs. national average (1980, 2006)

Sources: Wenling and Zouping County Annals and *China Statistical Yearbook 2007*.

Nonetheless, CBEs did not successfully develop in all rural locales, and Taizhou was one of those places in which CBEs, and therefore TVEs, never took root.

Despite the scarcity of reliable historical data, available evidence suggests that Taizhou—much like its cousin Wenzhou—was never known for its collective enterprises.[7]

Private enterprises clearly dominated the industrial sector in Taizhou prior to the 1950s. Only when the Maoist regime collectivized industries and prohibited private ownership in the mid-1950s did industrial production by private enterprises begin to fall (figure 5.4). But even during the Great Leap Forward, when collectivization and communal ownership were carried out to their extreme and private ownership was strictly banned, private enterprises did *not* completely fade out in Taizhou, as figure 5.4 indicates. Wenling county annals describe collective industries in 1976 as "paltry": though there were more than 800 production teams (*shengchan dadui*) in Taizhou, there were only 160 small-scale collective enterprises—a ratio of five production teams per enterprise.[8]

The market reform of the 1980s rejuvenated the historical entrepreneurial spirit in Taizhou and Wenzhou. Throughout the 1980s, when private enterprises were still shunned in the rest of China, industrial production by private entities had already began overtaking that of the state-owned enterprises and later of the collective enterprises (figure 5.5). Moreover, if Wenzhou is any guide, an overwhelming proportion of registered collective entities were not genuinely owned by local governments. Rather, they were "red hat" (*daihongmao*) firms—private enterprises registered as collective entities—or "hang on" (*guahu*) firms—those that paid a fee to collective or state-owned units to use their names, bank account numbers, and receipts—masquerading as collective to ward off hassles from central authorities.[9]

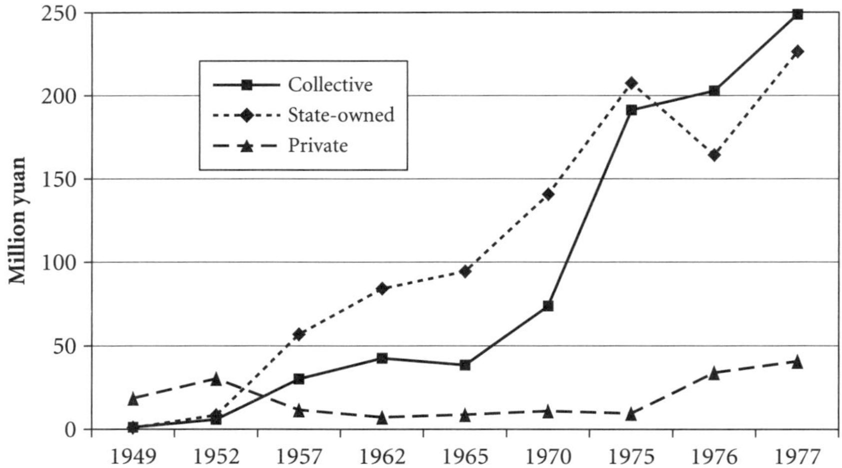

FIGURE 5.4 State-owned, collective, and private enterprises in Taizhou prefecture: Gross value of industrial production (1949–77)

Source: Taizhou Statistical Yearbook 2001, p. 86.

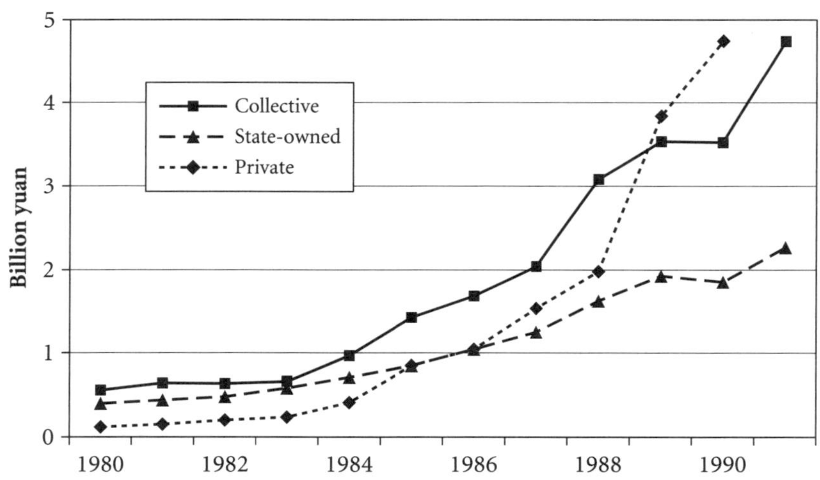

FIGURE 5.5 State-owned, collective, and private enterprises in Taizhou prefecture: Gross value of industrial production (1980–2000).

Source: Taizhou Statistical Yearbook 2001.

Local authorities in Taizhou were more amenable toward private capitalists than were authorities in most other locales. *Baolite*, a shoe manufacturer jointly established by a few households from Taizhou's Zen township in 1982, was China's first shareholding cooperative company (*gufen hezuozhi*). "Shareholding cooperative company" was a pseudonym for "private enterprise" in the early 1980s, when private ownership was still taboo.[10] Even more tellingly, it appears that the proprietors of the shoe manufacturer had initially wanted to register it as a collective enterprise. It was the local government that encouraged its registration as a shareholding cooperative, thereby flagging its status as a private enterprise. This was a considerable political risk for the local government at a time when non-state or non-collective ownership was strictly prohibited by the central government. This clearly indicates that the local government had tacitly recognized private firms and implicitly encouraged their growth, swimming against the political tide of that time.

Yet, in important respects, the actions of the Taizhou government were no different than those of local authorities in other parts of the country. Like other local governments, the Taizhou government was acting in self-interest, and its action was a survival strategy. Given low arable land per capita and low income levels, Taizhou authorities *had to* find alternative means of supplementing farm income expeditiously at the beginning of the liberal reform period. And all industrial enterprises, irrespective of the nature of their ownership, paid taxes and contributed to local-government coffers. Since there were people in this region who were astute entrepreneurs willing to take the lead, tacit encouragement of private enterprise growth was a rational response by the Taizhou government to its own dire financial straits.

Zen Township: Privately Led Industrialization and Prosperity

Today Zen is very much an exemplar of the highly industrialized rural township in China. Only 7 percent of the working population in Zen is employed in the agricultural sector, whereas 65 percent are in manufacturing. Zen hosts a large number of homegrown private enterprises, including clusters of shoe makers, air compressor manufacturers and scrap iron factories. Some of the manufacturers sell their goods under their own brand names, but a large number of them are original equipment manufacturers (OEMs), producing components for goods sold by other companies. Buyers of OEM products manufactured in Zen come from as far as Southeast Asia, Europe, and the Middle East.

The industrial sector in Zen has grown to such a scale that close to 40 percent of Zen's residents are migrant workers from various interior provinces (table 5.1), eager to make a living in the town's booming manufacturing and construction sectors. As we will see in chapter 6, this is the exact opposite of the situation in the impoverished and almost un-industrialized townships of Sichuan, where large-scale emigration is the norm.

TABLE 5.1 Basic indicators of Zen township

Province	Zhejiang	**Income per capita in township (yuan)**	8,255
Population	190,607 (120,000 local pop; 70,000 migrants)	**Avg. income of rural households in the province (yuan)**	7,335
Population density (per sq. km)	3,020	**Township GDP (million yuan)**	14,857.3
Working population, not incl. migrants	72,286	**Land area (sq. km)**	63.1
No. of migrant workers	57,230	**Distance to closest urban center (km)**	31

Sources: Wenling County Yearbook; interviews with township officials.

The Credit Sector in Taizhou

Prior to the Communist takeover in 1949, there were two private banks in Wenling county providing credit to the private industrial enterprises. These were the Wenling County Bank (*Wenlingxian Yinhang*), established in 1944, and the Zhejiang Local Bank (*Zhejiang Difang Yinhang*), Wenling branch, set up in 1936. Both banks were subsequently taken over by the Communist government in 1949. In the early 1990s Wenling became one of the first localities in the country to have established its own banks. Aside from Wenling's official RCC (now the Wenling Rural Cooperative Bank), there are two homegrown banks in Wenling. These are the Taizhou City Commercial Bank (*Taizhou shi shangye yinhang*) and the Tailong Urban Cooperative Bank (*Tailong chengshi shangye yinhang*), which were both formally urban credit cooperatives.[11] All three credit institutions are now privately owned.

These homegrown small and medium-sized credit institutions have played a prominent role in the growth of private enterprises in Taizhou. As indicated in figure 5.6, the three banks *each* accounted for one-fifth to one-quarter of market share throughout the 1990s and 2000s. This leaves the four state-owned banks as relatively small players in Taizhou, an unusual phenomenon given their size and national dominance.

By far most of the lending activities of these local credit institutions are directed toward private small and medium-sized enterprises (SMEs) and micro-enterprises (*getihu*). Four-fifths of Wenling Rural Cooperative Bank's lending went to micro-enterprises, while one-fifth went to SMEs.[12] Micro-enterprises or individual household businesses are typically petty commodity traders, neighborhood "mom and pop" shops selling nondurable consumer items, or small businesses running on push-carts. They can also be family businesses operating

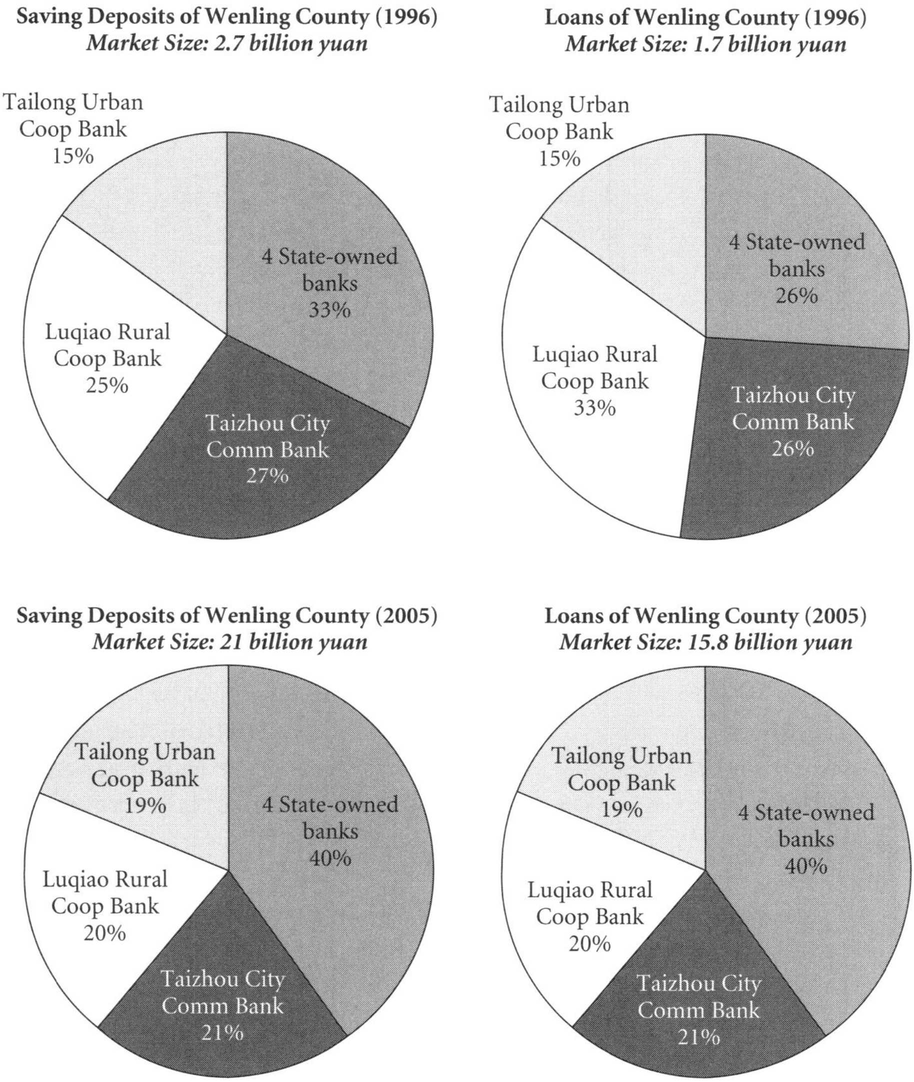

FIGURE 5.6 Total savings deposits and loans of Wenling county (1996, 2005)
Source: Wenling Rural Cooperative Bank.

from backyards and taking on support jobs outsourced by local SMEs. Loan default is a non-issue for these banks: their nonperforming loan ratios ranged between 0.5 and 2.2 percent in the first half of the 2000s.[13]

Unlike state-owned or collective firms, private enterprises have depended on financing from non-state credit institutions and on informal lending for their growth. Existing research on Wenzhou suggests that private firms there have relied on a variety of financing instruments. Such instruments include borrowing from friends and families, underground money houses (*dixia qianzhuang*), rotating credit associations (*hui*), and urban credit cooperatives.[14] Taizhou's official records show a long history of a similarly wide range of informal credit institutions.[15] However, my research in Taizhou during 2005–6 revealed a relatively inactive informal credit sector.[16] This is attributable to the fact that Taizhou's more developed formal credit institutions are now better able to satisfy local demand for credit. Two factors, in particular, have contributed to this. One is an innovative bank loan instrument (to be examined in detail later). The other is the increased central bank–sanctioned interest-rate flotation in recent years, which has allowed local lenders to raise lending rates to better reflect costs of capital.[17]

Indeed, lending activities in Taizhou have the telltale signs of a competitive credit market. Following the financial reform of the mid-1990s, banks elsewhere in China have centralized loan decisions. In contrast, grassroots loan officers in the rural cooperative banks in Taizhou have the power to approve loans up to 50,000 yuan, sufficient for funding micro-enterprise start-ups. This decentralization of loan approval is meant to enhance the bank's competitiveness, because delays in securing managerial approvals could cause clients to seek financing from other private banks.[18]

The relatively high and fluctuating lending rates of the formal banks in Taizhou are another sign of a fiercely competitive credit market. The rural cooperative banks adjust their lending rates at least four to five times a year. During seasonal peaks in consumer demand (such as before the Spring Festival, when businesses typically need capital to purchase goods), lending rates could go up to as high as 10–12 percent per annum (though they cannot go beyond 2.5 times the base-rate ceiling set by the central bank).[19] By contrast, banks' interest rates rarely fluctuate in the typical credit market in rural China. This also indicates the existence of profitable business ventures in Taizhou justifying such relatively high costs of borrowing.

An innovative lending scheme devised by a RCC manager in Taizhou to ameliorate rural borrowers' lack of security is yet another illustration of healthy market competition. As explained in earlier chapters, rural borrowers in China have difficulty providing collateral for bank loans, primarily because they cannot legally use the land they live on for this purpose.[20] However, a Taizhou RCC pioneered a scheme whereby a client's loan size is linked with the client's savings deposit. This allows an individual to take out bigger loans, up to three times the amount of his savings, the *more* and *longer* he parks his savings at the bank, despite having no collateral.[21] This innovative scheme has been instrumental in cultivating customer loyalty and in boosting savings deposits and ensuring regular loan repayments. This also underscores the fact that in Taizhou, unlike elsewhere in rural China, the RCC can ill afford to be complacent amid the keen competition since it is *not* the default market leader or lender. Since the scheme's debut in the late 1980s, other banks—including such competitors as Taizhou City Commercial Bank and the Tailong Urban Cooperative Bank—have copied it.

Local Government–Related Indicators

All indicators point to handsome payoffs for the local government from Zen's successful industrialization. The township government is debt-free, as indicated in table 5.2. Debt from the financing of collective enterprises has never been an issue because there were few local government–run enterprises to start with. As

TABLE 5.2 Revenue and expenditures of Zen township (2004)

REVENUE	MILLION YUAN	TOWNSHIP'S SHARE (MILLION YUAN)	EXPENDITURES	MILLION YUAN
Within-budgetary revenue	**319.7**	**15.0**	**Within-budgetary expenditures**	**18.0**
Value-added tax	171.0		Administrative expenses, including officials' salaries	14.0
Company income tax	82.0		Population control, education, and social welfare (paid for by intergovernmental transfer)	4.0
Consumption tax	0.4			
Sales tax	28.0		**Extra-budgetary expenditures**	**70.0**
Personal income tax	26.0		Urban development	34.0
City development tax	6.1		Rural development	14.7
Property tax	2.8		Education (building and salary bonus)	10.0
Stamp duty and land value tax	3.4		Social safety and welfare	6.3
			Environment	4.0
			Healthcare	1.0
Intergovernmental transfer		**4.0**		
Extra-budgetary revenue		**71.3**		
Land conversion income		71.3		
			Total expenditures	**88.0**
Total revenue		**90.3**		
			Balance	**2.3**

the fiscal data show, the township is highly self-reliant, with intergovernmental transfers accounting for merely 4 percent of its total income. Value-added taxes and company income taxes paid by private manufacturing firms constitute the bulk of the revenue collected by the township, but it gets to keep only a small portion of it. Because Zen is one of the richest townships in the county, an overwhelming proportion of its taxes—over and above the required level—is sent to Wenling county for redistribution to poorer townships.[22] Notably, this is done in accordance with a special deal struck between the county and the township.

Like most rapidly industrializing and urbanizing locales in rural China, land conversion income accounts for close to 80 percent of Zen's revenue. Rural land in China is collectively owned. The Land Management Law (*tudi guanlifa*) stipulates that collective lands have to be transferred to state ownership before land use rights are leased to private users.[23] This made it illegal (until this law was changed in 2008) for farmers to transact directly with real-estate companies or industrial developers regarding the land on which they live.[24] Instead of being converted from agricultural use to industrial or commercial use, farmland had to first be expropriated from farmers by local authorities, and the authorities lease the use rights to private developers.

Land conversion is highly lucrative for local authorities. The profit comes from the large gap between the low administratively determined prices at which local governments acquire land from farmers and the high market-determined prices at which they sell that land to private companies. While the law imposes a ceiling on the compensation at thirty times the value of agricultural production[25]; in practice, farmers usually obtain up to ten to fifteen times what they did previously in tilling, which is equivalent to 10,000–15,000 yuan for a *mu* (one-sixth of an acre) of farmland. Meanwhile, the prices at which local authorities sell to private companies are determined by market forces. In this rapidly developing region of rural China, where the number of enterprises is growing at a breakneck speed and demand for industrial and commercial-use land is skyrocketing, the selling price for commercial-use land (*shangye yongdi*) is around 300,000 yuan per *mu*, reaching as high as 600,000–800,000 yuan at times.[26] Commercial-use land is that used for building shopping malls and shop houses; it costs three to five times as much as industrial-use land (*gongye yongdi*), used for construction of factories.[27] Essentially, this translates to thirty to eighty times surplus for local authorities after the costs of land are taken into account![28] It is no wonder that local authorities in Zhejiang, as well as those as far-flung as in Yunnan, are fervently engaging in land development, and land-related issues have become the predominant source of peasant grievances since the early 2000s.[29]

Thanks to its substantial revenue from land sales, Zen is financially capable of providing public goods and services to its citizens. The township allocated close to 80 percent of its expenditures to rural and urban development, education, health care, social safety, and welfare (table 5.2). This contrasts starkly with most townships in rural China, particularly the "perished" ones examined in chapter 6, which can barely afford officials' salaries, let alone the provision of social services.

Successful industrialization also brings political rewards to party cadres. In 2006 Zen's party secretary was promoted from *zheng keji* to *fu chuji*, in recognition of his contribution to the township's economic development. The party rank of *fu chuji* is usually reserved for deputies of county governments, one level above the ordinary *zheng keji* rank of township secretaries. A year later, he was promoted to county party secretary.

Farmer-Related Indicators

Generally, Zen residents feel good about their lives. Per capita income in Zen is 8,255 yuan. This is almost three times the national average for rural residents (3,255 yuan) and approaches the national average for urban residents (10,493 yuan).[30] The affordability of the nine-year compulsory education, a major challenge for many rural townships, is a non-issue for Zen. It is not uncommon for households to send their children to technical institutes or universities in the provincial capital, Hangzhou; Shanghai; or even a developed Western country.

Neither the arbitrary extraction of fees and fines nor wage arrears has ever really been a concern for the residents of Zen. An average Zen resident is more preoccupied with return on real-estate and stock-market investments, and with non-essential consumption, such as buying a car or taking a vacation, than with procuring basic necessities, health care, or education. There is no notable incidence of land-related conflicts between local authorities and farmers. In general, farmers are keen to sell their land to the government in order to dispose of their farming obligations, since more profitable activities lie outside farming. In this increasingly prosperous and urbanized part of rural China, tilling is often considered a "backward" and "backbreaking" chore. Farming income is minuscule compared to wage employment or enterprise profits, particularly given the low arable land per capita in this region.

The Path of Successful Privately Led Industrialization

Taizhou's development stands out from other rural locales in the country. It is unique *because* of its tradition of strong private entrepreneurship (or *in spite of* its lack of state entrepreneurship). When the economy opened up in the early 1980s, the private sector boomed, though disguised in various forms owing to a restrictive regulatory environment at the time. Bank loans were going to private enterprises and micro-enterprises because of the absence of local government

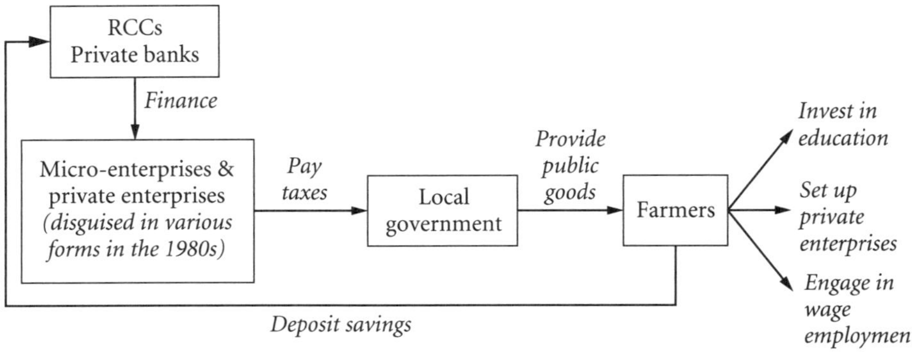

FIGURE 5.7 The path of successful privately led industrialization.
Source: Wenling Rural Cooperative Bank.

firms, rather than a fundamental change in the less-than-arm's-length relationship between local authorities and RCCs described earlier.

Taizhou authorities had allowed private firms to grow because they, too, contributed taxes to the coffers. This successful privately led path to township prosperity is shown in figure 5.7. Revenue from private firms allows the local government to carry out its function of providing social services, which in turn enables citizens to invest in education, to acquire health care when needed, and to set up further private enterprises, contributing to the cycle of wealth generation.

Han Township: Local Government–Led Industrialization and Prosperity

The privately led industrialization epitomized by Taizhou is not the only path to prosperity in rural China. Another successful path is illustrated by Zouping. In terms of its starting point, Zouping county was the antithesis of Taizhou. Unlike in Taizhou, few private enterprises existed in Zouping prior to the Communist takeover in 1949, and private enterprises had been visibly absent from the industrial sector from the 1950s through the 1980s (figure 5.8). Instead, throughout the period, the industrial sector was dominated by state-owned and collective enterprises, the latter emerging as the stronger of the two. In 1985, the collectively owned enterprises in Zouping not only out-produced the state-owned enterprises but also employed more workers, despite having a smaller asset size (figure 5.9). With private enterprises virtually nonexistent, local officials were the ones with experience managing industrial enterprises. It was therefore only rational for the local government to continue leading industrial development

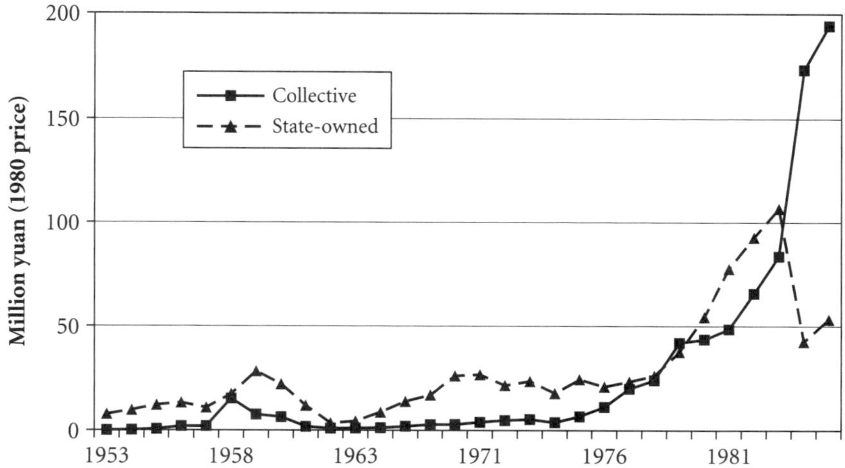

FIGURE 5.8 State-owned vs. collective enterprises in Zouping county: Gross value of industrial production (1953–85)
Source: Zouping County Annals, p. 491.

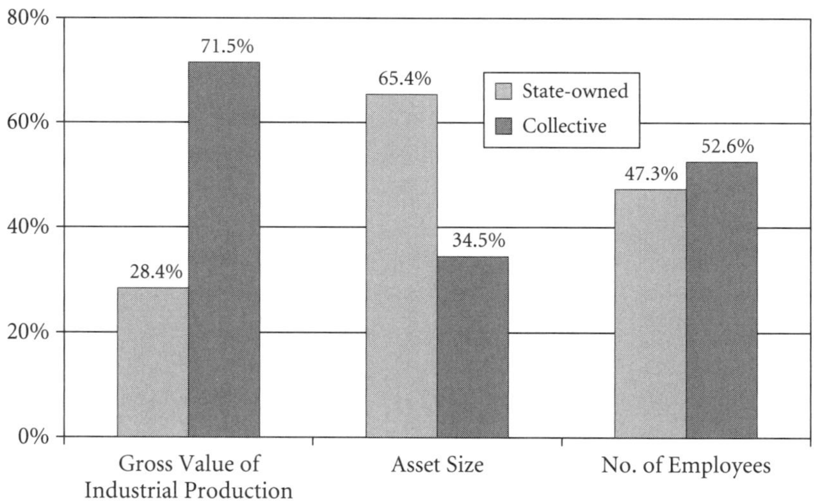

FIGURE 5.9 State-owned vs. collective enterprises in Zouping county: Gross value of industrial production, asset size, and number of employees (1985)
Source: Zouping Yearbook, 1985–95, p. 247.

even after the economic reforms of the late 1970s. The fiscal decentralization of the 1980s, which allowed local authorities to retain tax and enterprise surpluses for their own use, provided further impetus to the Zouping government's leadership role in local industrial development.

Zouping's development bears some resemblance to the widely studied Sunan model of development, originating from a region at the Yangtze River Delta in southern Jiangsu province near Shanghai.[31] Much like Sunan, the collective enterprise sector has a long history in Zouping, from the CBEs of the Maoist era to the TVEs of the 1980s and early 1990s. In Zouping as in Sunan, smaller collective enterprises acted as subcontractors to larger state-owned enterprises in the region. Similar to Sunan, which has benefited from technology and consumer markets in neighboring Shanghai, Zouping has benefited from easy access to the coastal city of Qingdao and major cities in northeastern China, such as Jinan.

Yet, this is only the first half of the story of Zouping. As Andrew Walder notes, private firms—either in the form of individual household businesses (*getihu*) or of shareholding cooperatives—started to emerge in Zouping in the early 1990s. By the mid-1990s these private firms began to surpass the collective enterprises in terms of production.[32] Of course, the collapse of the rural collective sector in the mid- to late 1990s was a widespread phenomenon, not unique to Zouping. As elaborated in earlier chapters, increased competition, combined with a shift in local governments' focus from enterprise revenue to enterprise profits caused a drastic transformation in the collective enterprise sector. Unprofitable TVEs were shut down, and the profitable ones were bought out at hugely discounted prices by their existing managers or contracted to private individuals.[33]

However, unlike in the rest of rural China, in Zouping vibrant private enterprises emerged to fill the void left by the fading out of the collective sector. As figures 5.10 and 5.11 illustrate, private enterprises overtook the collective sector both in terms of sheer number and industrial production after 2001. The industrial sector in Zouping, once dominated by the state-owned and collective enterprises, is now completely taken over by private firms.

The emergence of Zouping's private enterprises has coincided with rapid industrial development in Zouping. Since the mid-2000s, Zouping ranks in the top 100 counties nationwide in terms of industrial output. This is noteworthy because most of the other counties on the list are located in the coastal provinces of Zhejiang, Jiangsu, and Guangdong. Zouping is now home to the country's largest cotton spinning enterprise, Weiqiao Textile, with an annual turnover of 50.3 billion yuan in 2007. Weiqiao started off as a cotton supply and marketing cooperative (*gongxiaoshe*) in the Maoist era. In 1995 it expanded into weaving, dyeing, and the entire value chain of textile production.[34] By 2008, it was ranked the seventieth largest firm in China in terms of turnover, according to the China Enterprise Yearbook. Its contribution to the county government's coffers is huge: about 70 percent of Zouping's 1.4 billion yuan national-tax revenue came from the enterprise.[35] Its success has also spurred the growth of a cluster of downstream industries in dyeing, textile, and garment production in the county.[36]

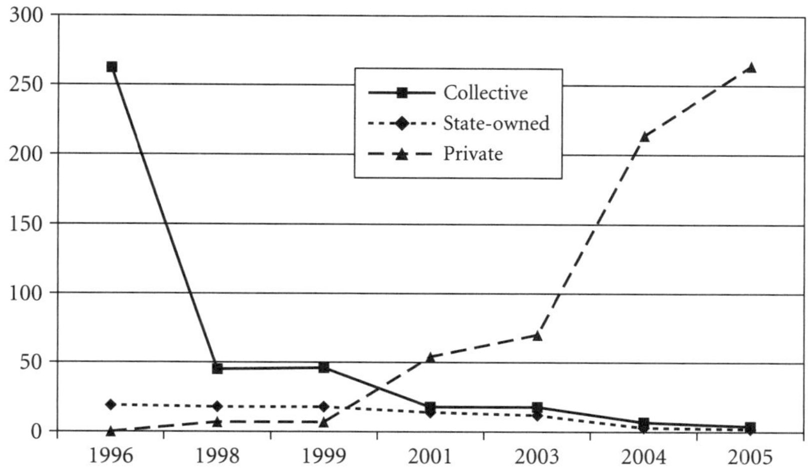

FIGURE 5.10 State-owned, collective, and private enterprises in Zouping county: Number of enterprises (1996–2005).

Source: Binzhou Statistical Yearbook 2007.

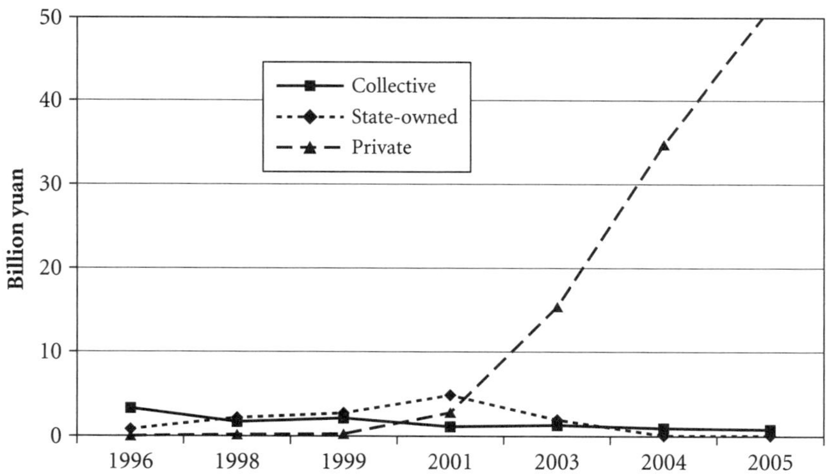

FIGURE 5.11 State-owned, collective, and private enterprises in Zouping county: Gross value of industrial production (1996–2005)

Source: Binzhou Statistical Yearbook 2007.

A prime example of industrial development in Zouping is the township of Han. A sleepy backwater township in the 1980s, Han is now the fastest growing township in the county. Its per capita income of 5,000 yuan is about 15 percent above the provincial average (though still considerably lower than that of Zen in Taizhou). It is relatively sparsely populated, with a population density of about 400 persons per square kilometer. Unlike in Zen, there is no massive influx of migrant labor into Han, reflecting the latter's relatively less robust industrial growth. Han's basic indicators are shown in table 5.3.

The emergence of successful private industrial enterprises in Han is even more remarkable because Han has no natural or mineral resources other than the corn grown by local farmers. Indeed, corn has become a major raw material for Han's rapidly developing manufacturing industry. One of the two largest enterprises in the township began in 1986 as a collectively owned flour mill processing locally grown corn. In 1996 the collective flour mill was bought out by its manager, with additional investment from his family members and with the township retaining a minority stake. The change in ownership turned the humble collectively owned mill into a major processor of corn starch and producer of glucose, corn oil, and animal feed.[37]

The success of the collective-turned-private corn company has, in turn, also aided the growth of de novo private firms, which further contributed to Han's economic rise. A major example is an indigenous private firm established in 1994 that started off as a family-run business to repair machinery at the flour mill. With the rapid expansion of the flour mill into a major food product manufacturer, this backyard repair business also grew to become a major manufacturer of agricultural machinery and equipment. It is today the largest producer of industrial corn processors in China, supplying 70 percent of the country's demand, with total assets valued at 310 million yuan and an annual turnover of 430 million yuan in 2003.

Why did a vibrant private sector emerge to replace the fallen collective enterprise sector in Zouping while other rural locales have seen little industrial growth after the collapse of their collective sector? The key reason for the success of privately led industrialization in Zouping is the county's location, which facilitates access to both domestic and overseas consumer markets and technical know-how. Zouping is not as commercially well-positioned as localities in the coastal provinces of Jiangsu and Guangdong. But it is also not hidden in

TABLE 5.3 Basic indicators of Han township

Province	Shandong	**Income per capita in township (yuan)**	5,000
Population	38,700	**Ave income of rural households in the province (yuan)**	4,368
Population density (per sq. km)	398	**Land area (sq. km)**	97.2
No. of migrant workers	—	**Distance to closest urban center (km)**	36

Source: Zouping County Yearbook; interviews with township officials.

mountainous regions like those "perished" townships discussed in chapter 6. Zouping is crossed by the Jinan-Qingdao highway, built in the late 1980s, which enables the transport of end products from Zouping county to Qingdao, a highly industrialized city and major seaport, and to the provincial capital, Jinan, home to an international airport. Qingdao has a population of 2.3 million with a per capita income of 12,919 yuan, while Jinan has a population of 5.9 million with per capita income of 13,578 yuan. These modern transportation links help facilitate information and technology flows into Zouping and connect its industries to large markets in neighboring urban centers and beyond.

Enterprises in Zouping were subject to competitive pressure, both nationally and internationally, even in the collective enterprise era. Writing about Zouping's economy during the 1980s, Walder remarks that almost all of the county's industrial products were marketed outside the locality and subject to intense competition.[38] Weiqiao's textile products were the first in the province to penetrate European and U.S. markets in the early 1990s and by 1995 were already sold to over thirty markets internationally.[39] This outward orientation of Zouping's industrial enterprises continues to this day, with one-third of the county's enterprise revenue of 13 billion yuan being generated from overseas markets in 2004.[40]

As a result of competitive pressure, enterprises in Zouping have adopted up-to-date technology and technical know-how from overseas. In an attempt to upgrade its technology base in the early 1990s, Weiqiao imported forty-four weaving machines from Hong Kong. In subsequent years, it also imported state-of-the-art technology from Japan, Germany, and the United States. Even small-scale indigenous private firms in Han started adopting agricultural technology from technical institutes in Wuhan and Zhengzhou in the early 1990s. Moreover, these firms focus on using local, household-grown raw materials, namely corn and cotton, as industrial inputs. In this way the acquired technological know-how is employed to maximize the utilization of readily available resources.

The Credit Sector in Zouping

The credit sector in Zouping reflects several salient features of Zouping's economy. First, unlike Taizhou, where local private banks populate the credit market, Zouping has never had private credit institutions. This suggests that the county has traditionally been dominated by government-linked enterprises, which obtained financing from credit institutions associated in one way or another with the government.

Further, it is the four state-owned banks rather than the local RCC that lead the credit market in Zouping. In 2005 the local RCC accounted for only a fifth of total market share, whereas the four state-owned banks collectively took up three-quarters of the market. The Agricultural Bank of China (ABC) is the leader, with a quarter share of the market.[41] This reflects the fact that Zouping's economy is dominated by large-scale enterprises that require big loans and are therefore best served by the state-owned banks—another economic feature of Zouping salient among locales in rural China. Indeed, while the state-owned banks have generally concentrated their economic activity in larger cities since the sectoral reform of the late 1990s, they have maintained their presence in Zouping. This is largely attributable to the presence of Weiqiao Textile, whose massive credit demand only the state-owned banks can meet. Weiqiao alone accounted for nearly 20 percent of the ABC's total loans, while the two large enterprises in Han took up another 16 percent of the bank's total loan portfolio in 2005.[42]

Even though Zouping's big enterprises have grown beyond the local RCC's capacity to serve, it was the main source of credit for the county's big enterprises during their humble beginnings. The county RCC continues to play a critical role in the development of private entrepreneurship in the county. Indeed, 70 percent of the RCC's loans finance individual household businesses and small-scale enterprises, with the remainder directed to agricultural households.[43]

Notably, interest rates for lending in Zouping do not fluctuate seasonally but differ according to borrowers' creditworthiness. This tends to discriminate against household businesses and small firms, which are generally deemed less creditworthy than state-owned firms simply because the state-owned banks lack the modern accounting techniques to evaluate their asset value. Therefore, in Zouping as in other parts of the country, private business owners pay significantly higher interest rates than large government-related enterprises.[44]

That loan decisions are more centralized in Zouping than in Taizhou reflects the fact that competition among lenders in Zouping is not as fierce as in Taizhou. The RCC loan officers in Zouping can approve loans of up to only 5,000 yuan, compared to 50,000 yuan in Taizhou.[45] Even the RCC branch managers in Zouping have limited loan-approval power, with any amount larger than 50,000 yuan having to be referred to the county union.[46] This underscores the fact that Zouping, especially in comparison with Taizhou, remains a lenders' market, the banks having more market power relative to borrowers.

Local Government–Related Indicators

The successful development of a private sector in Zouping is manifested in the fiscal structure of its townships. Han provides a telling example in this respect. To a large degree, Han is financially self-sufficient. Intergovernmental transfers account for only 14 percent of total revenue (table 5.4). Revenue per capita stood at 829 yuan, thanks to taxes paid by the food product manufacturer and corn

TABLE 5.4 Fiscal indicators of Zen vs. Han townships

	ZEN	HAN
Local-government revenue per capita (yuan)	753	829
Share of intergovernmental transfer in total fiscal revenue (%)	4%	14%
Debt-to-revenue ratio	0	0.9
Debt per capita (yuan)	0	646

Source: Author's calculation from fiscal data provided by township finance bureaus.

processor. Granted, the township keeps only a portion of the enterprise taxes, the rest being transferred upward to the county government for redistribution. Nonetheless, these tax revenues are still more than sufficient for the township to invest in infrastructure building and other public goods provisions.

Another notable benefit the local government accrues from hosting sizeable enterprises is co-investments by these enterprises in public education and infrastructure, otherwise the fiscal responsibility of local authorities. For instance, Zouping's food products manufacturer has invested in the construction of a secondary school in Han that boasts a swimming pool and an indoor gymnasium, largely for the benefit of its employees' children. High-rise workers' dormitories have also been built in Han in order to reduce workers' commutes. All this was done in order to retain the enterprises' large number of factory workers and to discourage them from leaving for factories in other localities. The enterprises have also co-invested with the township in constructing a major road connecting Han with the county seat and with some villages. This was done in order to improve the transportation of raw materials into Han from the villages and of end products from Han to the county seat. In other words, the private enterprises voluntarily contribute to the financing of services and infrastructure in their community. However, they do this not out of a "social obligation" (as the collective enterprises of the previous era were supposed to do) but because they deem such actions financially beneficial to them.[47]

Despite its economic leapfrogging of the last two decades, Han is still not debt free. However, its debt level is well under control. As we will see in chapter 6, most rural local governments that have attempted to spearhead industrialization still carry debts inherited from their failed RCFs, the local informal credit institutions set up by the township to finance collective enterprises by absorbing savings from farm households. In this respect, Han is no exception. It is saddled with 25 million yuan in debt, 20 million of which was borrowed from the county government and from private individuals to honor deposits in its RCF when it was shut down in the late 1990s. Also typically, the remaining 5 million yuan is owed to construction companies for some projects undertaken by the town-

TABLE 5.5 Revenue and expenditures of Han township (2004)

REVENUE	MILLION YUAN	EXPENDITURES	MILLION YUAN
Within-budgetary revenue	**27.5**	**Within-budgetary expenditures**	**32.1**
Value-added tax and enterprise income tax	24.1	Road construction	26.0
Agriculture tax	1.7	School construction	2.4
Fines and penalties	1.7	Social welfare	1.5
		Administrative expenses, including officials' salaries	1.0
Intergovernmental transfers	**0.0**	Population control	0.9
		Health care	0.3
Total revenue	**55.0**	**Total expenditures**	**32.1**
		Balance	**22.9**

Source: Han township finance bureau.

ship government. However, thanks to its rapidly growing revenue, Han's debt-to-revenue ratio stands at 0.9, and its debt per capita of 646 yuan is about two-thirds its local government revenue per capita (table 5.5).

Farmer-Related Indicators

There has been no known incidence of land-related conflicts between the local government and farmers in Han as in Zouping county as a whole. As with Zen in Taizhou, there are plenty of profiteering opportunities outside farming in Han. The farmers I interviewed were generally happy to get out of farming. They generally preferred to use their farmland compensation to pursue other profitable activities such as setting up household businesses selling consumer goods to meet growing demand in the township. Moreover, compensation to farmers who traded their land is over and above the norm for rural China. At times it has even exceeded the legally allowed maximum of thirty times the combined production value of the land and relocation compensation to the farmers.[48] According to the local land management office, this generous compensation policy (from a legal perspective) was based on the consideration that the traded lands were mostly used for production of cash crops, which fetch higher prices than the traditional staples used in the legislators' calculation.[49] In no small measure, this compensation policy accounts for the absence of land-related conflicts in Han.

Whereas most residents of rural China rely primarily on farming for their living, wage employment is the norm in Han, largely owing to the large number of factory workers. In this respect, there was little "surplus labor"[50] on Han farms. Furthermore, there is no emigration from Han, as the local enterprises are able to provide sufficient employment. Indeed, most of the working-age population works for the private companies, leaving their aged parents to look after their children. Yet, the enterprises have not developed to such a scale that a massive import of labor is needed to sustain their development, as was the case in Zen. The affordability of education and health care is not a concern for the average Han resident. Peasant burdens were not and are not a source of grievances. Wage arrears are nonexistent in the township.

The Path of Successful Local Government–Led Industrialization

Figure 5.12 depicts how local government–led industrialization brought prosperity to the township of Han. Before the mid-1990s, Han's revenue came predominantly from the profits and taxes of collective enterprises. The development of these TVEs was largely financed by the local RCC and RCF, whose capital came from farm households' savings. But even during this period, though the enterprises were assisted by local governments with cheap capital, they were not as shielded from competition as other TVEs elsewhere.

The turning point came in the mid- to late 1990s. When the collective sector faded out, uncompetitive TVEs exited the market, and the few profitable collective enterprises were bought out by their existing managers. The enterprises in Zouping performed better than their inland counterparts in remote or mountainous regions because of convenient access to large domestic and international markets.

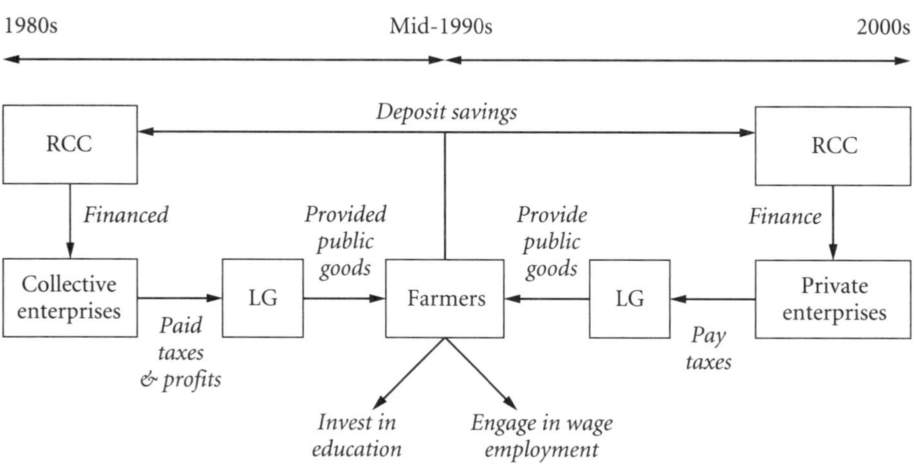

FIGURE 5.12 The path of successful local government–led industrialization
LG = local government.

To be sure, not all collective enterprises in Zouping successfully transformed into profitable private entities. At the peak of the collective enterprise era, Han had twelve township collective enterprises and six village collective firms.[51] Yet the survival of only a handful of them sufficed to make the township prosperous. Taking full advantage of readily available and locally grown industrial inputs, an enterprise manager turned a local flour mill into one of the largest manufacturers of food products in China. In the process, the enterprise boosted farmers' income by buying their produce for use as industrial inputs. The existence of a large corporation in the township in turn created spillover benefits by spurring the development of a cluster of supporting industries. One of these, an agricultural machinery repair business, itself managed to grow to become China's largest manufacturer of industrial corn-processing machines.

Private enterprises are now the engine of growth in Han, providing the local government with handsome revenue and subsidizing the provision of infrastructure in the locale. The local government is sufficiently well endowed financially to be able to invest in public goods and service that benefit its citizenry. Farm households gradually diversify from farming as they find better means of livelihood working in factories or running small businesses.

Therefore, strictly speaking, Zouping adheres to the local government-led Sunan model only in the first part of its industrialization process, which is prior to the mid-1990s. Thereafter, it is private entrepreneurs who have propelled the engine of growth in the county. Nevertheless, this is generally the case with the Sunan model since a significant proportion of collective TVEs, including those in southern Jiangsu where the model originates, were privatized by the late 1990s. In short, a time qualifier is needed to describe the model more accurately: the Sunan model was a local government–led industrialization strategy implemented during the 1980s and early 1990s.

Rapid local economic growth brings swift and direct political rewards for leading local party cadres, the bounties of the Communist Party cadre evaluation system. Since the take-off of the local economy in the early 2000s, leading cadres in Han were gradually promoted to higher levels. The township party secretary was promoted to become deputy head in Zouping county, and the assistant party secretary was promoted to replace him. This is the career path to which every local political leader aspires.

In a highly decentralized fiscal environment where local authorities are left to finance the provision of public goods and services, local residents' living standards depend critically on the fiscal health of local governments. Taizhou prefecture and Zouping county, exemplified by Zen and Han townships, have adopted two different industrialization strategies, both proving rather successful. Economic development has also brought significant political benefits to the township party leaders, leading them to higher positions in the political hierarchy.

The diverging pathways do not imply that the local authorities in Taizhou and Zouping are necessarily different. Rather, they were similar in that both acted out of institutional incentives to maximize revenue. They traversed separate paths simply because their starting points in terms of local conditions were dissimilar. In a locale where entrepreneurialism was already thriving, it was wise for local authorities to leave the monumental task of industrialization to creative and energetic private individuals. Conversely, where private enterprises were nonexistent and local officials had previous enterprise experience, it was only natural for local authorities to take on a leadership role in spearheading industrialization.

Yet, this begs another question: what differentiates Taizhou and Zouping from the many rural cases that have failed and "perished"? Much like Wenzhou, Taizhou champions the model of market capitalism in which only the fittest survives. Its firms are private enterprises established using personal savings or loans from relatives and friends and financing from profit-making credit institutions. In the presence of strong market competition, these enterprises were forced to utilize resources efficiently or risk going out of businesses and losing their owners' lifetime savings. By contrast, when local government–owned enterprises were funded by RCCs and other formal credit institutions, their budget constraints were not as hard as those of private enterprises. Notwithstanding that, for the enterprises in Zouping, competition in product markets—whether national or international—imposed a degree of discipline on enterprises' use of resources. This is illustrated by Weiqiao, the country's textile giant. Some collective enterprises in Zouping thus survived the collapse of rural China's collective sector in the mid- to late 1990s and were bought out by private individuals who continued to expand the scope of businesses.

Access to markets and time-to-market, which can often make or break a business, are critically determined by proximity to urban centers and transportation linkages. It is not necessary for the business to be located in a metropolitan area, however. Geographical isolation can be overcome, as it was in Zouping, by having good access to the provincial capital and coastal cities.

At the time of writing this manuscript in the late 2000s, private enterprises throughout China are reeling from the global financial crisis. The crisis has not only tightened the credit supply but also shrunk demand for manufactured goods. As we wait to see which enterprises will survive these hardships, the analysis of privately led and local government–spearheaded regional growth remains an important chapter in China's political-economic development.

6

THE LOCAL GOVERNMENT–LED PATH TO RURAL DECAY

I had been in this village in Sichuan province for a week now, but there was still no sign of any working-age adults. There were plenty of children and old folks, but no healthy young men or women. It was an "hourglass population pyramid" village, in which the population pyramid is hollowed out at the center. Nearly all working-aged adults—men and women alike—had left to become migrant workers in Guangdong, Beijing, and other coastal provinces and cities, in order to support their families back in the village. Men were typically construction workers. Women usually worked in the factories. Children were left behind to be taken care of by their grandparents. I wondered how these children would grow into emotionally healthy adulthood without the company of their parents. Unfortunately, this situation was common in China's hinterlands.

The prospering townships of the previous chapter do not represent the majority of rural China. This chapter tells a more sobering tale of rural townships, one that applies to vast swaths of the countryside. I vividly illustrate how failed attempts at industrialization by local governments drained their financial resources, leaving them paralyzed and unable to provide basic public services. In such "perished" locales, basic education and health care have become out-of-pocket expenses for the already destitute citizenry. Moreover, the loans that financed the local governments' failed ventures came predominantly from local residents' savings. The high rates of default suggest that a substantial portion of hard-earned rural household savings have been drained away. In addition, grassroots authorities scrambling for revenue have tried all means available to them to augment their income. Such measures, ranging from imposing arbitrary taxes and fees on farmers to illegally confiscating and trading farmland, have been immediate causes of popular discontent and unrest in rural China.

Perished Cases

This chapter draws on case studies of six townships located across three provinces—Sichuan, Hebei, and Shandong. These townships—Xiao, Cheng, Zhou, Zhang, Sun, and Fan—have perished as a consequence of failed local government–led industrialization.[1]

Socioeconomic Characteristics of the Cases

These perished townships do not share a common socioeconomic profile. They differ in geographical position, in population size and density, and in the characteristics and size of their economy. Situated in Sichuan province, Xiao, Cheng, Zhou, and Zhang are more densely populated than Fan in Hebei and Sun in Shandong. Except for Sun, which had an income per capita of 3,900 yuan in 2003, all the other townships had income levels below the national average of 3,255 yuan. That said, Sun is still poorer than the average township in Shandong province (table 6.1).

TABLE 6.1 Basic socioeconomic indicators of the perished townships

TOWNSHIP	XIAO	CHENG	ZHOU	ZHANG	SUN	FAN
Province	Sichuan	Sichuan	Sichuan	Sichuan	Shandong	Hebei
Average income of rural households by province (million yuan)	3002	3002	3002	3002	4368	3802
Income per capita (million yuan)	2,823	2,211	1,820	1,886	3,900	2,800
GDP (million yuan)	279.4	296.3	21.8	28.9	152.9*	19.6*
Population	5,173	9,000	12,027	18,000	39,200	7,000
Land area (sq. km)	51.7	17.2	20.7	31.0	98.5	57
Pop. density (per sq. km)	100	523	581	581	398	122
No. of migrant workers ("+/–" denotes net inward/outward)	–200	—	–3500 (80% of working pop)	–4500 (56% of working pop)	—	—
Distance to closest urban center (km)	170	140	300	300	70	108

*Estimated by author. Income per capita multiplied by population size.

The perished cases also differ in terms of population density, a characteristic unrelated to the provinces to which they belong. Zhou, Zhang, and Cheng in Sichuan are the most densely populated (523–81 people per sq. km), followed by Sun in Shandong (398 people per sq. km), Fan in Hebei, and Xiao in Sichuan (122 and 100 people per sq. km, respectively). Emigration is a distinguishing feature of the labor markets in Zhou and Zhang, where more than 60 percent of the working population makes a living outside the province. This is in stark contrast to the migrant-filled Zen and the emigration-low Han described in chapter 5.

Control Variables

All six townships similarly pursued local government–led industrialization and attained similarly dismal outcomes. Therefore control variables are introduced to allow for differentiation of the six case studies from each other. In addition, the control variables also allow for pair-wise comparisons with my other case studies, such as between Sun and Han, both of which adopted local government–led industrialization but ended up with different outcomes.

The three control variables are (a) whether the townships are located in coastal provinces; (b) whether they are near any urban center; and (c) whether they are endowed with any natural resource. All townships except Sun (in Shandong) are located in non-coastal provinces (Sichuan and Hebei). Two of the six locales are endowed with minerals or other natural resources used as raw materials in their industrial production. Xiao is richly endowed with such minerals as coal, sulfur, iron, and plaster stone and has a river that allows for a hydroelectric dam. Farmers in Sun, like those in Han, cultivate corn in the summer and cotton in the winter.

Moreover, all six townships are relatively distant from any urban center that can provide them with large consumer markets or with transportation links to markets in other regions of China or overseas. Xiao and Cheng are both located in a county in Ya'an prefecture, southwest of Sichuan's capital, Chengdu. Ya'an has a population of 1.54 million and a per capita income of about 8,000 yuan, about 70 percent of the national average urban income of 12,000 yuan. Since Ya'an is a relatively poor city, it cannot support all the industries in its vicinity. The major urban center closest to Xiao and Cheng is Chengdu, with a population of 10.3 million and a per capita income of 12,800 yuan. However, Chengdu is a 170-kilometer drive away from both Xiao and Cheng, with 30 kilometers of that being over treacherous country roads.

Zhou and Zhang are located in a county in Nanchong prefecture, in the northeast of Sichuan province, and even farther from Chengdu. Nanchong is both poorer and more populated than Ya'an, with a per capita income of 5,000 yuan and a population of 7.25 million. A few counties in Nanchong prefecture are officially designated as "poor counties" (*pinkunxian*), including the one in which Zhou and Zhang are located. The two townships are about 300 kilometers away from Chengdu, two-thirds of which are over treacherous and winding mountain roads covered in sandstone. Fan is located in Zhangjiakou prefecture, Hebei province. It is situated in between Beijing and Zhangjiakou, about 108 kilometers from each.

Sun, being from the same Zouping county as Han, fares the best among the six cases in terms of its proximity to urban centers. It is only 35 kilometers from the county seat of Zouping, which is en route to the provincial highway connecting the provincial capital, Jinan, with the major seaport of Qingdao. Still, there are at least three other neighboring townships closer to the county seat than Sun, putting Sun in a significantly worse position than competing townships.

The Pathway of Local Government–Led Industrialization and the "Withering Away" of Local Government Functions

As the case studies in this chapter illustrate, from the 1980s to the mid-1990s rural industrialization in China was driven predominantly by local government–owned collective enterprises. The prominence of the local government–led industrialization strategy in these rural regions is underscored by the provincial-level data in table 6.2. The table shows the shares of collective enterprises out of total TVEs in Shandong, Hebei, and Sichuan. TVEs are defined as including collective (*jiti qiye*) and private (*siying qiye*) enterprises and individual household businesses or micro-enterprises (*getihu*). Until the mid-1990s, collective enterprises employed between half and three-quarters of the total workforce in the sector. They also received more than 90 percent of total bank loans to the sector throughout the 1980s and the first half of the 1990s. Even in Hebei, where the share of collective enterprises was smaller than in Sichuan and Shandong, such enterprises still employed the majority of workers, produced the bulk of goods, and absorbed almost all of the bank loans to the sector, until 1995.

The rural landscape, however, changed drastically after the collapse of the collective enterprise sector in the mid- to late 1990s. The collapse was precipitated by the central government's 1994 shift in fiscal policy, from an emphasis on enterprise size to an emphasis on profitability. Once the VAT (calculated as a percentage of firms' revenue) was recentralized to the control of the central government, company income tax (based on firms' profit level) became the major source of tax income

TABLE 6.2 Shares of collective enterprises in total TVEs in Sichuan, Shandong, and Hebei provinces (1985–2002)

	SICHUAN				SHANDONG				HEBEI			
	NO. OF ENTPS.	NO. OF WORKERS	PROD. VALUE	BANK LOANS	NO. OF ENTPS.	NO. OF WORKERS	PROD. VALUE	BANK LOANS	NO. OF ENTPS.	NO. OF WORKERS	PROD. VALUE	BANK LOANS
1985	60%	70%	85%	89%	32%	70%	80%	100%	8%	41%	48%	100%
1986	60%	64%	72%	89%	19%	64%	77%	100%	7%	41%	46%	100%
1987	60%	63%	67%	90%	15%	63%	76%	100%	6%	38%	44%	100%
1988	60%	60%	66%	90%	13%	60%	76%	100%	6%	37%	43%	100%
1989	60%	58%	53%	89%	12%	58%	74%	95%	5%	36%	43%	100%
1990	60%	57%	53%	92%	11%	57%	73%	96%	5%	35%	41%	100%
1991	55%	57%	54%	92%	10%	57%	73%	96%	5%	35%	43%	100%
1992	50%	56%	53%	93%	10%	56%	71%	96%	5%	36%	46%	100%
1993	45%	53%	53%	91%	9%	53%	67%	90%	5%	37%	47%	100%
1994	45%	53%	45%	95%	9%	53%	73%	97%	4%	35%	29%	67%
1995	40%	52%	44%	88%	9%	52%	71%	88%	4%	34%	46%	88%
1996	6%	49%	40%	84%	7%	49%	64%	87%	4%	35%	45%	65%
1997	6%	54%	40%	76%	10%	54%	67%	86%	6%	33%	32%	42%
1998	4%	43%	29%	70%	5%	43%	57%	77%	5%	28%	29%	52%
1999	3%	36%	24%	62%	3%	36%	51%	69%	4%	25%	26%	54%
2000	2%	28%	20%	56%	2%	28%	42%	54%	3%	21%	23%	51%
2001	2%	22%	16%	42%	2%	22%	36%	44%	3%	18%	18%	47%
2002	1%	11%	18%	34%	1%	11%	33%	42%	2%	14%	15%	44%

Source: Township and Village Enterprise Statistical Information (1978–2002).

Note: Between 1979 and 1984, there were no statistics on non-collective enterprises. Hence the shares of collective firms were 100% of the total.

for local governments. As shown in chapter 4, this shift meant that keeping unprofitable collective firms afloat was no longer in local governments' interests. This prompted local governments to sell off or simply get rid of loss-making enterprises.

In addition, competition in the collective enterprise sector had intensified significantly by the mid-1990s, when the number of collective firms had grown to such a scale that they competed vigorously among themselves and with the private firms that also sprouted over time.[2] The initial recipes for collective firms' success—their agility and ability to offer consumer products that filled a market gap unmet by state-owned enterprises—gradually eroded. As competition in the product market intensified in the mid-1990s, collective firms that operated inefficiently and produced products of inferior quality incurred major losses.[3] From the mid- to late 1990s, local governments shut down loss-making collective enterprises, privatizing those for which they could find buyers, sometimes to insiders and at fire-sale prices.[4] This practice has been best described to me by an interviewee from the TVE management bureau as "Sell whatever enterprises you can sell, if not, give them away!"[5] As figure 6.1 indicates, the down cycle of the collective enterprises began in 1995, the first fiscal year for which the change in tax incentives was in effect. In 1995 alone, 61,812 collective enterprises were closed and 870,000 workers were laid off as a result.[6]

In most rural areas, the downturn in the collective enterprise sector was not accompanied by private sector growth. While local leaders were pressured into

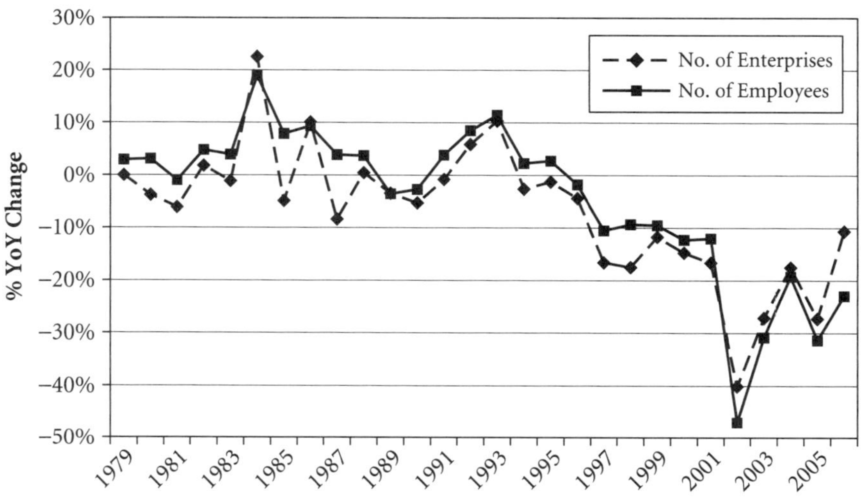

FIGURE 6.1 Changes in the number of collective enterprises and enterprise workers (1979–2006)

Source: China's Township and Village Enterprise Yearbook, various years.

competition with each other, there was little difference in the types of industrial companies they could promote or attract. Whether or not the industries were capital or labor-intensive, or high or low value-added, was of secondary concern as long as they were capable of bringing investment to the towns.[7] Rapid proliferation of factories from the same type of industry in neighboring townships, such as the cluster of coal and sulfur mining operations in SC1 county in Sichuan province, grew to such an extent that these factories competed merely on cost terms. Attracting investment is inherently more difficult in remote locations when every single town is pursuing an undifferentiated "me too" strategy.

In many central and western regions, the increase in private enterprises was insufficient to fill the vacuum left by the shut-down collective enterprises, as table 6.3 vividly illustrates. In Sichuan, the number of collective enterprises shrank on average 32.8 percent each year from 1996 to 2000 and 24.2 percent each year from 2001 to 2006. In Hebei, the number of collective enterprises fell by an average of 16.6 percent each year between 1996 and 2006. Private enterprises in both provinces, and household businesses in Hebei, also declined in number in the late 1990s. Private enterprises and household businesses in both provinces did expand after 2000, but at rates barely sufficient to offset the drastic declines in collective enterprises.

Shandong may appear to have been an exception to this story. In Shandong as a whole, the number of collective enterprises fell by less than 10 percent during 1996–2006, while the number of private entities in it rose significantly. However, Shandong province *as a whole* does not belong to the "perished" category. Han, for example, has prospered. Even Sun, covered in this chapter, is the best-off case in the "perished" category. Data regarding changes in the number of workers in the various types of enterprises (table 6.4) further support the proposition that growth in private enterprises and household businesses has failed to fill the void created by the TVEs' collapse since the mid-1990s.

Moreover, the actual drop in local-government revenue following the collapse of the TVE market was much worse than the sectoral growth data would imply, for several reasons. First, the change in the fiscal regime to one based on firms' profits, rather than revenue, has shrunk the pool of companies contributing taxes to local governments—from every existing firm to only the profitable ones. Second, aside from formally regulated taxes, collective firms also used to contribute "self-raised funds" (*zichou zijin*) to local governments' coffers. These "funds," consisting of profits and some other arbitrarily determined income, were *not* subject to sharing with higher-level governments and were sometimes a significant part of the local government's revenue. For instance, during the heyday of TVE development in Xiao in 1995, "self-raised funds" accounted for two-thirds of the total township income (table 6.5). "Self-raised funds," however, all but dissipated after the transformation of the collective enterprises in the township.

TABLE 6.3 Average changes in number of collective enterprises, private enterprises, and household businesses in Sichuan, Hebei, and Shandong provinces

	SICHUAN			HEBEI			SHANDONG		
	COLLECTIVE	PRIVATE	HOUSEHOLD	COLLECTIVE	PRIVATE	HOUSEHOLD	COLLECTIVE	PRIVATE	HOUSEHOLD
1986–90	11.8%	11.8%	11.8%	–5.8%	–2.7%	5.5%	–8.5%	8.4%	24.2%
1991–95	–2.2%	3.3%	28.4%	1.2%	2.4%	6.3%	–2.8%	–2.0%	3.1%
1996–2000	–32.8%	–13.5%	6.1%	–12.9%	–8.9%	–5.5%	–16.1%	23.0%	11.6%
2001–6	–24.2%	40.8%	–2.5%	–19.7%	3.7%	4.8%	0.1%	91.0%	9.3%
Average (1996–2006)	–28.1%	12.0%	1.8%	–16.6%	–2.0%	–0.3%	–7.3%	60.1%	10.5%

Source: *Township and Village Enterprise Yearbooks*, various years.

TABLE 6.4 Average changes in number of workers in collective enterprises, private enterprises, and household businesses in Sichuan, Hebei, and Shandong provinces

	SICHUAN			HEBEI			SHANDONG		
	COLLECTIVE	PRIVATE	HOUSEHOLD	COLLECTIVE	PRIVATE	HOUSEHOLD	COLLECTIVE	PRIVATE	HOUSEHOLD
1986–90	3.4%	8.7%	17.4%	0.7%	1.0%	9.4%	3.4%	6.7%	19.8%
1991–95	9.3%	10.6%	11.9%	5.1%	–7.9%	12.8%	4.5%	1.8%	10.6%
1996–2000	–20.1%	–1.6%	–0.7%	–8.1%	28.6%	1.2%	–10.6%	36.6%	6.0%
2001–6	–29.3%	20.1%	–1.1%	–9.5%	12.8%	6.5%	–25.4%	21.9%	2.2%
Average (1996–2006)	–25.1%	10.2%	–0.9%	–8.9%	20.0%	3.8%	–18.7%	28.6%	4.1%

Source: *Township and Village Enterprise Yearbooks*, various years.

TABLE 6.5 Revenue of Xiao township (1995)

	YUAN	% SHARE
Within-budgetary funds	81,081	*23.4%*
Extra-budgetary funds	37,522	*10.8%*
Self-raised funds	228,202	*65.8%*
Total income	346,805	*100.0%*

Source: Xiao township finance bureau.

Local Government–Related Indicators[8]

Since the mid-1990s, grassroots authorities in the perished locales have lost the bulk of their income. As the present section illustrates, the unabated fiscal pressure these governments faced made them resort to levying arbitrary taxes and fees from farmers. After the rural fiscal reforms, they generate income by fervently acquiring farmland—often with inadequate compensation to the land's residents—to convert and sell off for non-agricultural uses. Despite these revenue-generating activities, many local governments are still unable to provide basic public goods and services. Rural discontent and unrest stemming from these (sometimes illegal) activities has become increasingly commonplace in the countryside.

The data described in this section are summarized in tables 6.6 and 6.7. Detailed fiscal data for the townships are in the appendix to this chapter.

Fiscal data for Xiao and Cheng suggest that failed industrialization attempts have left both townships heavily in debt and largely paralyzed. Cheng is the county seat, and therefore has a relatively service-oriented economy. Even at the height of the industrialization push, Cheng was less industrialized than Xiao, with four collective enterprises to Xiao's five. Cheng also has no natural resource. As a result of these factors, two-thirds of Cheng's tax revenue comes from business tax paid by retail shops, an exception among the six perished townships. Still, Cheng's meager tax revenue of 400,000 yuan is sufficient to cover only 30 percent of its total expenditures (table 6A.2, in the appendix to this chapter). Then as today, Cheng's survival largely depends on transfers from higher-level governments, which account for 70 percent of its total income (table 6.7). The township owes the local RCC nearly 600 million yuan for financing its four collective enterprises (table 6.6), all of which are now collapsed.[9]

Xiao fared better than Cheng during the TVE era. At its height, the township even set up an agency, Xiao Township Private Limited, headed by a township party secretary's appointee, to manage its five collective enterprises. When the collective enterprise sector collapsed, three of Xiao's five TVEs were sold to their existing managers, while the other two were closed. One of the surviving enterprises is a processing plant for sulfur, a mineral found locally. The other

TABLE 6.6 Creditors of the perished townships

TOWNSHIPS	TOTAL DEBT (THOUSANDS YUAN)	CREDITORS	DEBT (THOUSANDS YUAN)
Xiao	2,960	RCC	2,960
Cheng	590	RCC	590
Zhou	5,580	RCF, of which:	1,380
		RCC	*1,380*
		WB Development Aid	1,200
		Private lenders	3,000
Zhang	2,200	Construction companies	2,100
		RCF, of which:	*2,700*
		Households	*1,500*
		County and prefecture governments	*1,200*
		RCC	1,000
Sun	1,100	RCF, of which:	1,100
		County government	*1,100*
Fan	5,000	RCC	2,200
		ABC	800
		Private lenders	2,000

Source: Author's calculation from fiscal data provided by township finance bureaus.

TABLE 6.7 Fiscal indicators of the perished townships

	XIAO	CHENG	ZHOU[1]	ZHANG	SUN	FAN
Local-government revenue per capita (yuan)	186	59	33	123	326	244
Share of intergovernmental transfer in total fiscal revenue (%)	48%	70%	N/A	58%	52%	37%
Share of agriculture-related tax revenue in total tax revenue (%)	13%	17%	74%	87%	55%	51%
Debt-to-revenue ratio[2]	11.6	0.9	16.4	6.2	0.2	4.6
Debt per capita (yuan)	572	23	464	322	28	714

[1]Figures for Zhou exclude intergovernmental transfer.
[2]Revenue includes within- and extrabudgetary revenue.

Source: Author's calculation from fiscal data provided by township finance bureaus.

two enterprises are a cement factory and a hydroelectric company, generating electricity from the river that runs through the township.[10]

Notwithstanding the survival of three of its TVEs, Xiao is still highly in debt, even more so than Cheng. Xiao's debt-to-revenue ratio stood at 11.6, suggesting the township would need at least eleven years of revenue generation without incurring any expenditures or interest expense to repay its debt! Xiao's per capita debt of 572 yuan was nearly three times its per capita local revenue of 186 yuan (table 6.7). Xiao has not been able either to repay the 3 million yuan loan that it took out from the local RCC to finance collective enterprises *or* to pay for township cadres' salaries. This underlines the fact that Xiao is indebted to such an extent that it has been stretching its resources—well beyond its capacity—to simply function as a unit of government.

The dire straits of perished townships are even better illustrated by Zhang and Zhou, located in the same county in Nanchong prefecture, in Sichuan's remote mountainous northeastern region. In the early 1990s, Zhang had six collective enterprises and Zhou had five, which in both townships were a combination of silk factories, brick factories, and fish farms. None of these enterprises, however, had been particularly successful.[11] Neither of these townships has any natural resource endowment.

Notably, Zhang and Zhou's county (SC2 county) is officially designated as a "poor county by the provincial standard" (*shengji pinkunxian*). However, this designation does not necessarily mean it is poorer than other locales without the designation. Being officially "poor" entitles the county to a range of subsidies from the central and provincial governments. As a result, almost every marginally poor locale aspires to receive this designation, which is therefore sometimes acquired through lobbying and political connections.[12]

The enormous costs of unsuccessful industrialization are borne out in the fiscal situations of both Zhang and Zhou. Zhou owed 1.4 million yuan to the now-defunct RCF, the (bad) assets of which were transferred to the local RCC in the late 1990s (table 6.6).[13] The RCC was then instructed by the central government to help the financially distressed township meet the RCF's obligations to its individual depositors, as was common in locales where local governments were destitute. Thus, Zhou now owes the 1.4 million yuan to the RCC. In addition, Zhou has borrowed 3 million yuan from private individuals to help pay for cadres' salaries and meet its tax revenue targets. Its debt-to-revenue ratio stands at 16.4 (see table 6.7), making its debts almost impossible to amortize given its meager income!

Zhang faces a similarly dismal reality. Zhang is 5.8 million yuan in debt, more than *six times* its tax revenue (tables 6.6 and 6.7). Half of Zhang's financial liabilities come from the RCF it had set up: 1.2 million yuan is owed to higher-level governments for loans taken to repay the RCF's creditors, while 1.5

million yuan worth of RCF deposits remain unhonored (table 6.6). Zhang also owes the local RCC 1 million yuan for collective enterprise financing. Finally, it owes some construction companies about 2 million yuan for the refurbishment of its town hall (table 6.6).

Fan, a township in Zhangjiakou prefecture in Hebei province, is still struggling to repay its debt of 3 million yuan. This debt consists of 2.2 million yuan to the local RCC and 800,000 yuan to the ABC, both from loans used to finance Fan's three collective enterprises (table 6.6). In addition, Fan also borrowed 2 million yuan from private individuals to meet its tax revenue targets and build schools in order to meet the compulsory nine-year education target (table 6.6).[14] Its debt per capita is thrice its revenue per capita (table 6.7).

Sun, in Shandong, is the best performer in the perished pool, carrying a small debt burden and deficit. However, Sun has no spending allocated to public goods and service provision. The only expenditure items on its budget are personnel salaries and government administration (table 6A.5 in the appendix to this chapter). Moreover, half of the township's fiscal income comes from intergovernmental transfer (table 6.7).

A defining characteristic of these perished townships, with the exception of Xiao and Cheng,[15] has been their overwhelming reliance on the agriculture tax. At the time of my fieldwork, the agriculture tax accounted for about half of the income of Sun and Fan and almost all of the income of Zhang and Zhou (table 6.7). This income is now largely lost owing to the central government's abolition of the agriculture tax in the mid-2000s. The central government did promise to compensate grassroots authorities for their loss of agricultural tax revenue through intergovernmental transfers. However, as shown in chapter 4, intergovernmental transfers in China are inherently opaque, and the hoarding of transfer payments by county governments is commonplace.[16] It is therefore almost certain that the fiscal health of these already struggling townships has deteriorated even more since I collected my fiscal data in 2004 and 2005.

From the perspective of rural development, the most critical concern with regard to these six townships is their lack of spending on public goods and services such as education, health care, and social welfare. In China's decentralized fiscal environment, these essential social services are largely financed by township authorities. As a result, lack of government financing means farmers have to pay for these services themselves. In a majority of these perished townships, the only budget expenditure items are officials' salaries and administrative and government office expenses (see the appendix to this chapter). The expenditures on education and health care shown in some of these townships were paid for directly by county governments via intergovernmental transfers, in a desperate attempt to help the impoverished townships. But the county governments in these regions are just as destitute, so that residents are not getting full services even with the subsidies. The farmer-related indicators, to which we turn next, are further evidence of this harsh reality.

Farmer-Related Indicators

Farmers' dismal livelihood prospects in Zhang and Zhou is best illustrated by the emigration of the working-age population. As shown in table 6.1, 56 percent of the adult workforce in Zhang, and a whopping 80 percent of the adult workforce in Zhou, are making a living in other provinces! During my visits to these townships, almost all the people I met were either younger than fifteen or older than fifty. The young and physically able—men and women alike—had taken up jobs as construction or factory workers in the eastern coastal cities to help support remaining family members in the villages.[17] When contrasted to the influx of migrant labor in Zen and the high proportion of wage laborers in Han, the costs of failed local government–led industrialization and absence of private enterprises become abundantly clear. Without successful local industrialization, and with low arable land per capita, local agriculture cannot provide for farmers' sustainable livelihood, forcing them to seek employment elsewhere.[18]

Wage arrears are the norm for government officials in this part of rural China. Routinely, cadres in Zhang and Zhou were paid only six to nine months' salaries in a year. Ironically, a cadre working in the township finance bureau, in charge of collecting taxes, revealed to me that the local government had owed her close to 10,000 yuan over the last five years, a substantial amount given her monthly wages of 700 yuan.[19] Indeed, the issue of wage arrears for grassroots cadres had grown to such a serious scale that in 2003 the central government made the financing of township cadres' salaries a county government responsibility. But this policy only somewhat ameliorated the problem because in the parts of the countryside in which wage arrears are most common, county governments are just as bereft of income as township authorities.

Farmers' additional taxes and fees, known as "peasant burdens" in the literature, were also exorbitant in these townships before 2002. These "peasant burdens" ranged from the agriculture tax, the agricultural specialty tax (*nongye techanshui*), and corvee labor, to more arbitrary components, such as communication fees (*guangbo fei*), slaughter fees, vaccination fees, and fines for population control. My survey findings indicate that at their peak these arbitrarily imposed financial burdens were equivalent to a 25–30 percent tax on peasants' income (figures 6.2 and 6.3). Notably, across townships with different income levels in the sample, it was Zhang and Zhou, the poorest townships, that bore higher levels of "peasant burdens."

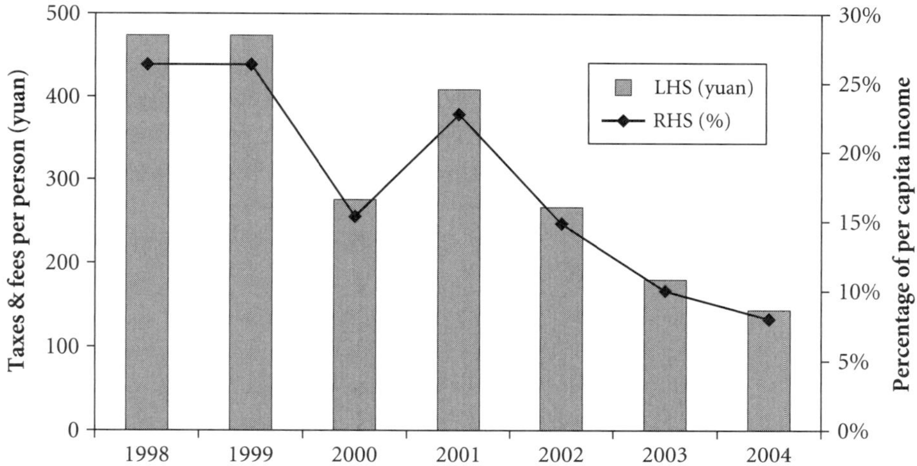

FIGURE 6.2 Taxes and fees paid by Zhou township residents (N = 8)
LHS = left-hand side; RHS = right-hand side.
Source: Author's survey.

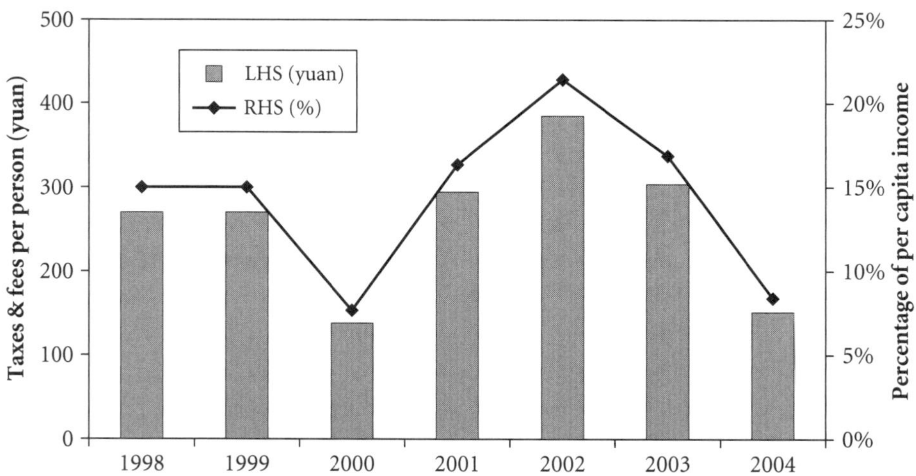

FIGURE 6.3 Taxes and fees paid by Zhang township residents (N = 52)
LHS = left-hand side; RHS = right-hand side.
Source: Author's survey.

Not surprisingly, these "peasant burdens" were the *most serious cause* of rural discontent and unrest from the late 1990s to the early 2000s. In response, the central government implemented the Tax-for-Fee reform in 2002, converting these arbitrarily imposed fees into more transparent taxes in order to reduce farmers' tax burdens. The agriculture tax and other agriculture-related taxes were then altogether abolished in 2005. These rural tax reforms have helped appease farmers by reducing their payments to local governments. However, they have also drastically reduced the income of local authorities directly responsible for providing services to the rural citizenry.[20]

Moreover, many peasants were forced to take out loans from the local RCC to pay the arbitrary taxes and fees. The household survey suggests the payment of taxes and fees was the single most important use of farmers' loans from the RCCs in Zhang and Zhou, accounting for more than 40 percent of total borrowing (figure 6.4).[21] According to the farmers I interviewed, this was due to the fact that local tax collectors were usually accompanied by RCC loan officers. When farmers could not make payments, they were forced to borrow the needed money from the credit cooperative.

This underscores the blurring of the line between uses of banking resources (*jinrong*) and fiscal resources (*caizheng*) in China. The two systems are intended to serve different purposes. The banking system is intended to improve the efficiency of capital allocations through the reinvestment of household savings in high-return projects. The fiscal system is intended to allow for government spending on public projects and centrally determined social priorities through the redistribution of taxes. However, in China, household savings end up being channeled to meet local governments' fiscal obligations. This results in a significant compromise of the goals of the banking system and in the introduction of systemic risk into both systems, as household savings will eventually have to be

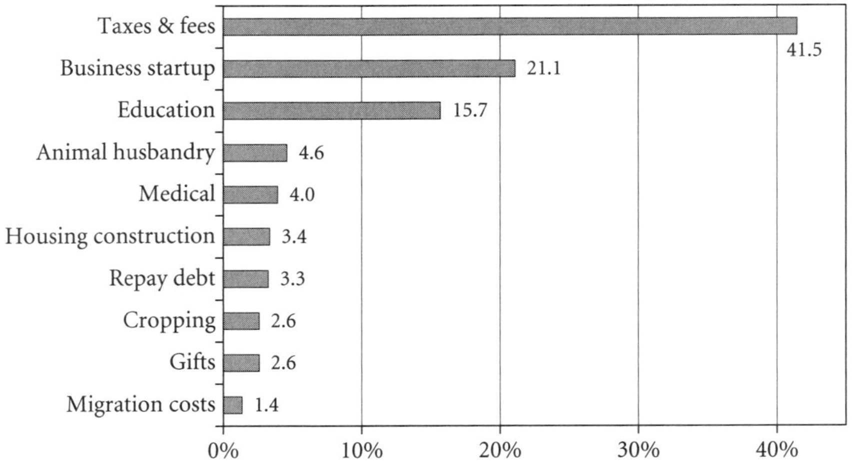

FIGURE 6.4 Uses of RCC loans in Zhang and Zhou townships ($N = 60$)

Source: Author's survey.

honored. This was already evidenced in the analysis of the widespread insolvency of RCFs in chapter 3 and will be further analyzed with regard to RCCs in the Conclusion.

Another major component of farm households' expenditures is education. Under the central government's compulsory education policy, children are supposed to receive nine years of education for free.[22] However, my survey findings highlight the fact that basic education in these poor areas is essentially user-paid. Indeed, annual tuition fees are as high as 360 yuan per student for kindergarten, 490 yuan per student for the first grade of primary school, and 740 yuan per student for primary year six. In addition, every student has to pay some miscellaneous examination, textbook, and insurance fees totaling about 100 yuan. Education expenditures account for 16 percent of total RCC loans in Zhang and Zhou (figure 6.4). The share of education expenditures as a proportion of household income ranges from 15 percent in Cheng and 23 percent in Fan to 29 percent in Zhou (figure 6.5). Moreover, tuition fees in these areas cover only teachers' salaries. As a result, rural households also had to pay an educational surplus fee (*jiaoyu fujia fei*) to finance school construction and renovation, before the central government abolished such fees in the mid-2000s. Since then, no funding has been available for the purpose of school construction and renovation.[23]

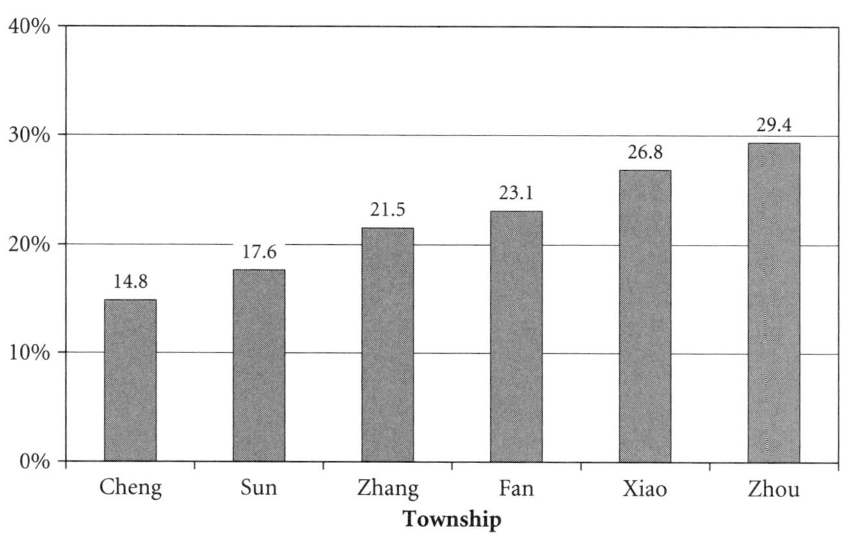

FIGURE 6.5 Education expenses as a percentage of household income (N = 257)

Source: Author's survey.

Similarly, because these revenue-starved local authorities are unable to provide subsidized medical services, health care has also become an out-of-pocket expense item for farmers. As a proportion of household income, medical expenses in the perished townships range from 2 percent in Zhang to 16 percent in Fan and 21 percent in Xiao (figure 6.6). As a result, the combined share of education and medical expenses out of household income is at least a quarter in Sun and Zhang and as high as half in Zhou and Xiao. For families already stretching their financial resources to pay for children's education expenses, household finances can often be crippled by a family member's falling ill and requiring medical treatment. In this situation, it is not uncommon for farmers to either sell off whatever assets they have (usually poultry, cows, or motorcycles) or incur tremendous debt by getting a loan from the RCC (or, for the desperate, do both).

The dismal fiscal situation of grassroots authorities is therefore a major reason for the lack of health-care provision in rural China.[24] This was meant to be addressed by a new rural medical insurance system, the Cooperative Medical Scheme, based on copayments between farmers and various levels of governments. This scheme is designed to extend health insurance coverage for rural residents while requiring them to make only a nominal payment of 10–20 yuan per person.[25] Nonetheless, this scheme, which had yet to be implemented when I was conducting my fieldwork in 2004 and 2005, is fraught with several design

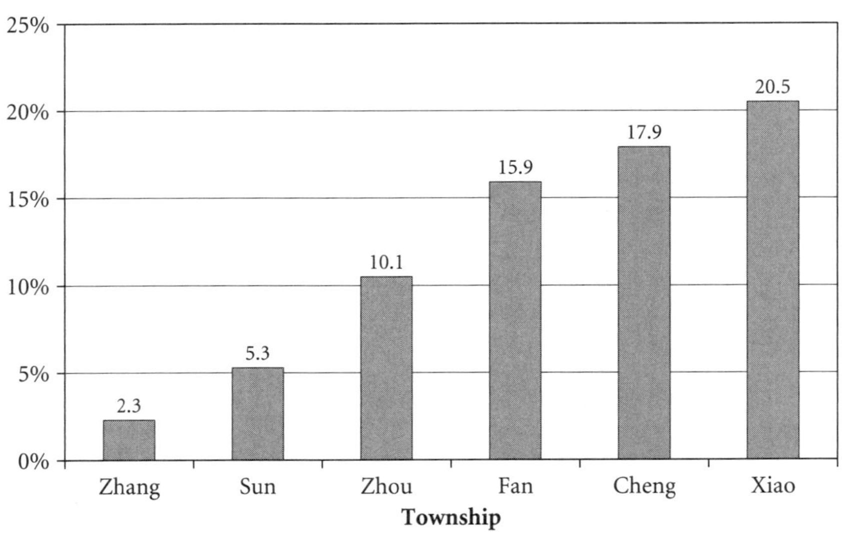

FIGURE 6.6 Medical expenses as a percentage of household income ($N = 257$)

Source: Author's survey.

problems. In particular, this scheme entails significant copayments by grassroots governments. But as my case studies show, the local governments in those destitute locales in which this health insurance scheme is needed the most are the ones that can least afford such payments.[26]

Aside from arbitrarily imposed taxes and fees, and exorbitant education and medical expenses, peasant discontent has also increasingly stemmed from perceived inadequate compensation for land requisitioning. Land takings happen most frequently in peri-urban areas where demand for converting land into industrial and urban usage is high. However, as land-leasing income has become the most significant source of local revenue, local governments also expropriate farmland for urban development purposes, even when no clear demand for urbanization exists, particularly when easy finance from banking institutions is readily available.[27] While local governments throughout the country have been actively engaging in land requisitions, the case studies suggest that land-related grievances are disproportionately higher in perished townships where local governments are more revenue deprived, which negatively affects their ability to provide adequate compensation.[28] In such locales, local authorities often resort to evicting farmers if they refuse to vacate their homes or to acquiring land without providing proper compensation to farmers. This is not to say that farmers in prosperous areas are always well compensated or that corruption, a common trigger of land grievances, does not exist in such places. But these governments are somewhat able to compensate adequately given their improved financial capacity. One such example is Zouping county government's decision to compensate landless peasants at a rate over and above that stipulated by the Land Management Law. At the township level, the pressure to scour for funding is particularly immense after the Tax-for-Fee reform in 2002 and the abolition of remaining taxes and fees in 2005.

For example, Cheng, a peri-urban county seat, has seen a flurry of land-trade activity as the township tried to convert farmland for use in the construction of retail stores.[29] During my fieldwork there, I came across some residents who were forced to leave their homes as part of an "old town refurbishment" (*jiucheng gaizao*) project launched by the township. The residents refused to move out of the premises because they felt the compensation the township offered was grossly inadequate to allow for the purchase of new and thus considerably more expensive houses. In order to force the residents to leave their homes, the township shut off electricity and water to the housing complexes. After a protracted struggle with local authorities, the residents vacated their homes, largely out of despair. The underlying social sentiment in Cheng was anger and outrage at the local authorities' total disregard for their basic livelihood.[30]

The pathway to local-government indebtedness and rising rural discontent as a result of failed local government–led industrialization attempts is depicted in figure 6.7. During the 1980s and early 1990s, in response to fiscal decentralization incentives, local authorities utilized two major channels to finance their industrialization efforts: RCCs and RCFs. As explained in chapter 3, local governments could borrow directly from RCFs but not from RCCs. However, local party secretaries had veto power over hiring, firing, and other decisions regarding credit cooperative managers until the reform in the late 1990s. As a result, most RCC loans were allocated to collective enterprises established by local governments, which contributed taxes and profits to local governments and provided public goods to residents. Loans from RCFs served the same purposes, but some RCF loans also went directly to filling local governments' budgetary deficits.

Collective TVEs served local governments' interests as long as they could contribute to local governments' coffers. It mattered little whether the enterprises were making profits because their tax contributions were based on their revenue. It therefore made sense for local authorities to grow the number *and* scale of collective enterprises, since loans were cheap and readily available. The turning point came when the central government recentralized the revenue-based VAT in 1994, leaving grassroots authorities with the profit-based enterprise tax. From that point onward, *only* profitable enterprises were of benefit from local governments' fiscal standpoint. Local authorities therefore began shedding unprofitable TVEs, some through privatization, but most through massive closures.

However, the downfallen collective sector was not replaced by a thriving private sector in most of the hinterlands, as exemplified by case studies in this chapter. This led to shrinking revenue bases for grassroots governments, which are responsible for financing the bulk of public goods and services under the highly decentralized current fiscal arrangement. Faced with dwindling income, local leaders began imposing and extracting arbitrary taxes and fees from farmers. The central government–introduced tax reform which prohibited most such taxes and fees further incapacitated the fiscal health of local authorities. This tax reform alleviated the symptoms of the problem ("peasant burdens") while leaving its root causes (poor local governance and weak fiscal capacity) unsolved. Instead of demanding payments from farmers, local governments now raise revenue by confiscating or expropriating farmland and leasing it to commercial users, setting off a new range of rural governance issues. Meanwhile, local governments continue to be deeply indebted to the local credit institutions whose loans financed their fallen collective enterprises. Consequently, local credit institutions remain highly leveraged due to the mounting nonperforming loans that resulted.

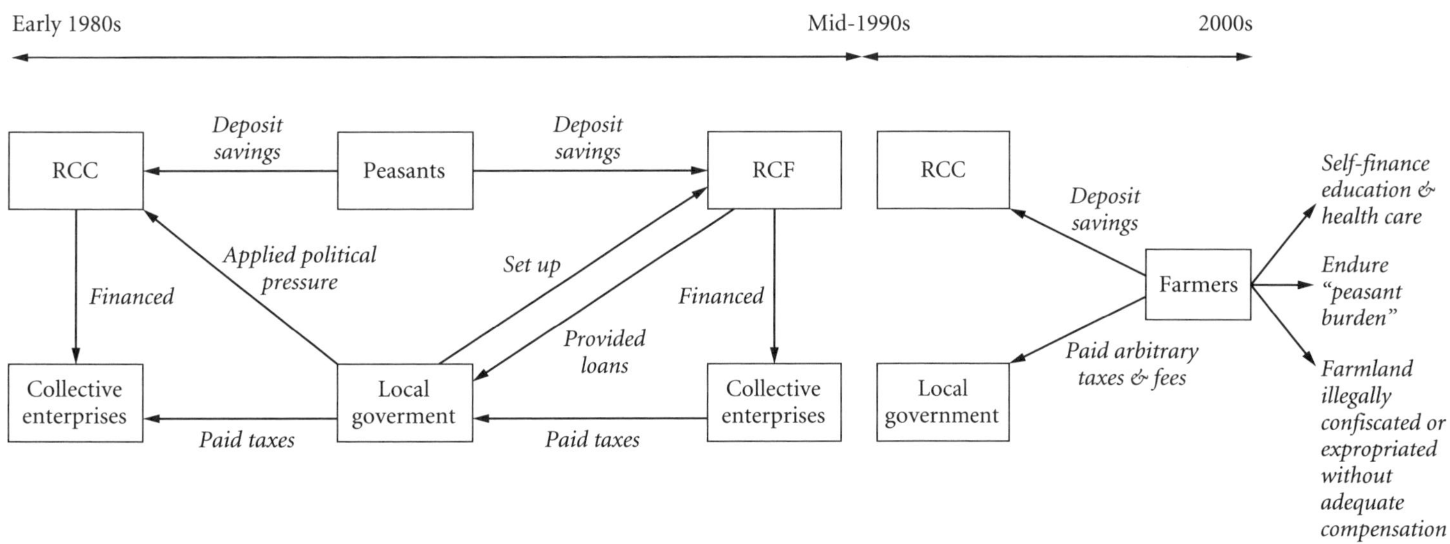

FIGURE 6.7 How local government–led industrialization led to rural decay

Prospered and Perished Cases and the Control Variables

What factors differentiate the prospered cases analyzed in chapter 5 from the perished cases analyzed in the present chapter? Contrary to the common perception that locales in coastal provinces (Zhejiang, Jiangsu, Guangdong, Fujian, and Shandong) perform better economically than locales in inland regions, my findings suggest that the location of the province is not a *determining* factor in successful industrialization. Both Han and Sun are located in the same county in Shandong province, but the former has prospered while the latter has not. Similarly, natural resource endowment contributes to economic success in some locales but not others. Han is able to utilize its locally grown corn for successful industrialization. By contrast, Xiao has been far less successful despite its mineral resources, and Zen's lack of natural resources has not prevented it from successful industrialization (see table 6.8).

My analysis suggests that proximity to an urban center is the key determinant for successful rural industrialization. Non-coastal Zouping county, where Han and Sun townships are located, is geographically well positioned, with excellent transport networks linking it to nearby urban centers to allow for transportation of products to large consumer markets. However, while Han is 5 kilometers from the county seat, through which the state highway passes, Sun is 35 kilometers away, and there are at least three townships in between Han and Sun. Moreover, because all the townships in the county are fervently developing similar industries—the processing of cotton and the production of corn oil, starch, and other corn by-products—only a few can become successful. When each of the sixteen townships in the county tries to set up its own corn oil, starch, and cot-

TABLE 6.8 Studied cases and variables

		CONTROL VARIABLES			OUTCOME	
CASE	INDUSTRIALIZATION	LOCATION OF PROVINCE	PROXIMITY TO URBAN CENTER	NATURAL RESOURCES	PROSPERED	PERISHED
Zen	P	C	×		×	
Han	G	C	×	×	×	
Xiao	G	I		×		×
Zhang	G	I				×
Zhou	G	I				×
Cheng	G	I				×
Fan	G	I				×
Sun	G	C		×		×

P = privately led; G = government-led; C = coastal; I = inland.

ton processing factories, the townships' products are virtually undifferentiated except on the basis of prices, which makes speed-to-market—a factor facilitated by geography—a determinant for success. It is noteworthy that this "me too" strategy is not exclusive to Zouping, but prevalent throughout rural China, as with the cluster of scrap iron factories in Zen and the cluster of now-collapsed silk producers in Zhou and Zhang.

Even though neighboring townships have industrialized more successfully than Sun, there is a resulting benefit to Sun's economy: the cotton growers and corn farmers in Sun derive income from supplying agricultural raw materials to the factories in Han. Their income may not be as high as that of the factory workers in Han, but they are doing much better than residents of the perished townships in rural Hebei and mountainous Sichuan, where successful industrial enterprises are virtually nonexistent. In addition, the factories in Han provide wage employment to some people from Sun, which has supplemented agricultural income in the township.

A large majority of the industrialization efforts spearheaded by local governments across rural China have failed miserably. Local governments ended up mired in debt and financially incapable of providing any social services. These rural townships borrowed heavily to finance the development of collective enterprises before the mid-1990s, but the collapse of the collective sector has *not* been replaced by profitable private companies.

Farmers in these townships bore substantial financial burdens as local authorities resorted to extracting arbitrary fees and fines from households to supplement their income. Though the recent rural fiscal reforms have helped reduce peasant burdens, they have also exacerbated local governments' financial straits. Most of these rural locales survive *solely* on fiscal transfers from higher-level governments. Consequently, the formal functions of grassroots governments—such as the provision of basic infrastructure, education, and health care—have largely withered away. These governments are no longer able to fulfill their most basic functions, such as paying the wages of their own cadres, teachers, or health-care workers. The result is that these public officials often cannot carry out their jobs or they commonly face massive wage arrears.

Other scholars have similarly pointed out that grassroots governments' fiscal crisis has paralyzed their functions.[31] However, this book disagrees with other studies on the primary cause of the fiscal crisis. Undoubtedly, the series of rural fiscal reforms implemented during the mid-2000s to reduce peasant burdens have heightened the fiscal crisis across vast swaths of rural China. But while the fiscal reforms have been rolled out in similar fashion throughout rural China, why are the fiscal crisis and peasant burdens concentrated in the central and western regions? The reason for this is that in these regions, local government–led industrialization failed miserably, resulting in massive debt, while private firms competing under market conditions have also failed to grow. Hence, it was unsuccessful rural industrialization that impoverished these local authorities, and the recent fiscal reforms have merely made the symptoms worse.

The key determinant of successful private enterprises for rural locales boils down, simply, to market interconnectedness and competition enabled by geography. Imagine that there are about forty thousand townships in China, and each and every one tries to industrialize. Where are the markets for their products? How do they reach consumers? The present study suggests that the location of the province matters less than does proximity to urban centers. Indeed, not all townships in eastern provinces have successfully industrialized, though a majority of them have.

As my case studies amply illustrate, an overwhelming proportion of the financing of local government–led industrialization during the 1980s and 1990s came from local RCCs and the RCFs. This implies that rural savings have financed the bulk of local government–led industrialization attempts. But more importantly, the mounting local-government debt resulting from the futile industrialization attempt means that rural savings have been bled profusely, resulting in insolvent rural credit institutions. Since savers—unlike taxpayers—expect to have their savings honored, this is not merely a problem of the banking sector but one that has immense political consequences. The political implications of the insolvent credit institutions will be explored further in the Conclusion.

What role does corruption play in this story? Obviously, corruption contributes to governance problems in the countryside, such as "peasant burdens" and land-related conflicts. Nevertheless, instead of attributing every malaise to corruption, this inquiry takes an institutional approach by asking what an upright and uncorrupt government official might have done given the systemic incentives and constraints. This is not to deny the existence of corruption or cronyism. It is to stress that local governments behave as they do because of the incentives embedded in the system. I contend that an upright official would have behaved in the same manner in order to get his job done. If he happened to be corrupt, the outcome might or might not be worse, but that falls outside the scope of this study and has already been addressed elsewhere.[32]

What do the successful and unsuccessful case studies tell us about the Sunan model? A large majority of local governments in China adopted the local government–led industrialization strategy during the 1980s and early 1990s. Nevertheless, they were not adherents of the Sunan model, strictly speaking. This is because the model describes only successful local government–led industrialization; it does not generally account for unsuccessful cases.[33] Yet a more productive exercise than picking apart the Sunan model is to ask why local government-led strategy has been successful in some locales but not in others.

That is, what differentiates Han from the perished townships? The answer is exposure to competition and access to technical know-how, which its geographical position provides for. Most local governments might not have been as farsighted as those in Zouping to introduce new technologies to the enterprises and to subject them to competition, especially when cheap credit was available and excess demand existed for consumer goods prior to the mid-1990s. Local government's caliber—specifically, its ability to formulate strategies to preempt future challenges—matters. Notwithstanding that, strong government capability does not guarantee success. Even under the guidance of the most farsighted local party leaders, neither competition nor new technologies could be introduced to industries in remote locations. To be sure, geography, on its own, is an insufficient condition for growth. It is geography coupled with infrastructure capacity that provides a conducive environment for market competition and interconnectedness, which are the key ingredients for regional industrial growth.

Since the mid-2000s, the Hu-Wen administration has invested enormous resources in the construction of a "new socialist countryside" (*shehui zhuyi xinnongcun*), with money being poured into infrastructure development and improvements in the provision of public goods and services, such as health care and education. When I conducted my field studies in the mid-2000s, the program, which was still in its infancy, had yet to produce results. Recent surveys indicate that the pro-rural policy and the 2008 fiscal stimulus have improved the plight of some rural populations and helped improve rural sentiments.[34] The policies include abolition of the agriculture tax, massive investment in infrastructure development in rural areas, a rural cooperative medical scheme, and various rural subsidies.

While these recent policies and developments may have improved conditions in some parts of the countryside, they vindicate this study's findings rather than refute them. By improving public goods and service provisions, the policies are intended to prevent festering rural discontent from threatening social stability and the party's legitimacy. This is a profound recognition by the center that many local governments, when left to their own devices, are financially incapable of providing the most basic public services to the rural citizenry. Such is the premise of my argument about how failed local government industrialization and deprivation of revenue could lead to rural decay with self-finance of farmers for basic health care and education, and local governments' predatory behaviors aimed at augmenting revenue. See figure 6.7 for the chain of causation to rural decay.

Overall, these pro-rural policies and fiscal stimulus have achieved dubious success. Poverty alleviation funds rarely end up in the hands of the intended recipients or those who need them the most. This is a classic problem with the handouts from the central government described in chapter 2. The fiscal stimulus program largely funded by local governments' borrowing from financial institutions, including RCCs, have worsened the local government debt situation—a pertinent issue that will be dealt with in the Conclusion. Some observers have also questioned whether it is really the policies per se that are making the difference or whether it is migrant workers' remittance that is keeping poor villagers afloat.[35] While an evaluation of the success of the policies falls outside the scope of this study, the motivation and numerous consequences of the policies are at the heart of this inquiry.

Appendix

Revenue and Expenditures of the Perished Townships

TABLE 6A.1 Revenue and expenditures of Xiao township (2003)

REVENUE	(THOUSANDS YUAN)	EXPENDITURES	(THOUSANDS YUAN)
Within-budgetary revenue	**254.4**	**Within-budgetary expenditures**	**917.2**
Sales tax	153.4	Agricultural expenses	53.7
Company income tax	54.9	Culture and media fees	39.1
Personal income tax	0.8	Educational expenses	447.0
Resources tax	10.9	Medical and healthcare expenses	134.6
Stamp duty	0.1	Social welfare fees	41.9
Agriculture tax	33.6	Administrative and management fees, incl. officials' salaries	108.2
Agricultural specialty tax	0.3	Other expenses	92.8
Other income	0.4		
Intergovernmental transfer	**606.7**		
Repatriation of consumption tax & VAT	204.5		
Earmarked grant allocations	65.0		
Subsidies for agricultural tax reforms	66.6		
Subsidies for wage increment	252.0		
Other	18.6		
Extrabudgetary revenue	**260.2**	**Extrabudgetary expenditures**	**271.0**
Previous year balance	148.5	Budgeted fund expenditures	13.4
Budgeted fund revenue	6.7		
Total revenue	**1,276.5**	**Total expenditures**	**1,201.6**
		Balance	74.9

Source: Xiao township finance bureau.

TABLE 6A.2 Revenue and expenditures of Cheng township (2003)

REVENUE	(THOUSANDS YUAN)	EXPENDITURES	(THOUSANDS YUAN)
Within-budgetary revenue	**402.5**	**Within-budgetary expenditures**	**1,323.8**
Sales tax	252.0	Educational expenses (paid for by intergovernmental transfer)	611.2
Individual income tax	73.3	Administrative expenses, including officials' salaries	358.5
Agriculture tax	68.0	Health care	129.2
City and town land use tax	8.1	Social welfare fees	95.5
Other	1.2	Agricultural expenses	50.9
		Culture and media fees	41.2
Intergovernmental transfer	**1,035.4**	Other	35.2
Subsidies for wage increment	306.6		
Subsidies for agricultural tax reforms	117.5		
Other	611.2		
Previous year revenue	(210.4)		
Extrabudgetary revenue	**258.8**	**Extrabudgetary expenditures**	**251.4**
Total revenue	**1,486.3**	**Total expenditures**	**1,575.2**
		Balance	(88.9)

Source: Cheng township finance bureau.

TABLE 6A.3 Revenue and expenditures of Zhang township (2003)

REVENUE	(THOUSANDS YUAN)	EXPENDITURES	(THOUSANDS YUAN)
Within-budgetary revenue	**820.0**	**Within-budgetary expenditures**	2,880.7
Agricultural tax	710.0	Education expenses (paid for by intergovernmental transfer)	1,280.0
Business tax	110.0	Office expenses	680.8
		Officials' salaries	370
		Social welfare fees	211.0
Intergovernmental transfers	1,300.0	Agricultural expenses	106.9
Subsidy income from higher-level govts	650.0	Culture and media fees	81.6
Transfers from central govt	650.0	Other expenses	82.9
Extrabudgetary revenue	110.0		

TABLE 6A.3—*cont.*

REVENUE	(THOUSANDS YUAN)	EXPENDITURES	(THOUSANDS YUAN)
Additional agriculture tax	110.0		
Total revenue	**2,230.0**	**Total expenditures**	**2,880.7**
		Balance	(650.7)

Source: Zhang township finance bureau.

TABLE 6A.4 Revenue and expenditures of Fan township (2004)

REVENUE	(THOUSANDS YUAN)	EXPENDITURES	(THOUSANDS YUAN)
Within-budgetary revenue	**1,079.0**	**Within-budgetary expenditures**	**1,867.0**
Value-added tax	130.0	Officials' salaries	1,612.0
Sales tax	399.0	Administrative expenses	240.0
Agriculture tax	550.0	Welfare payments	15.0
Intergovernmental transfer	**630.0**		
Transfer payment	630.0		
Total revenue	**1,709.0**	**Total expenditures**	**1,867.0**
		Balance	(158)

Source: Fan township finance bureau.

TABLE 6A.5 Revenue and expenditures of Sun township (2004)

REVENUE	(MILLIONS YUAN)	EXPENDITURES	(MILLIONS YUAN)
Within-budgetary revenue	**6.2**	**Within-budgetary expenditures**	**13.0**
Company income tax	0.3	Officials' salaries	9.0
Value-added tax	1.0	Administrative expenses	3.5
Sales tax	0.3	Infrastructure building	0.5
Stamp duty, land utilization tax	1.2		
Agriculture tax	2.4		
Additional agriculture tax	1.0		
Intergovernmental transfer	**6.7**		
Transfer payment	3.2		
Labor subsidies	1.0		
Agricultural tax subsidies	2.5		
Total revenue	**12.9**	**Total expenditures**	**13.0**
		Balance	(0.1)

Source: Sun township finance bureau.

TABLE 6A.6 Revenue and expenditures of Zhou township (2003)

REVENUE	(THOUSANDS YUAN)	EXPENDITURES
Within-budgetary revenue	**341**	**unknown**
Agricultural tax	250	
Sales tax	90	
Extrabudgetary revenue	**55**	
Corvee labor fees	55	
Total revenue (excluding intergovernmental transfers)	**395**	

Source: Zhou township party secretary.

CONCLUSION

I start these conclusions by updating the RCC reform in the late 2000s, analyzing the costs of soft budget constraint and bailout by the central government. I then compare the political-economic dynamics of the rural credit sector with the surge in local-government borrowing and debt as a result of the 2008–9 fiscal stimulus program. I then situate the book's findings in the broader theoretical contexts of local development-oriented and predatory states, central-local government relations, and market-preserving federalism. I conclude by drawing normative implications for China's development policies and its growth model.

Moral Hazard, Central Government's Bailout of Credit Institutions, and Local Governments

The chief of China's central bank, Zhou Xiaochuan, revealed that RCCs' nonperforming loan rate reached more than 50 percent at the end of the 1990s, according to official estimates.[1] At the end of 2002, official estimates were that 19,542 (about 55 percent) of RCCs had a negative net worth—that is, their liabilities exceeded their asset values.[2] Moreover, it is likely that the actual negative net worth and nonperforming loan rates were even significantly higher, given deceptive bookkeeping practices such as "ever-greening" of loans (see p. 64 for further details), which were frequently employed by banking institutions in China to lower nonperforming loan rates. Under market conditions, any corporation with negative net worth will be closed before its shareholders' equity is usurped by losses. Notwithstanding that, the central bank has not allowed RCCs to fold, out of fear that such a collapse would lead to widespread economic and social instability. This made them, politically, "too big to fail" (TBTF), leading to the central government's bailout.[3]

The central bank's financial assistance amounted to a bailout because it did not harden RCCs' budget constraint in any fundamental way. Furthermore, because local governments were major debtors of the credit institutions, the RCC bailout was therefore in fact a bailout of local authorities. Various grassroots governments were already heavily indebted in the early 2000s, which was a manifestation of their soft budget constraint, despite the Budget Law (*yusuanfa*) prohibition on local-government debt financing. In effect, township and village authorities had raised capital from various local credit institutions and shifted the lion's share of repayment costs to the central government.

The TBTF argument for interventionist government action is by no means limited to communist regimes. The bailout of giant mortgage companies Fannie Mae and Freddie Mac in the United States in 2008 was justified on similar grounds. The domestic housing market, and potentially the global capital market, it was argued, would be destabilized should these colossal intermediaries—providing guarantee for millions of individual homeowners' mortgages—fold.[4]

RCCs are TBTF because they collectively hold more than 80 percent of deposits by individual rural households. Had the central government let RCCs fold, millions of rural depositors would have lost their hard-earned savings to mismanagement at the local credit cooperatives. Bank runs of a massive scale have inconceivable consequences for social stability in the countryside, which is the top concern of the Communist regime. Xie Ping, a former leading official at the central bank, concedes that "with a large amount of deposits from low-income farmers and the absence of explicit deposit insurance, closures (of RCCs) are expected to cause serious political and social unrest. Therefore, RCC bankruptcy is almost 'out of the question.'"[5]

The threat of social instability posed by RCCs' potential failure, and therefore their TBTF nature, was heightened by their quasi-state nature. As revealed by the survey results in chapter 3, a major reason many rural depositors had chosen to bank with RCCs was the widespread perception that RCC deposits had a central-government guarantee. This perception exists even though central authorities have no formal legal obligation to RCC depositors. On the one hand, RCCs are unlike state-owned banks, in which profits and losses are borne by the central government. On the other hand, they are also unlike privately owned banks, in which shareholders are responsible for the bank's bottom line.

Moreover, RCCs fulfill centrally prescribed policy functions. RCCs were essentially the only existing formal credit providers in the countryside prior to the liberalization of the rural credit sector in 2007. And their closure would deny millions of rural residents any access to formal loans and force them to turn to illegal sources of lending. Further, during the high inflation years of the late 1980s, the central government required RCCs to guarantee their depositors real positive interest returns. In the absence of these subsidies, depositors would have been paid interest rates lower than the rate of inflation.[6]

The TBTF nature of RCCs made it imperative that the central government come to their rescue.[7] As part of the 2003–5 reform package, the central bank handed out two forms of financial subsidies to help RCCs with negative net worth dispose of their bad assets and historical losses. The main subsidy, largest in magnitude and most popular among RCCs, was the 165.6 billion yuan conditional debt-for-bills swaps (*zhuanxiang piaoju*). The second and much more limited form of subsidy was the 830 million yuan earmarked central bank loans (*zhuanxiang daikuan*). These loans had no conditions and were intended to inject immediate liquidity into cash-strapped RCCs. Together, the bailout accounted for about 10 percent of RCCs' loan portfolio in 2003. In addition, the central government also cut RCCs' corporate income tax and business turnover tax rates to help raise their profitability.

The magnitude of the largest of these subsidies—the debt-for-bills swaps—was determined on the basis of half of total liabilities-in-excess-of-assets value (*zibudizhai*) of RCCs nationwide at 2002 year-end. The central bank bought bad assets from RCCs at book value, which has undeniably inflated the market value of the toxic assets. The credit cooperatives were supposed to hold the bills for two to four years, during which they were paid an annual interest rate of 1.89 percent. Upon maturation, RCCs could swap the bills for cash, subject to them fulfilling certain criteria that I will turn to next.

Notably, this arrangement differs from the central government's arrangements for ridding the four big state-owned banks of their bad assets. In the latter case, government-established asset management companies purchased the bad assets and subsequently restructured and sold them to recover some losses for the state.[8] In the case of RCCs, the central bank in effect paid the technically bankrupt institutions the book value of their toxic assets in order to allow them to write the losses off their balance sheets.[9] Predictably, this policy was hugely popular among RCCs. The policy was rolled out in stages beginning in late 2003. As of June 2008, 120.6 billion yuan, or 73 percent of all bills, had been cashed by credit cooperatives in 1,771 counties and cities.[10]

The central government's assistance did *not* harden RCCs' budget constraints in any fundamental sense. This was the case even though the central authority had made cashing out the bills conditional on certain criteria—namely, improvement in corporate governance structure and increases in capital adequacy ratios. The financial rewards were intended to be a quid pro quo for RCC restructuring, termed *huaqian mai jizhi*. Nevertheless, RCCs had been allowed to cash their bills even though there had been no real substantial improvement in either their corporate governance or their capital adequacy.

None of the changes to their corporate governance structure have incentivized RCC credit officers to be more accountable to members or shareholders. The reform required all RCCs to set up three major internal institutions—a board of directors (BoD), a board of supervisors (BoS), and a member or shareholder representative meeting. Members of the supreme decision-making body—the BoD—are supposed to be elected in the shareholder representative meeting. The BoS has a supervisory function over the BoD to prevent any abuse of power by the head or members of the board of directors.

Nonetheless, it is difficult to execute such separation of powers or checks and balances in an institutional environment where there is a superimposing Communist Party hierarchical structure. The head of the BoD, the top decision maker, is also the internal party secretary. The BoS typically consists of one man, a member of the party disciplinary committee (*jilv jiancha weiyuan*), who could also be a deputy head or the secretary of the BoD. In terms of either party ranking or corporate hierarchy, the head of the BoS answers to the party secretary and head of the BoD. It is inconceivable that the oversight function can be carried out impartially when the supervisor's career is being determined by the supervision subject.[11]

The shareholder or member representative meeting is still nothing more than a rubber stamp. Despite being nominally the highest governing body, it has no effective power in electing members of the BoD, deliberating, or making any major decisions. Further, owing to the large base of members or shareholders, the member representative meeting is persistently plagued by a collective action problem, as no individual has any real incentive to monitor the executives' behavior.[12] By RCC rules, each shareholder is permitted to hold only a small proportion of the organization's shares. My own research into the post-reform rural cooperative banks suggests there are as many as fourteen thousand shareholders in the shareholder representative meeting. Therefore, each individual (and employee) shareholder owns less than 0.5 percent, and each company shareholder owns less than 1.5 percent, of the credit institution. In a post-reform rural cooperative bank in Shandong I have studied, the top ten shareholders collectively hold merely 11 percent of the shares.[13] As a result, the benefits accrued to each individual in terms of either dividend payouts or improved profitability is too insignificant to justify the exertion of the supervisory effort.

As explained in chapter 2, as part of the 2003–5 restructuring, RCCs were also put under the management of provincial governments. For this purpose, new provincial-level administrative units, known as provincial credit unions, were created. However, it is not clear whether these provincial unions contribute to better governance or improved profitability of RCCs. Their highly interventionist role, often overriding RCCs' decisions in various areas, even further distances RCCs from accountability to their shareholders or members. Some post-reform RCC managers I have interviewed, particularly from profitable RCCs in developed regions, see this as problematic. They believe that provincial unions, having little knowledge of local credit markets, often set province-wide rules that stifle local innovation and adaptation. Traditionally, experienced credit officers, who have good knowledge of local borrowers' creditworthiness, were given substantial loan approval rights. This practice has brought RCCs handsome profits combined with low nonperforming loan rates. As RCC managers have convincingly argued, a uniform province-wide rule on loan approval rights deprives the credit cooperatives of their local advantage and competitive edge over the centrally managed state-owned banks.[14]

Another requirement for cashing in the central bank's bills is improvement in RCCs' capital adequacy ratio, a measure of financial soundness. The Basel Accord recommends an international standard for a minimum capital adequacy ratio to ensure banks' ability to absorb a reasonable level of losses before becoming insolvent. The central bank monitors this ratio to prevent RCCs from falling into negative net worth. Since a bank's ability to absorb losses is better the larger its capital or equity base is, augmenting equity provides a quick—but imperfect—solution for raising the bank's capital adequacy ratio. Thus, RCCs have employed several tactics in order to draw equity participation. Some have promised dividend payouts higher than existing interest rates to attract new shareholders, when in fact the payouts are unjustified by their profitability level. Others have used higher-than-savings-rate payouts to lure prevailing depositors to turn their savings into equity without informing them that equity participation, unlike savings, cannot be freely withdrawn.[15]

The total RCC bailout may have cost a fraction of the financial rescue of the state-owned banks in the early 2000s, but its stakes are just as high. The central bank's financial subsidies did not result in any fundamental change in the ways RCCs operate or in their incentive structure. These subsidies therefore encouraged credit officers to continue making unjustifiably risky decisions and engaging in other financially irresponsible behavior. The consequence of this "moral hazard" is that RCCs *expect* to be bailed out again in the future since they have managed to get away with prior bad financial decisions. The expectation of financial rescue thus discourages RCCs from adopting meaningful institutional changes as well as from making financially sound decisions.

The central government's financial rescue amounts to an indirect bailout of local authorities, and this has also allowed local governments to shirk their financial responsibility. Mounting levels of local-government debt are a manifestation of soft budget constraints they face. A 2004 study put village debt alone at 370 billion yuan, township debt at 215 billion yuan, and county debt at 410 billion yuan.[16] The unsustainability of these debt levels is further underlined by a recent World Bank study. Using a modest estimate of village liabilities at 250 yuan per villager (equivalent to 240 billion yuan in total village debt), this liability level is still about double the size of the current village income per capita of 140 yuan.[17] My own field research paints a similarly grim—and unsustainable—picture of grassroots government financial liabilities, even prior to the launch of the fiscal stimulus in 2008. In a Sichuan county I studied, the average debt per capita was about 5,400 yuan, almost three times the size of its 2003 average tax revenue of 1,900 yuan or average per capita income of 1,800 yuan. All the townships in the county had some degree of financial liabilities, with the debt-to-tax revenue ratio ranging from 0.7 to 6.6.[18]

Given the severity of grassroots government debt problems prior to 2004, the rescue of local authorities could have been in the central government's calculus when devising the financial subsidies. However, such a rescue had a similar "moral hazard" impact on local governments, since it did not deter government officials from borrowing from RCCs again even if they have no repayment ability. Indeed, local governments had gone all-out to assist their local credit cooperatives in reaching the central bank–required capital adequacy ratios that qualify them for the subsidies. Many had also gone to the extent of subsidizing dividend payouts in order to attract new equity members.[19] This fact suggests local authorities saw RCCs' cashing out of the central bank's bills as serving their own interests.

Aside from this one-off transfer from taxpayers, an even larger looming question is the stability of the rural banking system itself. On the eve of the financial rescue, it was evidently clear that had bank runs occurred, RCCs—the majority of which were technically bankrupt at the time—would not have been able to honor all deposits. The central government's financial rescue has put out the fire this time, albeit with taxpayers' money, through the central bank's picking up the tab for badly managed local credit institutions. But the lack of fundamental changes in RCCs' corporate governance structure and the persistence of soft budget constraints mean that the possibility of another fire looms large. After all, the arsonists are still around.

Rising Local-Government Borrowing and Debt and the 2008–10 Fiscal Stimulus Package

At the end of 2008, faced with a sluggish export market and a global financial meltdown, China announced a 4 trillion yuan (US$538 billion) fiscal stimulus package to prevent the economy from sinking into recession. The stimulus package consisted of infrastructure investments, such as construction of railways, highways, airports, and power grids, and redistributive social spending, such as low-cost housing for low-income families. As mentioned in chapter 6, some of the stimulus spending has improved infrastructure development in the countryside and facilitated the provision of public services in some areas. However, of the 4 trillion yuan, the central government was funding 30 percent of the total cost, with local governments expected to pay for 30 percent, with the remaining 40 percent funded by bank lending.

Given that regional authorities that had insufficient funding were also turning to banks for assistance, the banks' share in funding the stimulus package arguably exceeded 40 percent.[20] Therefore, bank lending was the single largest source of the fiscal stimulus package by any estimate. As a result, all banks in China, ranging from the policy banks, such as the China Development Bank, to the commercial banks, such as the Industrial and Commercial Bank of China and the Bank of China, were under immense pressure to support the central government's efforts to pump-prime the economy. Between 2008 and the first half of 2010, the four state-owned commercial banks and policy banks were funding railway investments and other large-scale infrastructure projects.[21] The city commercial banks were ramping up lending to local government–related companies. And the rural cooperative banks and credit cooperatives were key financiers of lower-level governments' projects in localities where other banks are not present, namely, in county-level cities.

Not surprisingly, bank lending has surged dramatically since the announcement of the fiscal stimulus package in late 2008.[22] As a result, RCCs have experienced rapid growth in lending, over and above financially prudent levels.[23] This is especially troubling because a substantial proportion of the stimulus program bank loans are not expected to be repaid, for several reasons. First, rapid increases in bank lending mean the banks did not carry out thorough evaluations of the projects' riskiness and profitability. Moreover, most loans issued were for infrastructure projects that yield no tangible financial returns. They have been approved simply because they are used for pump-priming the economy and are therefore perceived to carry an implicit central government guarantee. Some lending has reportedly been siphoned off by local officials for speculative investments in the stock market or jockeyed for private gains.[24] Perhaps, most importantly, local governments have been servicing interest payments based on revenue from land sales. This is feasible as long as land prices keep rising, but in the event of a fall or crash of property prices, most local authorities will conceivably have difficulties servicing the loans, pushing up the banks' nonperforming loan rates.[25]

Indeed, by March 2011, the conduit companies set up by local governments or the so-called local government financing vehicles (LGFVs, or *difang rongzi pingtai*) had racked up 7.7 trillion yuan in debts, more than the fiscal stimulus package itself.[26] An audit conducted by the National Audit Office in 2010 revealed that local-government debt totaled 10.7 trillion yuan, about half of which came from LGFVs.[27] It was estimated that debts carried by LGFVs were already 3.5 times that of local-government revenue by the second quarter of 2010.[28] Hence, it has been widely speculated that banking institutions, including state-owned banks and RCCs, will need to be bailed out—again—by the central government in the near future.[29] To err on the side of caution, even if a bailout is unnecessary, it is beyond doubt that the fiscal stimulus package has raised bad loan levels, reversing the painstaking accomplishments of the banking sector restructuring in the late 1990s and 2000s. From the perspective of RCCs, recent events provide glaring evidence that nothing has fundamentally changed with the 2003–5 reform: soft budget constraint and local-government interference in lending are still very much the reality of China.

The political-economic mechanisms operating in the fiscal stimulus package are inherently similar to those revealed by the present inquiry into the rural credit sector, larger magnitude and higher administrative levels involved notwithstanding. To a large extent, these LGFVs function similarly to the TVEs of the past. Both act as conduits between local governments and banking institutions to bypass the law prohibiting direct lending to government entities. Local officials then utilize the funds in the conduit companies to finance desired infrastructure projects. This, again, is not unlike the TVEs de facto owned by township and village governments, which in turn helped finance the provision of public goods and services, as described in chapter 6. Because most loans to TVEs and financing vehicles alike were/are guaranteed by local governments, they become implicit government debt that could potentially threaten fiscal sustainability.

Government finance, however, is only one side of the equation, as I have shown. The other and equally—if not more—disturbing thing is the debts local governments owe to the banking sector. If local governments default en masse, central authorities will be forced to recapitalize the banks because—just like RCCs—they are "too big to fail." The political-economic issues highlighted in this volume, such as the institutional causes of local-government interference in banks' lending decisions, and the implications of utilizing banking resources for fiscal purposes, are applicable to the broader financial system and intergovernmental fiscal relationship at large.

Summary and Addressing the Broader Literature

Political-economic institutional design explains the bias in RCCs' lending patterns toward local government–related firms and projects across all locales, even though RCCs' mandate was to serve the agricultural/rural community. The dual accountability system entails RCC managers reporting to functional superiors in the vertical hierarchy and to regional party bosses. Of the two principals, local party secretaries wielded stronger control over the RCC, the agent, because they had veto power over use of personnel and financial resources. This was particularly the case when RCCs were under the leadership of the state-owned ABC from 1979 to 1996, during which TVEs grew most rapidly.

Additionally, the fiscal system and cadre evaluation system make it imperative for local officials to augment revenue collection and to promote industrial enterprises that contribute to their coffers. The 1994 fiscal recentralization did not reduce local incentive to collect revenue. It strengthened the need for income because expenditure assignments had remained unchanged. The cadre evaluation system rewards industrial promotion and revenue increase, reinforcing the incentive created by the fiscal system.

Despite the general lending pattern, there is local variation in the outcome of rural industrialization. Both privately led and local government–led industrialization can be successful, to which the cases of Taizhou prefecture and Zouping county have attested. When funded by private savings and local private banks, firms are subject to hard budget constraints and financial resources are used more efficiently. In the decentralized environment where local governments are tasked with financing public goods and services, successful industrialization brings income essential to basic governance.

Notwithstanding that, not all local government–led industrialization has prospered. The difference lies in whether the locales have the geography-enabled market exposure and interconnectedness for enterprises to prosper. When lacking this crucial factor, enterprises were not able to withstand competition once market conditions became unfavorable like they did against the collective TVE sector in the mid-1990s. In these perished locales, the downfall of local government–led enterprises has not been replaced by private sector growth. This deprives local authorities of much-needed revenue. Consequently, public goods and services that are largely funded by local authorities become seriously deficient, resulting in a series of local governance issues. Failed government-led industrialization proves to be a far more widespread phenomenon compared to the successful cases.

Developmental, Corporatist, or Predatory Local States?

Scholars studying local states in China are divided into two camps, conjuring up starkly contrasting images of China's rural development, primarily due to their different foci. One camp examines the role of local states in rural industrialization and TVE promotion and generally lauds local states' role in economic development. In this vein, Walder describes a county government in Shandong as operating like a profit-oriented corporation.[30] Jane Duckett, who studies government agencies in Tianjin, depicts local states as "entrepreneurial" for their engagement in profit-seeking business activities.[31] And the work of Marc Blecher and Vivienne Shue in a municipality in Hebei province suggests the local state is more "developmental" than "entrepreneurial" because local officials work for the "collective good" as opposed to maximize profits for themselves.[32] The most influential researcher in this camp is Jean Oi, who has coined the term "local state corporatism" to depict local government's corporate-like behavior in running enterprises.[33] Oi's work has defined studies of local governments in China for nearly two decades since the early 1990s.

On the other end of the spectrum is the camp that sees the nature of local states through the lenses of "peasant burdens" and corruption. Prominent among these researchers are Xiaobo Lü and Thomas Bernstein, who study "peasant burdens" and local officials' preying on enterprise revenue.[34] This body of literature depicts local bureaucracies as having weak capacity and facing many "unfunded mandates," which drive them to extract revenue surpluses from peasants and local enterprises. Through this lens, local states are portrayed as "predatory" and "booty socialist."

How do we reconcile these two opposing views? I argue that each perspective is valid only given the *time period* and *locality* in question. Much like the analogy of "the elephant and the blind men," it is futile to typecast China's local states into one category or another. China is a gargantuan country with each region having its own distinctive characteristics. The fact that a variety of local states coexist in the Middle Kingdom should come as no surprise.

A re-examination of the "local state corporatism" literature, written at the peak of the collective TVE development in the early 1990s, is warranted. As described in this volume, since the mid to late-1990s TVEs have largely disappeared, having either folded or been privatized. Consequently, local governments are *no longer* directly involved in the running of local enterprises, which is the underpinning of the "local state corporatism" concept. In hindsight, it was not the corporatist nature of local governments that promoted rural industrial development. In the post-TVE era, some local authorities are still collecting handsome revenue by taking a hands-off approach and leaving the private sector to steer industrial development. It is the institutional incentives that either drive industrial growth or stymie it. (See my other work for an analysis of the transformation of the Sunan-type local government from the pre- to post-collective TVE eras.[35])

I therefore argue against a "one-size-fits-all" approach in studying local states and local governance in general. All local governments are similarly driven by fiscal and political incentives to maximize revenue collection. However, the specific actions they take and the outcome depend on the conditions and characteristics of the locales they govern. Thus, in regions with an entrepreneurial tradition and proximity to metropolitan centers, successful industrialization generates handsome fiscal resources. By contrast, in remote areas where resources are scarce and infrastructure underdeveloped, local governments have their hands tied with regard to revenue generation. They either could not build profitable enterprises or have tried to do so but have failed miserably. Hence, they *had to* extract whatever surpluses they could from rural residents. Local officials in poor areas are thus not necessarily more predatory than their counterparts in resource-rich locales.

The problem is that institutional (fiscal and political) incentives are the same for all local governments, without taking into account their intrinsically diverging circumstances. In other words, the diverging outcome—corporatist, developmental, and predatory local states—is *not* a consequence of the innate characteristics of the officials per se. Rather, it is a consequence of the interplay of uniform systemic demands with diverse local conditions.

Who Holds the Balance of Power in Central-Local Relations?

In post-reform China, which is stronger: central or local government? This question has been debated since Deng Xiaoping implemented economic decentralization and market reforms in the late 1970s. Both sides of the debate are best represented by the works of Yasheng Huang vs. Shaoguang Wang and Angang Hu as summarized in chapter 1.

I have shown in this book that the power and influence the central leadership has over local officials is overestimated. Beijing and higher-level governments can determine who will become party secretaries at lower levels through the *nomenklatura* or personnel appointment system. They can also influence local leaders' behavior by setting evaluation targets. But they are incapable of dictating *how* local leaders actually carry out tasks. In other words, even though political institutions allow the center to effectuate desired end results, such as 8 percent GDP growth per annum or zero petition, the authoritarian leadership is powerless to determine the process through which the targets are attained.

The process matters for several reasons. Most obviously, results can be faked and numbers can be fudged. Local leaders can hire bounty hunters to intercept petitioners from traveling to Beijing or from staging a protest, but this does not imply that social discontent is nonexistent.[36] During the Great Leap Forward, Mao's grandiloquent and naive project of overtaking the developed world, local officials fervently reported great harvests while having bad crops, as such reports were music to the ears of their political superiors.[37] False reporting and information asymmetry further exacerbated the food shortages that culminated in the loss of thirty million to forty-five million lives.[38]

The process matters for another important reason. As I have illustrated in this volume, local leaders are able to mobilize financial resources in order to fulfill center-imposed hard targets. Consequently, local authorities racked up huge debts, and the bad debt problem grew so immense that central leadership was forced to bail out the savings institutions. Accordingly, ordinary Chinese ended up footing the bill for local authorities' callous efforts to keep their jobs and advance their political careers. The banking institutions' integrity is compromised to the effect that loans do not reach those whose projects yield the highest returns, and enormous inefficiency in banking resource allocations ensues. Savers or ordinary Chinese become the main losers. In sum, central leadership may be able to make local governments achieve specific quantifiable targets, but at the huge expense of the center and of ordinary people, which is neither intended nor desired by central leadership.

Market-Preserving Federalism, Chinese Style

My findings cast doubt on the influential concept of "market-preserving federalism" (MPF), which proposes China's fiscal federalist arrangement as a primary explanation for its impressive growth. In a widely cited paper, Montinola, Qian, and Weingast argue that "federalism, Chinese style" is a set of institutions that constrains the government from encroaching on the market. It therefore has a limiting effect on state predation, similar to the effect of the rule of law and horizontal separation of powers in democracies.[39] Along with the eighteenth-century United Kingdom and the nineteenth-century United States, China is held up as an exemplar of the way fiscal federalism has created a market-preserving institutional structure that underlay its impressive growth, despite the palpable absence of the typical political institutions limiting state predation.

I beg to differ. China's fiscal arrangements, together with its political institutions, have made it imperative for local officials to augment revenue while allowing them to tap savings resources. This results in undisciplined local-government borrowing and mounting local-government debt, the lion's share of which is unrepaid loans owed to local credit institutions, putting these credit institutions at risk of bankruptcy. The situation forces the central government to bail them out, which in effect financially rescues the indebted grassroots governments. This gives rise to soft budget constraints and fiscal indiscipline among subnational governments, leading to macroeconomic instability.[40] Put simply, Chinese-style fiscal federalism neither preserves the market nor promotes economic growth. It is not a substitute for the typical political institutions constraining state predation either.

Normative Implications

Are all state-owned rural financial institutions doomed to fail? If they were, there is nothing surprising about the loss-making rural credit institutions in this study. International experience suggests otherwise, however. The Bank Rakyat Indonesia (BRI)'s Unit Desa, the micro-credit unit of a state-owned bank in Indonesia, is a prime example of a successful government-run institution.[41] The Unit Desa began in the 1970s as the rural agents for the government's subsidized credit for the rice self-sufficiency program, BIMAS. After government deregulation of interest rates in 1984, the institution underwent restructuring: each Unit Desa became an independent profit center, and it became a commercially oriented micro-credit institution as a whole. At the peak of the Asian financial crisis in 1998, while the NPL rate for the parent company BRI stood at 53 percent, that for the Unit Desa was only 5.7 percent.[42]

While a whole range of factors might have contributed to Unit Desa's success,[43] a few of them are particularly instructive for RCCs. The Unit Desa has a far more stringent monitoring and reporting system to prevent collusion between loan officers and borrowers. Branch managers are responsible for cross-checking the units' loan and deposit records with clients and for meeting with clients whose loans are overdue. All these measures serve to identify and deter potential collusion between grassroots credit officers and borrowers.

Additionally, Unit Desa credit officers are given strong incentives to improve the performance and profitability of the units they work for. To reward good performance, all employees can receive a bonus up to 10 percent of each unit's annual profits. However, employees can also lose their jobs if their unit fails to attain profitability. For instance, when loan arrears exceed 5 percent, unit managers will lose their authority in lending decisions and their career prospects can be in jeopardy. This reward and punishment system has been far more doggedly enforced than in RCCs.

The Indonesian microcredit institution is arguably more commercially oriented than RCCs given there is no imposed requirement for it to serve the poor segments of the population. Its clientele is also more urbanized and resides in more densely populated areas, which lowers its operating costs. My rough calculation indicates the Unit Desa operates on a more cost-effective basis compared to RCCs: there are twenty-six thousand people per township RCC compared to thirty-three thousand people per subdistrict Desa unit.[44]

Most importantly, the institution is not subject to any administrative or operational interference from local authorities. This allows the savings institution to operate based on its commercial principle and to allocate resources accordingly. It also enables the branch and regional offices to effectively supervise and manage grassroots units without any external interference. Unit managers—unlike township RCC managers—do not answer to local political leaders, even though they work in a state-owned institution.

The importance of strengthening the corporate governance structure of credit institutions in China cannot be overemphasized. The country's growth in the last few decades has been attained at massive expense to banking sector efficiency, which ultimately puts the savings of ordinary Chinese at risk. A bank run is not unimaginable if ordinary savers had better knowledge of the system's vulnerabilities and if public confidence in the regime was shaken. It is not unimaginable that the Jishou incident described in chapter 1 may happen on a much wider scale if these issues remain unaddressed.

Competition, market exposure, and interconnectedness facilitated by geography are pivotal to successful local industrialization, as evidenced in chapters 5 and 6. This justifies a reassessment of China's growth strategy, which has so far been a "one-size-fits-all" approach: industrialization for all. Not all locales have the indispensable geographical ingredients to become successfully industrialized. To do more of the same will result in more wastage of fiscal and banking resources and further redistribution from the rural poor and the peasantry to the rural elite. This will widen the existing gap between the "haves" and the "have-nots" and fuel simmering rural discontentment.

The cadre evaluation system, which perpetrates the "one-size-fits-all" approach, needs an overhaul. Evaluation criteria need to be tailored to local conditions and income levels. Industrial growth needs to be made a less universal goal. Industrialization as a rigid target is suitable only for places with the requisite conditions for success. Targets such as provision of health care and education are just as worthy of attention and effort from local officials, if not more so.

The implication of this differentiated political assessment system is locales that are not conducive to industrialization cannot be left to finance public goods and service themselves, but have to be subsidized by the central government. This necessitates a redesign of the fiscal system that pays greater attention to interregional equity in revenue and expenditure assignments and intergovernmental transfers. While the 1994 fiscal recentralization was implemented on the premise that the center's share of tax revenue could be augmented in order for it to redistribute wealth to poor regions and areas, it has achieved the former but not the latter objective.[45] China's status as the most decentralized nation in the world in terms of expenditure responsibilities—while not being accompanied by corresponding revenue assignments—has serious negative implications for rural-urban divide and interregional inequality that sow the seeds of social instability.

What are the potential solutions to harden local-government soft budget constraint? International experience suggests that in countries with vertically integrated party systems, such as Germany and Australia, when voters hold national political parties responsible for bailout costs, local governments controlled by the national government's party that press for bailouts will be punished in the electoral system.[46] Alternatively, the central governments in Norway, Canada, and Hungary have successfully employed hierarchical mechanisms, such as tight monitoring of local budgets and strict controls over local spending and borrowing, to regulate local fiscal decisions.[47]

However, the existing literature is drawn from the experience of countries with institutions such as multiparty structure and competitive elections, which are nonexistent in China. Yet this does not mean there is no solution to the problem of subnational government soft budget constraints in China. It means merely that any potential institutional remedy will have to be one embedded within the communist system. The cadre evaluation system, the critical instrument of evaluating and monitoring lower-level cadres, is a case in point. As chapter 4 has argued, the system has been effective in creating revenue-generating incentives for lower-level officials but has also resulted in short-term opportunistic behavior. Local cadres are fixated on attaining quantitative targets without much consideration for the resources consumed to achieve the goals.

The scope of evaluation criteria could be broadened to include the amount of resources used in attaining the outcome (for example, the magnitude of bank lending to local enterprises and other government-related projects), so that local leaders are *not* judged solely on their results. Reducing the size of local-government debt can also be made a "hard target" to ensure local officials give it due consideration. Accurate measuring of the size of debt may be problematic because the system is based on cadres' self-reported values, and it is not in their inherent interest to declare the actual magnitude of debt.[48] However, it should not pose a bigger problem than declarations of other quantitative targets, such as industrial production and amount of investment attracted, do.

A larger issue with incorporating the size of debt into cadre evaluation is that it contradicts the center's priorities of maximizing revenue collection and local economic growth. Much like combating environmental pollution, restraining the scale of loans taken and debt accumulated entails compromising the relentless pursuit of economic growth.[49] The two sets of targets cannot be given equal weight at the same time; one must be given priority over the other. Ultimately, the success of reducing local-government debt critically hinges on the central authority's resolve to sacrifice some degree of economic growth for better governance in the long term.

The issues touched on in this inquiry are emblematic of the larger problems confronting China's growth model. A healthy corporate governance structure presupposes a functioning rule of law. An effective political evaluation system requires genuine public accountability and institutional checks and balances. To boost household consumption and achieve domestic rebalancing, interest rates will have to be liberalized. To harden local budget constraint, the central authority will have to cease making local governments provide matching funds for central policies that the center knows they could ill afford. To completely sever the nexus between politics and finance, the government cannot count on banks to supply resources to fulfill its fiscal functions. All these will entail slower economic growth and require the Communist regime to readjust its growth model. Notwithstanding that, painful as it may be in the short term, better governance is essential to a healthy and functioning system in the long run.

Perhaps this study could be improved if more cases were examined. We might or might not be able to find a case of unsuccessful privately led industrialization. A well-designed survey coupled with the existing detailed qualitative interviews might enhance our understanding of why some locales succeed and others fail. Notwithstanding that, given the breadth of this inquiry—from accounting for the bias in lending pattern, untangling the functions of the banking and fiscal systems, to explaining the regional variation in industrialization outcome and an update on the RCC bailout—there is no space for such an analysis, which would require almost an entire book devoted. On this note, this volume opens the door to the next step that future researchers should take.

Appendix

LIST OF NON-SURVEY FIELD INTERVIEWS, 2003–6

INTERVIEW NO.	DATE	LOCATION	ADMIN. LEVEL	PROVINCE	COUNTRY	INSTITUTION	POSITION
1	11-Aug-03	Canberra	–	ACT	Australia	Victoria University of Technology	Research fellow
2	15-Aug-03	Beijing	Municipality	–	PRC	World Bank	Economist
3	15-Aug-03	Beijing	Municipality	–	PRC	RDI, CASS, Beijing	Research fellow
4	20-Aug-03	Beijing	Municipality	–	PRC	Chinese Academy of Agricultural Sciences	Research fellow
5	20-Aug-03	Beijing	Municipality	–	PRC	China Foundation for Poverty Alleviation	Director
6	22-Aug-03	Beijing	Municipality	–	PRC	RDI, CASS, Beijing	Research fellow
7	22-Aug-03	Beijing	Municipality	–	PRC	RDI, CASS, Beijing	Research fellow
8	29-Aug-03	Beijing	Municipality	–	PRC	Rabobank Beijing	Chief representative
9	2-Sep-03	Beijing	Municipality	–	PRC	China Agricultural University	Professor
10	2-Sep-03	Beijing	Municipality	–	PRC	Planet Finance	Chief representative
11	4-Sep-03	Beijing	Municipality	–	PRC	World Bank, Beijing	Financial sector specialist
12	6-Sep-03	Beijing	Municipality	–	PRC	University of California, Davis	Agricultural economist
13	8-Sep-03	Beijing	Municipality	–	PRC	CCER, Peking University	Economist
14	9-Sep-03	Beijing	Municipality	–	PRC	Institute of Sociology & Anthropology, Peking University	Professor
15	31-May-04	Chengdu	Provincial	Sichuan	PRC	PBoC, Chengdu office	Deputy director

Appendix—*Cont.*

INTERVIEW NO.	DATE	LOCATION	ADMIN. LEVEL	PROVINCE	COUNTRY	INSTITUTION	POSITION
16	31-May-04	Chengdu	Provincial	Sichuan	PRC	RCC union, Sichuan	Deputy director
17	3-Jun-04	Chengdu	Provincial	Sichuan	PRC	Association for Rural Dev. of Poor Areas, Sichuan	Director
18	Jun-04	SC1	County	Sichuan	PRC	Local tax bureau	Director
19	Jun-04	SC1	County	Sichuan	PRC	County finance bureau	Deputy director
20	Jun-04	SC1	County	Sichuan	PRC	Poverty alleviation office	Director; Deputy director
21	Jun-04	SC1	County	Sichuan	PRC	Ex-county senior official	–
22	Jun-04	SC1	County	Sichuan	PRC	Forestry bureau	Deputy director
23	Jun-04	SC1	County	Sichuan	PRC	Agricultural Bank of China	Deputy manager
24	Jun-04	SC1	County	Sichuan	PRC	Postal Savings	Director
25	Jun-04	SC1	County	Sichuan	PRC	County RCC union	Manager
26	Jun-04	SC1	County	Sichuan	PRC	Township enterprise management bureau	Director; Deputy director
27	Jun-04	Q	Village	Sichuan	PRC	Q village, Xiao township	Village party secretary
28	Jun-04	Xiao	Township	Sichuan	PRC	Xiao Enterprise Pte Ltd	Managing director
29	Jun-04	Xiao	Township	Sichuan	PRC	Xiao township RCC	Manager
30	Jun-04	S	Village	Sichuan	PRC	S village, Xiao township	Village party secretary
31	Jun-04	Xiao	Township	Sichuan	PRC	Xiao township government	Township head
32	Jun-04	B	Village	Sichuan	PRC	B village, Cheng township	Village head
33	Jun-04	B	Village	Sichuan	PRC	B village, Cheng township	Village party secretary
34	Jun-04	Cheng	Township	Sichuan	PRC	Cheng township RCC	Manager
35	Jun-04	Cheng	Township	Sichuan	PRC	Cheng township RCC branch	Manager
36	Jun-04	Cheng	Township	Sichuan	PRC	Cheng primary school	Principal
37	Jun-04	Cheng	Township	Sichuan	PRC	Cheng party committee	Township party secretary
38	Jun-04	Cheng	Township	Sichuan	PRC	Civil affairs office	Director
39	Jun-04	D	Village	Sichuan	PRC	D village, Cheng township	Village secretary

40	Jul-04	SC2	County	Sichuan	PRC	SC2 county village development office (UNDP micro-credit office)	Director
41	Jul-04	SC2	County	Sichuan	PRC	SC2 county ABC branch	Manager
42	Jul-04	SC2	County	Sichuan	PRC	SC2 county poverty alleviation office	Director
43	Jul-04	SC2	County	Sichuan	PRC	SC2 county township enterprise management bureau	Director
44	Jul-04	SC2	County	Sichuan	PRC	SC2 county RCC union	Manager
45	Jul-04	J	Village	Sichuan	PRC	J village, Zhang township	Village party secretary
46	Jul-04	Zhang	Township	Sichuan	PRC	Zhang township finance bureau	Director
47	Jul-04	Zhang	Township	Sichuan	PRC	Zhang township RCC branch	Manager
48	Jul-04	Zhang	Township	Sichuan	PRC	Zhang township government	Township head
49	Jul-04	B	Village	Sichuan	PRC	B village, Zhang township	Village party secretary
50	Jul-04	Zhou	Township	Sichuan	PRC	Zhou township RCC branch	Manager
51	Jul-04	Zhou	Township	Sichuan	PRC	Zhou township government	Township head
52	9-Jul-04	Chengdu	Provincial	Sichuan	PRC	RCC union, Sichuan	Chief accountant
53	10-Jul-04	Chengdu	Provincial	Sichuan	PRC	Poverty alleviation office, Sichuan province	Director
54	11-Jul-04	Chengdu	Provincial	Sichuan	PRC	CASS, Sichuan	Director
55	12-Jul-04	Chengdu	Provincial	Sichuan	PRC	CASS, Sichuan	Graduate student
56	12-Jul-04	Chengdu	Provincial	Sichuan	PRC	Agricultural Economy Station, Ministry of Agriculture	Director
57	18-Jan-05	Hong Kong	SAR	–	PRC	City University of Hong Kong	Professor
58	23-Feb-05	Beijing	Municipality	–	PRC	Center for Chinese Agricultural Policy, CAS	Professor
59	8-Mar-05	Beijing	Municipality	–	PRC	China Agricultural University	Professor
60	9-Mar-05	Beijing	Municipality	–	PRC	Shanghai Pudong Development Bank, Beijing	Director
61	11-Mar-05	Beijing	Municipality	–	PRC	RDI, CASS, Beijing	Research fellow
62	Mar-05	CS	County	Jiangsu	PRC	CS rural commercial bank	HR manager
63	Mar-05	CS	County	Jiangsu	PRC	CS rural commercial bank	BoD secretary
64	Mar-05	CS	County	Jiangsu	PRC	CS rural commercial bank	Researcher

Appendix—*Cont.*

INTERVIEW NO.	DATE	LOCATION	ADMIN. LEVEL	PROVINCE	COUNTRY	INSTITUTION	POSITION
65	Mar-05	CS	County	Jiangsu	PRC	CS rural commercial bank branch	Manager
66	Mar-05	WJ	County	Jiangsu	PRC	WJ rural commercial bank	Office manager
67	Mar-05	WJ	County	Jiangsu	PRC	WJ rural commercial bank	Deputy head BoD
68	Mar-05	WJ	County	Jiangsu	PRC	WJ rural commercial bank	BoD secretary
69	Mar-05	SZE	Township	Jiangsu	PRC	SZE rural commercial bank branch, WJ county	Manager
70	Mar-05	TY	Township	Jiangsu	PRC	TY rural commercial bank branch, WJ county	Manager
71	Mar-05	TY	Township	Jiangsu	PRC	TY township government	Township Head
72	Sep-05	Beijing	Municipality	–	PRC	A private share-holding bank	Independent BoD
73	Sep-05	Fan	Township	Hebei	PRC	Township ABC branch	Manager
74	Sep-05	Fan	Township	Hebei	PRC	Fan township party committee	Township party secretary
75	Sep-05	Fan	Township	Hebei	PRC	Fan township RCC	Manager
76	Sep-05	M	Village	Hebei	PRC	M village, Fan township	Village head
77	Sep-05	Taizhou	Prefecture	Zhejiang	PRC	Taizhou Office, Zhejiang provincial RCC union	Director
78	Sep-05	FJ	Township	Zhejiang	PRC	FJ branch, LQ rural cooperative bank	Manager
79	Sep-05	LQ	District	Zhejiang	PRC	LQ district rural cooperative bank	Head of BoS
80	Oct-05	Shanghai	Municipality	–	PRC	Bank of Shanghai branch	Manager
81	Oct-05	Shanghai	Municipality	–	PRC	Bank of Shanghai branch	Director
82	Oct-05	Hangzhou	Provincial	Zhejiang	PRC	Retired PBoC research	
83	Oct-05	Hangzhou	Provincial	Zhejiang	PRC	University of Zhejiang	Economics professor
84	Oct-05	HY	District	Zhejiang	PRC	HY district RCC union	Head of BoS
85	Nov-05	Zouping	County	Shandong	PRC	County agricultural bureau	Deputy director
86	Nov-05	Zouping	County	Shandong	PRC	County national resource bureau (formerly land office)	Director
87	Nov-05	Zouping	County	Shandong	PRC	County ABC branch	Manager

88	Nov-05	Zouping	County	Shandong	PRC	County CBRC office	Director & Researcher
89	Nov-05	Zouping	County	Shandong	PRC	County local tax bureau	Director
90	Nov-05	Zouping	County	Shandong	PRC	County administration for industry & commerce	Director
91	Nov-05	Zouping	County	Shandong	PRC	County national tax bureau	Director
92	Nov-05	Zouping	County	Shandong	PRC	County Industrial Commerce Bank of China (ICBC) branch	Manager
93	Nov-05	Zouping	County	Shandong	PRC	County PBoC office	Director
94	Nov-05	Zouping	County	Shandong	PRC	County personnel bureau	Director
95	Nov-05	Zouping	County	Shandong	PRC	County RCC union	Manager
96	Nov-05	Zouping	County	Shandong	PRC	County SME management office	Deputy director
97	Nov-05	Zouping	County	Shandong	PRC	County finance bureau	Director
98	Nov-05	B	Village	Shandong	PRC	B village, Han township	Village bookkeeper
99	Nov-05	Han	Township	Shandong	PRC	Han township finance bureau	Director
100	Nov-05	Han	Township	Shandong	PRC	Han party committee	Township party secretary
101	Nov-05	Han	Township	Shandong	PRC	Han township RCC	Manager
102	Nov-05	Y	Village	Shandong	PRC	Y village, Han township	Village party secretary
103	Nov-05	Sun	Township	Shandong	PRC	Township finance bureau	Director
104	Nov-05	Sun	Township	Shandong	PRC	Sun township RCC	Manager
105	Nov-05	Sun	Township	Shandong	PRC	Sun township government	Township head
106	Nov-05	F	Village	Shandong	PRC	F village, Sun township	Village party secretary
107	Nov-05	H	Village	Shandong	PRC	H village, Sun township	Village committee
108	Nov-05	Jinan	Provincial	Shandong	PRC	Shandong Agricultural University	Professor
109	Nov-05	Jinan	Provincial	Shandong	PRC	RDI, CASS, Shandong	Professor
110	Nov-05	Jinan	Provincial	Shandong	PRC	Shandong provincial RCC union	Deputy directors

Appendix—*Cont.*

INTERVIEW NO.	DATE	LOCATION	ADMIN. LEVEL	PROVINCE	COUNTRY	INSTITUTION	POSITION
111	Dec-05	Wenling	District	Zhejiang	PRC	Wenling district rural cooperative bank	Head of BOS
112	Dec-05	XH	Township	Zhejiang	PRC	XH national resource bureau (formerly land management bureau)	Director
113	Dec-05	XH	Township	Zhejiang	PRC	XH township finance bureau	Director
114	Dec-05	XH	Township	Zhejiang	PRC	XH branch, Wenling rural coop bank	Manager
115	Dec-05	MY	Township	Zhejiang	PRC	MY branch, Wenling rural cooperative bank	Manager
116	Dec-05	XH	Township	Zhejiang	PRC	XH township party committee	Township party secretary
117	Dec-05	XH	Township	Zhejiang	PRC	XH township organization dept	Director
118	Dec-05	Zen	Township	Zhejiang	PRC	Zen township finance bureau	Director
119	Dec-05	Zen	Township	Zhejiang	PRC	Zen ABC branch	Manager
120	Dec-05	HK	SAR	–	PRC	Asian Corporate Governance Association	Director
121	Jun-06	Canberra	–	ACT	Australia	Peter Peterson Institute for International Economics	Economist

Notes

1. LOCAL GOVERNMENTS, RURAL CREDIT, AND REGIONAL DEVELOPMENT IN CHINA

1. BBC, "Protests in Two Chinese Cities," September 5, 2008, http://news.bbc.co.uk/2/hi/asia-pacific/7600762.stm. Changping Luo and Hongliang Ouyang, "Huge Lending Racket Unravels in Jishou," *Caijing Magazine*, September 10, 2008, http://english.caijing.com.cn/2008–09–10/110011443.html.

2. 100 Chinese yuan was equivalent to about US$14.60 in September 2009.

3. This assertion, which is contrary to a popular study by Yasheng Huang, will be defended in chapter 2. See Yasheng Huang, *Capitalism with Chinese Characteristics: Entrepreneurship and the State* (New York: Cambridge University Press, 2008).

4. This was based on the traditional four-tier NPL classification based on loans' maturity dates. The new five-tier classification based on loan risks replacing the previous four-tier system was introduced to the state-owned banking sector in 2002 and to the RCCs only in 2006. To illustrate the difference between the two classifications: if a borrower takes out two loans, and he fails to repay one of them, the other loan would be classified as "nonperforming" under the new risk-based five-tier classification, since his repayment ability is now in doubt. Nonetheless, under the old maturity date–based classification, the other loan would still be "performing" until the maturity date. Since the adoption of the more stringent risk-based classification, Chinese banking institutions have adjusted their nonperforming loan rates upward.

5. International Fund for Agricultural Development, *Rural Financial Services in China: Thematic Study, Volume I—Main Report* (International Fund for Agricultural Development [IFAD], December 2001). Loren Brandt, Albert Park, and Sangui Wang, "Are China Financial Reforms Leaving the Poor Behind?" in *Financial Sector Reform in China*, ed. Yasheng Huang, T. Saich, and E. Steinfeld (Cambridge, MA: Harvard University Asia Center, 2005). Albert Park, Loren Brandt, and John Giles, "Competition under Credit Rationing: Theory and Evidence from Rural China," *Journal of Development Economics* 71 (2003): 463–95.

6. The estimate is based on the 50 percent official NPL rate and the ratio of the RCCs' lending to TVEs, households, and other commercial and industrial entities in 1999.

7. Xiaochao Li, ed., *China Statistical Yearbook 2007* (Beijing: Zhongguo tongji chubanshe, 2007).

8. World Bank, *World Development Indicators 2007*, http://data.worldbank.org/products/data-books/WDI-2007.

9. Author's calculation of data in United Nations Development Program, *China Human Development Report, 2007–2008: Basic Public Services Benefiting 1.3 Billion Chinese People* (Beijing: China Translation and Publishing Corporation, 2008).

10. Despite the inconsistent definition of "mass incidents" or "incidents of public disorder," it is indisputable that the frequency of social unrest has been on the rise in China. All figures, except that for 2010, are from the Ministry of Public Security. The latest number is from Liping Sun, "China's Challenge: Social Disorder," *Economic Ob-*

server (Jingji guancha bao), February 28, 2011, http://www.eeo.com.cn/Politics/by_region/2011/02/28/194539.shtml.

11. Xiaolin Guo, "Land Expropriation and Rural Conflicts in China," *China Quarterly* 166 (2001): 431. Yongshun Cai, "Collective Ownership or Cadres' Ownership? The Non-agricultural Use of Farmland in China," *China Quarterly* 175 (2003): 662–80. Kathy Le Mons Walker, "From Covert to Overt: Everyday Peasant Politics in China and the Implications for Transnational Agrarian Movements," *Journal of Agrarian Change* 8 (2008): 473. Jianrong Yu, "Land Disputes: The Focus of Rights-Defending Activities of Peasants (tudi wenti yi chengwei nongmin weiquan kangzheng de jiaodian)," *Survey and Study (diaoyan shijie)* (2005): 22–23.

12. The bailout cost a total of 4 trillion yuan, which was ultimately paid for by peasant households. Guonan Ma, "Sharing China's Bank Restructuring Bill," *China and World Economy* 14, no. 3 (2006): 19–37.

13. c.f. Victor Shih, *Factions and Finance in China: Elite Conflict and Inflation* (Cambridge: Cambridge University Press, 2008), which uses elite political dynamics to provide explanations for the inflationary cycle and persistent lack of banking reforms in China. Power struggles between the two factions, the technocrats versus party generalists, each of which have their own distinct policy objectives, have resulted in stagnation in the banking sector reforms. Ibid.

14. Nicholas Lardy, *China's Unfinished Economic Revolution* (Washington, DC: Brookings Institution Press, 1998).

15. Harry W. Blair, "Agricultural Credit, Political Economy and Patronage," in *Undermining Rural Development with Cheap Credit*, ed. Dale W. Adams, Douglas H. Graham, and J. D. Von Pischke (Boulder, CO: Westview Press, 1984), 183–93. Avishay Braverman and J. Luis Guasch, "Rural Credit Markets and Institutions in Developing Countries: Lessons for Policy Analysis from Practice and Modern Theory," *World Development* 14, no. 10/11 (1986): 1253–67. Timothy Besley, "How Do Market Failures Justify Interventions in Rural Credit Markets?" *World Bank Research Observer* 9, no. 1 (1994): 27–47.

16. Kellee S. Tsai, *Back-Alley Banking: Private Entrepreneurs in China* (Ithaca, NY: Cornell University Press, 2002). In localities where local governments are more supportive of the private sector, such as Wenzhou in Zhejiang province and Quanzhou in Fujian province, informal finance tends to be more diverse than in areas where local authorities are ambivalent or unsupportive of the non-state sector.

17. This inquiry provides evidence that formal institutions matter, in contrast to Lily Tsai's work that shows that solidary groups and informal accountability systems explain differences in the levels of public goods provision among locales with the same level of development. See Lily Tsai, *Accountability without Democracy: Solidary Groups and Public Goods Provision in Rural China*, Cambridge Studies on Comparative Politics (New York: Cambridge University Press, 2007).

18. There are two case studies from Zouping county. Both are local government–led, but one is successful while the other is not.

19. Jean C. Oi, "Fiscal Reform and the Economic Foundations of Local State Corporatism in China," *World Politics* 45, no. 1 (1992): 99–126.

20. Jane Duckett, *The Entrepreneurial State in China: Real Estate and Commerce Departments in Reform-Era Tianjin* (London and New York: Routledge, 1998).

21. Marc Blecher and Vivienne Shue, *Tethered Deer: Government and Economy in a Chinese County* (Stanford, CA: Stanford University Press, 1996).

22. Jean C. Oi, "The Role of the Local State in China's Transitional Economy," *China Quarterly* 144 (1995): 1132–49. Andrew Walder, "Local Governments as Industrial Firms:

An Organizational Analysis of China's Transitional Economy," *American Journal of Sociology* 101, no. 2 (1995): 263–301.

23. Jiahua Che and Yingyi Qian, "Institutional Environment, Community Government, and Corporate Governance: Understanding China's Township-Village Enterprises," *Journal of Law, Economics, and Organization* 14, no. 1 (1998): 1–23. The positive role of local government in development also inspires the idea of "federalism, Chinese style" by Gabrielle Montinola, Yingyi Qian, and Barry R. Weingast, "Federalism, Chinese Style: The Political Basis for Economic Success," *World Politics* 48, no. 1 (1996): 50–81.

24. Shaoguang Wang and Angang Hu, *The Political Economy of Uneven Development: The Case of China* (Armonk, NY: M. E. Sharpe, 1999).

25. Yasheng Huang, *Inflation and Investment Controls in China: The Political Economy of Central-Local Relations during the Reform Era* (Cambridge: Cambridge University Press, 1996). Yasheng Huang, "Central-Local Relations in China during the Reform Era: The Economic and Institutional Dimensions," *World Development* 24, no. 4 (1996): 655–72. Yasheng Huang, "Managing Chinese Bureaucrats: An Institutional Economics Perspective," *Political Studies* 50 (2002): 61–79. Using similar logic, Kai-yuen Tsui and Youqiang Wang assert that the central and higher-level governments can still influence local authorities through the cadre evaluation system despite fiscal decentralization; see "Between Separate Stoves and a Single Menu: Fiscal Decentralization in China," *China Quarterly* 177 (2004): 71–90.

26. Pierre Landry, *Decentralized Authoritarianism in China: The Communist Party's Control of Local Elites in the Post-Mao Era* (New York: Cambridge University Press, 2008).

27. Montinola, Qian, and Weingast, "Federalism, Chinese Style." There has been increased skepticism about the contribution of "market-preserving federalism" to China's economic growth. Yang challenges the institutional durability assumption of "market-preserving federalism," arguing that the central government has backpedaled on its promise by regaining fiscal power from the subnational governments with the Tax-Sharing System implemented in 1994. Dali Yang, *Remaking the Chinese Leviathan: Market Transition and the Politics of Governance in China* (Stanford, CA: Stanford University Press, 2004). In a similar vein, Tsui and Wang argue that despite fiscal decentralization, the central government has been able to exert control over local officials using the Communist Party cadre evaluation system. Hence, the central government is not as weak and local authorities are not as strong as has been portrayed in the Chinese federalism literature. Using the case of the automobile sector, Eric Thun, in "Keeping Up with the Jones': Decentralization, Policy Imitation, and Industrial Development in China," *World Development* 32, no. 8 (2004): 1289, argues that although decentralization has provided the incentive for local authorities to promote growth, actual changes may be impeded by the inertia of local institutions. Meanwhile, Hongbin Cai and Daniel Treisman, in "Did Government Decentralization Cause China's Economic Miracle?" *World Politics* 58 (2006): 505–35, contend that fiscal decentralization did not contribute to economic growth because local economic activities began in the late 1970s, before the launch of the fiscal policy, and continued through the 1990s, when the fiscal policy was recentralized.

28. Montinola, Qian, and Weingast, "Federalism, Chinese Style," 79. The central idea is that along with the rule of law and horizontal fiscal structure, fiscal federalism can provide incentives for a more "credible commitment" by the state to secure economic rights and to preserve markets, hence the name "market-preserving federalism." See Barry R. Weingast, "The Economic Role of Political Institutions: Market-Preserving Federalism and Economic Development," *Journal of Law, Economics & Organization* 11, no. 1 (1995): 1–31. Yingyi Qian and Barry R. Weingast, "Federalism as a

Commitment to Preserving Market Incentives," *Journal of Economic Perspectives* 11, no. 4 (1997): 83–92.

29. János Kornai, "The Soft Budget Constraint," *KYKLOS* 39, no. 1 (1986): 3–30. János Kornai, *Economics of Shortage* (Amsterdam: North-Holland, 1980).

30. For an example of how local authorities are able to raise extrabudgetary funds to supplement their budgetary revenue, see Jing Jin and Heng-fu Zou, "Soft Budget Constraints and Local Government in China," in *Fiscal Decentralization and the Challenge of Hard Budget Constraints* (Cambridge, MA: MIT Press, 2003).

31. David E. Wildasin, *Externalities and Bailouts: Hard and Soft Budget Constraints in Intergovernmental Fiscal Relations* (Washington, DC: World Bank, 1997). Wildasin describes Brazil's experience in the early 1990s, when São Paolo borrowed heavily from a few state-owned banks to finance its public expenditures and racked up a debt level amounting to almost half of all state-government debt. The major state banks were forced into bankruptcy when São Paolo ceased to service its loans. In order to avoid a banking crisis, the central government in Brazil was forced to bail out the state banks—and by implication absorb São Paolo's debt.

32. The "too big to fail" justification of the RCCs' bailout is akin to those provided by the U.S. government for its bailouts of banking institutions during the Savings and Loans Crisis in the late 1980s and the Great Recession in the late 2000s. For an analysis of "too big to fail" and bailouts in the 1980s crisis, see Gary H. Stern and Ron J. Feldman, *Too Big to Fail: The Hazards of Bank Bailouts* (Washington, DC: Brookings Institution Press, 2004).

33. Tony Saich, "The Blind Man and the Elephant: Analysing Local State in China," in *East Asian Capitalism: Conflicts, Growth and Crisis*, ed. Luigi Tomba (Milan: Feltrinelli, 2002), 75–100. For positive characterization of the local states, see Walder, "Local Governments as Industrial Firms." Andrew Walder, "The County Government as an Industrial Corporation," in *Zouping in Transition: The Process of Reform in Rural North China* (Cambridge, MA: Harvard University Press, 1998), 62–85. Oi, "The Role of the Local State in China's Transitional Economy." Oi, "Rural China Takes Off," *China Quarterly* 144 (1995): 1132–49. Duckett, *The Entrepreneurial State in China*. Blecher and Shue, *Tethered Deer*. For negative role of local states, see Thomas Bernstein and Xiaobo Lü, *Taxation without Representation in Contemporary Rural China* (New York: Cambridge University Press, 2003).

34. David Collier and James Mahoney, "Insights and Pitfalls: Selection Bias in Qualitative Research," *World Politics* 49, no. 1 (1996): 56–91. Barbara Geddes, *Paradigms and Sand Castles: Theory Building and Research Design in Comparative Politics* (Ann Arbor: University of Michigan Press, 2003). Gary King, Robert O. Keohane, and Sidney Verba, *Designing Social Inquiry: Scientific Inference in Qualitative Research* (Princeton, NJ: Princeton University Press, 1994). Henry E. Brady and David Collier, *Rethinking Social Inquiry: Diverse Tools, Shared Standards* (Lanham, MD: Rowman & Littlefield, 2004).

35. World Bank, *The East Asian Miracle: Economic Growth and Public Policy* (New York: Oxford University Press, 1993).

36. Barbara Geddes, "How the Cases You Choose Affect the Answers You Get: Selection Bias in Comparative Politics," in *Political Analysis: An Annual Publication of the Methodology Section of the American Political Science Association*, ed. James A. Stimson, vol. 2 (Ann Arbor: University of Michigan Press, 1990).

37. There were probably a host of factors that may affect industrialization outcome that I could have taken into consideration, such as cadre qualifications and average education levels of the residents. However, it is difficult to obtain this information before visiting the locales, and I have no a priori reason to suspect that any of the sites has a particularly skewed distribution of data pertaining to these variables.

38. I have avoided using the real names of some of the locales for the purpose of protecting the interviewees' identities.

39. The control variables are introduced in order to answer these questions: Are the rural townships in the coastal provinces more likely to industrialize successfully compared to those in the inland provinces? Are those closer to urban centers, such as provincial capitals, more likely to succeed due to their better access to a large consumer market? Are the townships with natural resource endowments, such as raw materials and minerals, more likely to industrialize successfully because the availability of natural resources facilitates the growth of processing industries?

40. Ethan Michelson, *Public Goods and State-Society Relations: An Impact Study of China's Rural Stimulus* (Indiana University Research Center for Chinese Politics & Business, 2011).

41. World Bank, *China: Deepening Public Service Unit Reform to Improve Service Delivery* (Washington, DC: World Bank, 2005). Poverty Reduction Office, "Evaluation Report on the Implementation Results of the 'China Rural Poverty Reduction and Development Outline (2001–2010)'" (Unpublished internal report, 2010).

42. The Yangtze River Delta accounts for over 40 percent of total foreign direct investment and 37 percent of total exports in China even though it has less than 10 percent of the nation's population. Source: Tom Orlik, "Yangtze River Delta: Stalled Dynamo," *China Economic Quarterly*, March 2009, 52–56.

43. The print media have widely reported immense financial difficulties faced by giant firms in Taizhou, a prefecture in southern Zhejiang province, during the global economic downturn. For instance, see Jiangning Yan, Haipeng Yang, and Binbin Yang, "Patchy Prospects for Sewing Machine Giant," *Caijing Magazine*, November 13, 2008.

44. China's indigenous firms, established primarily since the liberal market reforms of the 1980s and 1990s, are still run and managed by founders' family members. They therefore lack the sophisticated management expertise required once firms expand to a certain size and face business challenges that traditional management styles are too ineffective to handle.

45. The Chinese government has been criticized for blindly pursuing economic growth in its grand development strategy, while neglecting other "softer"—but no less important—aspects of the people's lives. If this study were to employ only one indicator in the analysis, it would be making the same strategic mistake for which commentators criticize the Chinese government.

46. This term is first used in China studies by Bernstein and Lü, in *Taxation without Representation*, to describe the numerous mandated responsibilities of local governments for which they have little formal funding.

2. THE RURAL FINANCIAL SYSTEM AND RURAL DEVELOPMENT IN CHINA

1. Huang, *Capitalism with Chinese Characteristics.*

2. The total number of townships nationwide is 41,600.

3. It was subsequently abolished and restored a few times during the tumultuous 1960s and 1970s. In 1957, the ABC was merged with the People's Bank of China (PBoC) to become the only bank in China at that time (there was no central bank in China until the early 1980s). After the implementation of the disastrous Great Leap Forward, initiated by Mao to jump-start the industrial sector but resulting in widespread famine in the countryside, the ABC was restored in 1963 to provide credit support to farmers and to supervise the use of central government budgetary funds in rural areas. Nonetheless, it was abolished again two years later and was restored only with the launch of economic reforms in the late 1970s.

4. Zhongfu Ma, "The Evolution of the Rural Financial System and Policies," in *Rural Financial Markets in China*, ed. Christopher Findlay, Andrew Watson, Cheng Enjiang, and Zhu Gang (Canberra: Asia-Pacific Press, 2003), 36.

5. Interviews no. 17 and 53.

6. The director of the poverty alleviation office justified the allocation of poverty loans to the power plant instead of poor households by arguing that the power plant will contribute tax revenue to the local government coffers. Source: Interview with the county poverty alleviation office (interview no. 42).

7. Ma, "The Evolution of the Rural Financial System and Policies," 38.

8. RCCs could not remit funds from one city to another because they are county-based financial institutions with independent computer and accounting systems.

9. However, the profits were so lucrative the Postal Savings had been able to cross-subsidize its parent company, the China Post, before becoming an independent banking entity in 2007.

10. The conclusions here are consistent with a study on household savings by Aart Kraay, "Household Saving in China," *World Bank Economic Review* 14, no. 3 (2000): 545–70.

11. Jikun Huang, Scott Rozelle, and Honglin Wang, "Fostering or Stripping Rural China: Modernizing Agriculture and Rural to Urban Capital Flows," *Developing Economies* 44, no. 1 (2006): 1–26.

12. Author's calculation based on figures from Huang and Rozelle (2003) and *China Statistical Yearbook 2001*. The gross value of production in the agricultural sector was 2491.6 billion yuan in 2000.

13. Huang, *Capitalism with Chinese Characteristics*, 71–81.

14. Data between 1979 and 1985 has been excluded in the figures for this reason.

15. Huang (2008) has taken into account only the number of enterprises and number of workers employed. See table 2.1 on p. 28.

16. Xiaobo Xu et al., *Reform and Development of Rural Finance in China (Zhongguo Nongcun Jinrong de Biange yu Fazhan)* (Beijing: Dangdai Zhongguo chubanshe, 1994). Ibid., 49–50.

17. Yuanhong Zhang, *Theories and Practicalities of Contemporary Rural Financial Developments (Dangdai Nongcun Jinrong Fazhan de Lilun yu Shijian)* (Nanchang: Jiangxi Renmin Chubanshe, 2002).

18. Andrew Watson, "Financing Farmers: The Reform of Rural Credit Cooperatives and Provision of Financial Services to Farmers," in *Rural Financial Markets in China*, ed. Christopher Findlay, Andrew Watson, Cheng Enjiang, and Zhu Gang (Canberra: Asia-Pacific Press, 2003).

19. Xu et al., *Reform and Development of Rural Finance in China*.

20. The "Cultural Revolution" was a tumultuous period during Mao's rule in which he embarked on a class struggle to get rid of ideological impurities, at least in rhetoric. The revolution resulted in intense political infighting within the upper echelons of the Chinese Communist Party and the deaths of hundreds of thousands, often for arbitrary reasons.

21. On-Kit Tam, "Rural Finance in China," *China Quarterly* 113 (1988): 60–76.

22. Ibid.

23. Watson, "Financing Farmers."

24. Tam, "Rural Finance in China."

25. In August 1996, the central government established the Inter-Ministry Coordination Group for Rural Finance Reform at the State Council, with its head office located at the headquarters of the PBoC in Beijing. In addition, the local leading groups for rural financial reform (*nongcun jinrong tizhi gaige lingdao xiaozu*) were established at the provinces and prefectures, and they subsequently became the rural credit cooperative manage-

ment offices (*nongcun xinyongshe guanli bangongshi*) that were put in charge of managing the county credit unions. The local leading groups reported to the heads of the PBoC's local branches. Source: Interview no. 77.

26. There were various conflicts of interest between the central bank's role as the manager of credit cooperatives and its supervisory role. For further details, see Ping Xie, "Debates on the Reforms of China's Rural Credit Cooperatives' System (Zhongguo Nongcun Xingyonghezoushe Tizhi Gaige de Zhenglun)," *Jinrong Yanjiu (Journal of Financial Research)* 1 (2001): 1–13.

27. Xianqun Yu, "Reforms of the RCCs Should Be Pushed Forward (Nongxinshe gaige ying quanti tuijin)," *China Economic Times (Zhongguo Jingji Shibao)*, August 6, 2003.

28. Ping Xie and Lei Lu, "Principle of Party Cadre Management, System of 'Officials are Omnipotent', and China's State-owned Commercial Banks' Corporate Governance Structure (Dangguan ganbu yuanze, guanbenwei zhidu yu zhongguo guoyou shangye yinghang de gongsi zhili jiegou)," in *Special Discussion on State-owned Commercial Banks' Corporate Governance Structure* (Beijing: China Finance and Economics (Zhongguo caizheng jingji chubanshe), 2002). Ping Xie, "Reforms of China's Rural Credit Cooperatives and Policy Options," *China Economic Review* 14 (2003): 438.

29. In the late 1990s, the central bank shut down many trust and investment companies and informal credit institutions that violated rules of financial prudence. These financial institutions included the Hainan Development Bank, China New Tech Venture Investment Corporation, Guangdong International Trust and Investment Corporation, Guangdong International Lease Company, and the Rural Cooperative Foundations (the latter will be discussed further in chapter 3).

30. Lending rates for the micro-loans in the survey sites range from 7 to 11 percent per annum, while the subsidized interest rate was 3.5 percent per annum for loans with a six-month term.

31. People's Bank of China, *Increasing the Effects of Agricultural On-lending to Support the Construction of the New Socialist Countryside* (Beijing: Author, 2006).

32. This micro-loan scheme differs in substance from Grameen Bank-pioneered microfinance because it lacks group guarantee, market interest rates, focus on women clients and regular repayments, which are the essential features of the Grameen model.

33. Even though there is no comparative data to compare with loan access prior to the implementation of the micro-loan scheme, the survey results appear to support the existing findings that poor households' access to credit has improved with the introduction of the micro-loan scheme. For examples of the existing studies, see Ping Xie et al., *Establishing a Framework for Sustainable Rural Finance: Demand and Supply Analysis in Guizhou Province of the People's Republic of China* (Beijing: Asian Development Bank, 2005).

34. The bar for households in relatively rich locales to become eligible for the subsidized scheme is naturally higher.

35. Xie et al., *Establishing a Framework for Sustainable Rural Finance.*

36. Since the nonperforming loan rate is a division of the scale of nonperforming loans by total loan size, an increase in the denominator will lower the rate when the numerator remains unchanged. For the eight pilot provinces (municipalities) undergoing the reform, the after-tax profits of 77 million yuan in 2004 come from 60 million yuan in company income tax exemption and 17 million yuan in income from the central bank's bonds, according to Ping Xie, Xu Zhong, and Minggao Shen, *RCC Reforms: What Have We Done? What Do We Still Need to Do?* (Beijing: The Ford Foundation (China), 2006).

37. Xie, "Reforms of China's Rural Credit Cooperatives and Policy Options."

38. The pilot sites were Zhejiang, Shandong, Jiangxi, Guizhou, Jilin, Shaanxi, and Jiangsu provinces and Chongqing municipality.

39. Xie, Zhong, and Shen, *RCC Reforms*. That said, the transfer of financial responsibility remains a policy intention, as no provincial government has yet been put to the test on this.

40. Interview no. 110.

41. China Banking Regulatory Commission, *Policies on Relaxing Entry Requirements of Rural Banks* (Beijing: Author, 2006).

42. Economist Intelligence Unit, "A Stillborn Scheme for Microfinance," April 26, 2007. Financial Stability Analysis Group, *China Financial Stability Report 2007 (Zhongguo Jinrong Wending Baogao)* (Beijing: People's Bank of China, 2007).

43. The minimum registered capital requirement for a county-based bank is 3 million yuan, while that for a township-based bank is 1 million yuan.

44. Zhenghua Wang, "Hubei Gets First Foreign Rural Lender," *China Daily*, December 14, 2007, http://www.chinadaily.com.cn/bizchina/2007–12/14/content_6322102.htm. Daisy Ku, "HSBC Gets Approval for Rural Bank in China," Reuters (Beijing, August 9, 2007), http://www.reuters.com/article/2007/08/09/idUSL0930628220070809.

45. In addition to the micro-credit companies approved by the CBRC, the central bank can also issue licenses for micro-credit companies whose business functions are similar to the CBRC-approved ones. They are called "micro-credit" companies for the small amount of lending conducted, not for following the practices of the Grameen model.

46. Man Zhang and Yuze Zhang, "Policies on New Rural Financial Institutions Soon Announced," *Caijing*, April 22, 2008. In addition to those approved by the CBRC, there were reportedly seven micro-credit companies approved by the PBoC at the end of 2006, operating in five provinces.

47. Joseph Stiglitz, "Peer Monitoring and Credit Markets," *World Bank Economic Review* 4, no. 3 (1990): 351–66.

48. Tsai, *Back-Alley Banking*, 39.

49. Minggao Shen and Xu Zhong, "Informal Finance and Domestic Financial Liberalization," *Caijing*, February 20, 2006. When the lender does not know the likelihood of repayment, interest rate can be used as a screening mechanism. A borrower with a risky project is likely to be willing to take out a high-interest loan, while one with a low-risk or low-return investment is more likely to stick with a low-interest loan. See Joseph Stiglitz and Andrew Weiss, "Credit Rationing in Markets with Imperfect Information," *American Economic Review* 71 (1981): 393–410.

50. The repayment rates of the earlier NGO programs were close to 100 percent. For further information, see Albert Park and Changqing Ren, "Microfinance with Chinese Characteristics," *World Development* 29, no. 1 (2001): 39–62.

51. Tony Saich, *Governance and Politics in China* (New York: Palgrave, 2001), 170–75.

52. All programs must be approved by local authorities. Additionally, organizations that do not have necessary manpower in the program sites may require assistance from local officials. When borrowers fail to repay loans, persuasion or influence by village elders may be useful to induce desirable behavior.

3. THE DESIGN OF CHINA'S RURAL CREDIT INSTITUTIONS

1. Currently, all commercial banks, including the rural commercial banks, are free to adjust their lending rates, while RCCs are only allowed to adjust their lending rates up to 2.5 times of the base lending rates. Saving rates are still fully controlled by the central bank.

2. Stephan Haggard, Chung H. Lee, and Sylvia Maxfield, *The Politics of Finance in Developing Countries* (Ithaca, NY: Cornell University Press, 1993). J. D. Von Pischke, *Finance at the Frontier: Debt Capacity and the Role of Credit in the Private Economy* (Washington, DC: World Bank, 1991). J. D. Von Pischke, Dale W. Adams, and Gordon Donald, *Rural Financial Markets in Developing Countries: Their Use and Abuse* (Balti-

more: Johns Hopkins University Press for the Economic Development Institute of the World Bank, 1983).

3. This was an initiative led by former president Jiang Zemin that resulted in an amendment of the PRC Constitution.

4. Alan P. L. Liu, "The 'Wenzhou Model' of Development and China's Modernization," *Asian Survey* 32, no. 8 (1992): 696–711. Yia-Ling Liu, "Reform from Below: The Private Economy and Local Politics in the Rural Industrialization of Wenzhou," *China Quarterly* 130 (1992): 293–316.

5. This phenomenon is also mentioned in Albert Park, Loren Brandt, and John Giles, *Giving Credit Where Credit Is Due: The Changing Role of Rural Financial Institutions in China* (Ann Arbor: William Davidson Institute, University of Michigan Business School, 1997).

6. Collective ownership means neither state nor private ownership. It means that land is owned by the local community.

7. Karla Hoff and Joseph E. Stiglitz, *Imperfect Information and Rural Credit Markets: Puzzles and Policy Perspectives* (Oxford: Oxford University Press for the World Bank, 1993).

8. A cooperative is a user-owned, user-controlled business that distributes benefits proportionally, on the basis of use. Source: Marvin A. Schaars, *Cooperatives: Principles and Practices in the 21st Century*, vol. 4 (Madison: University of Wisconsin Extension–Madison, 1980).

9. The coexistence of the board of directors and board of supervisors is unique in China. The idea of a supervisory board is borrowed from Germany.

10. The Fisher's exact test indicates that a statistically non-significant relationship between the two variables is rejected at less than 0.1 percent significance level.

11. Though villages are the lowest administrative level in China, they are not a formal level of government as defined in China's constitution.

12. See K. G. Lieberthal, *Governing China: From Revolution through Reform*, vol. 2 (New York: W. W. Norton, 2004), 186–88.

13. Elizabeth Economy, *The River Runs Black: The Environmental Challenge to China's Future* (Ithaca, NY: Cornell University Press, 2004). Abigail R. Jahiel, "The Organization of Environmental Protection in China," *China Quarterly* 156 (1998): 757–87.

14. To illustrate these two concepts, consider an employer (principal) who hires a technician to work on a factory floor (agent). Before hiring the technician, the employer will want to find out as much as possible about the technician's skills and level of competence. This gives the agent an informational advantage over the principal, as he may choose to hide pertinent information from the employer. This will give rise to "adverse selection" in that someone whose skills do not meet the job requirements is selected for the job. After the technician is hired, he will have better knowledge of how the machinery operates and how long it takes to get the job done than the employer does. The technician (agent) may choose not to disclose certain information to the employer (principal) in order to get the boss to reward him for his "efforts" or to hire a coworker to share his workload. Therein lies the problem of "moral hazard."

15. D. Roderick Kiewert and Mathew D. McCubbins, *The Logic of Delegation: Congressional Parties and the Appropriations Process* (Chicago: University of Chicago Press, 1991). William F. West and Joseph Cooper, "Legislative Influence vs. Presidential Dominance: Competing Models of Bureaucratic Control," *Political Science Quarterly* 104, no. 4 (1990 1989): 581–606. Thomas H. Hammond and Jack H. Knott, "Who Controls the Bureaucracy?: Presidential Power, Congressional Dominance, Legal Constraints, and Bureaucratic Autonomy in a Model of Multiinstitutional Policy-making," *Journal of Law Economics & Organization* 12, no. 1 (1996): 119–66. Susan K. Snyder and Barry R. Weingast, "The

American System of Shared Powers: The President, Congress, and the NLRB," *Journal of Law Economics & Organization* 16, no. 2 (2000): 269–305.

16. Mathew D. McCubbins and Thomas Schwartz, "Congressional Oversight Overlooked: Police Patrols versus Fire Alarms," *American Journal of Political Science* 28, no. 1 (February 1984): 165–79.

17. The exceptions are these ministries/organizations that were centralized by the central government over the last two decades: the Administration for Industry and Commerce, local tax bureaus, land management bureaus, the four state-owned banks, and the PBoC.

18. Andrew Mertha, "China's Soft Centralization: Shifting Tiao/Kuai Authority Relations," *China Quarterly* 184 (December 2005): 791–810.

19. Kjeld Erik Brodsgaard, "Institutional Reform and the Bianzhi System in China," *China Quarterly* 170 (2002): 363. Maria Edin, "Remaking the Communist Party-State: The Cadre Responsibility System at the Local Level in China," *China: An International Journal* 1, no. 1 (March 2003): 1–15.

20. Tam, "Rural Finance in China."

21. Watson, "Financing Farmers."

22. Shih, *Factions and Finance in China*, 44.

23. Meanwhile, the widespread establishment of county unions since 1996 helped consolidate the credit cooperatives' capital within counties so that funds could flow from areas of excess supply to those of excess demand, improving overall resource efficiency.

24. Supervision of the securities and insurance industries was also transferred to newly established agencies, the China Securities Regulatory Committee (CSRC) and the China Insurance Regulatory Committee (CIRC), respectively.

25. The PBoC is a ministry under the State Council, China's Cabinet. It is therefore not independent of the central government.

26. Susan L. Shirk, *China, Fragile Superpower: How China's Internal Politics Could Derail Its Peaceful Rise* (New York: Oxford University Press, 2007), 57. Jianrong Yu, "Maintaining a Baseline of Social Stability", 2010, https://caonima.ws/2010/03/yu-jianrong-maintaining-a-baseline-of-social-stability.

27. Xiaochuan Zhou, "The Central Bank's Role in the Rural Credit Cooperatives' Reforms (Zhongyang yinhang zai Nongxinshe gaige zhong de jueshe)," *21 Century Economic Report (21 shiji jingji baodao)*, 2004.

28. Bank runs occur when many depositors rush to withdraw their savings from a bank at the same time, and the financial institution cannot honor all requests for withdrawal because it is inadequately capitalized or some of its capital is locked in investment projects or is lent out.

29. It should be noted that some economists are of the view that the higher interest rates in the informal credit market reflect market-clearing rates when excess demand for loans exists. The excess demand comes from the fact that lending rates in the formal market are artificially kept low by the government and this makes more borrowers chase after the amount of loans available.

30. The base salary could be as low as 250 yuan a month for junior officers and increase modestly with seniority. Together with the variable component, total monthly salary could reach 1,000 yuan for loan officers and 2,500 yuan for managers. The salaries of those in economically developed regions are higher than those in relatively underdeveloped areas.

31. State-owned and other commercial banks are subject to regulations such as the PBoC's "Interim Method of Recognizing Non-performing Loans" (*buliangdaikuan zanxingbainfa*), which bans such practices. For an analysis of how state-owned banks have used these tactics to inflate their profitability, see Lardy, *China's Unfinished Economic Revolu-*

tion. Haining Zhang, *Bank Against Bank: The New Basel Capital Accord and China's Credit Risk Analysis (Yinhang fandui yinhang)* (Beijing: Tshinghua Daxue Chubanshe, 2004).

32. A lender may reschedule loan payments for reasons unrelated to "cooking the books," such as when a loan term does not synchronize with the cycle of the borrower's economic activity. For instance, if a loan to a pig farmer has a six-month maturity term, but it takes nine months for the farmer to raise his pigs before he could sell them off, the loan may be rescheduled to allow the borrower to earn a profit.

33. For further details on "bullet" loans, see International Fund for Agricultural Development, *Rural Financial Services in China: Thematic Study, Volume I—Main Report*. Lardy, *China's Unfinished Economic Revolution*.

34. Anyu Tao, "Weaknesses and Solutions of Central Bank's Financial Supervision at the Grassroots Level," *Shanghai Finance Press (Shanghai Jinrong Bao)*, May 14, 2002.

35. Andrew Sheng, *Bank Restructuring: Lessons from the 1980s* (Washington, DC: World Bank, 1996).

36. Interviews with some household borrowers, June–July 2004.

37. Interviews with a county PBoC researcher (interview no. 93) and several RCC managers (interviews no. 25, 29, 101, and 103).

38. Interviews no. 79 and 111.

39. Jun Ma, *Macroeconomic Management and Intergovernmental Relations in China* (World Bank, 1995).

40. Ning Yu, "An Investigation of the Repayment Situations of the Central Bank's On-lending (Yanghang zaidaikuan changhuan qingkuang diaocha)," *Finance and Economics (Caijing)*, August 5, 2003.

41. For further analysis of the post-reform RCCs, see Lynette Ong, "Communist Party and Financial Institutions: Institutional Design of China's Post-Reform Rural Credit Cooperatives," *Pacific Affairs* 82, no. 2 (2009).

42. For instance, see Eric Girardin, *Banking Sector Reform and Credit Control in China* (Paris: Organization for Economic Co-operation and Development, 1997).

43. Interviews no. 23, 73, 87, 92, and 119.

44. In an industrialized Zhejiang county where I conducted field study, the township RCC that has lost its independent legal status since becoming a rural cooperative bank is allowed to approve loans up to 1 million yuan. The township ABC branch has no rights to approve loans. The county-level branch can sign for loans up to 3 million yuan. And the prefecture branch can sign loans between 3 million and 10 million yuan. In a poor Sichuan county where the township RCCs were still independent cost centers when I conducted fieldwork, they could approve loans up to 20,000 yuan, but any loan greater than that had to be referred to the county union. Meanwhile, the township ABC branch has no approval rights and the county branch could approve any loan up to 300,000 yuan.

45. Tiejun Wen, "The Rise and Fall of the Rural Cooperative Foundations: 1984–1999 (Nongcun hezou jijinghui de xingshuai: 1984–1999)," *China's Reforms (Zhongguo gaige)*, December 30, 2000, http://forum50.cei.gov.cn/newwork/cyfx_wtj_20010060704.htm.

46. Ibid. That said, RCFs were believed to have stemmed the outflows of financial resources from rural to urban areas to some extent and facilitated rural households' access to credit in some localities.

47. Carsten Holz, "China's Monetary Reform: The Counterrevolution from the Countryside," *Journal of Contemporary China* 10, no. 27 (2001): 195.

48. Cheng Enjiang, Christopher Findlay, and Andrew Watson, "Institutional Innovation without Regulation: The Collapse of Rural Credit Foundations and Lessons for Further Financial Reforms," in *Rural Financial Markets in China*, ed. Christopher Findlay, Andrew Watson, Cheng Enjiang, and Zhu Gang (Canberra: Asia-Pacific Press, 2003). Wen, "The Rise and Fall of the Rural Cooperative Foundations."

49. Cheng, Findlay, and Watson, "Institutional Innovation without Regulation."

50. Holz, "China's Monetary Reform," 200.

51. Lu Bo, "Debt Crisis of Xiangyi County in Hebei," *Jingji Magazine*, March 22, 2004. Cheng, Findlay, and Watson, "Institutional Innovation without Regulation."

52. Wen, "The Rise and Fall of the Rural Cooperative Foundations."

53. Cheng, Findlay, and Watson, "Institutional Innovation without Regulation."

54. Xiaoming Guo, *In the Name of Farmer's Cooperatives: Milestones of RCFs in Sichuan Province, 1986–1999 (Yi nongmin hezuo de mingyi: sichuansheng nongcun hezuo jijinghui qunwang licheng, 1986–1999)*, 2001, http://www.usc.cuhk.edu.hk/wk_wzdetails.asp?id=920.

55. Bo, "Debt Crisis of Xiangyi County in Hebei."

56. Holz, "China's Monetary Reform."

57. Park, Brandt, and Giles, *Giving Credit Where Credit Is Due*. Holz, "China's Monetary Reform."

58. Interviews with some township officials who used to manage the RCFs in Sichuan and Shandong provinces (interviews no. 46, 99, and 103).

59. Interviews with the Sichuan Ministry of Agriculture, which was the base of the former Sichuan Rural Cooperative Management Station (interview no. 56). Some interviewees indicated to me that the corporate governance structure existed only nominally. Irrespective of whether the corporate governance structure took effect in reality, RCFs were essentially run, managed, and supervised by local party cadres.

60. During the interview (interview no. 56), I probed to ask why borrowings had come from these particular sources. The interviewee, who used to be in charge of the Sichuan Cooperative Management Station, provided no direct answer. However, I was given the impression that at those times, local authorities were in such dire straits that they had to borrow from whoever had surplus funds and was willing to lend.

4. THE IMPLICATIONS OF CADRE EVALUATION AND FISCAL SYSTEM FOR LOCAL-GOVERNMENT BEHAVIOR

1. Hon S. Chan, "Cadre Personnel Management in China: The Nomenklatura System, 1990–1998," *China Quarterly* 179 (2004): 703–34.

2. The other leading cadres in a township typically include the chairman of the local people's congress, the assistant party secretary, and deputy township heads.

3. On the difference between the *bianzhi* and *nomenklatura* systems, see chapter 3.

4. Landry, *Decentralized Authoritarianism in China*, 43–45. Landry argues that the system was intended to reduce local opposition to rehabilitation of cadres prosecuted during the Cultural Revolution and to lessen the reliance of local officials on their immediate superiors.

5. That said, some corruption does occur during cadre recruitment when party leaders "sell" political posts to their patrons. Obviously, when this occurs, the priorities of central leadership may not be carried out at the local level. For more information on the practice of "selling official appointments" (*maiguan*), see Minxin Pei, *China's Trapped Transition: The Limits of Developmental Autocracy* (Cambridge, MA: Harvard University Press, 2006). Yan Sun, *Corruption and Market in Contemporary China* (Ithaca, NY: Cornell University Press, 2004).

6. Bill Chou, "Implementing the Reform of Performance Appraisal in China's Civil Service," *China Information* 19 (2005): 49.

7. Bernstein and Lü, *Taxation without Representation in Contemporary Rural China*, 48–83. Since the abolition, poor local governments have largely relied on transfers from higher-level authorities for their finances.

8. Chou, "Implementing the Reform of Performance Appraisal in China's Civil Service," 51.

9. Interview with the township organization department committee (interview no. 94).

10. Several studies have documented the strong bias of cadre evaluation criteria toward economic growth and industrial performance, but they have not compared the criteria across locales with differing economic conditions and level of development. For instance, see Maria Edin, "State Capacity and Local Agent Control in China: CCP Cadre Management from a Township Perspective," *China Quarterly* 179 (March 2003): 35–52. Susan Whiting, *Power and Wealth in Rural China: The Political Economy of Institutional Change* (New York: Cambridge University Press, 2001).

11. Though "number of large industrial enterprises" and "number of industrial parks" are only listed as "hard targets" in Zen, they reinforce the target of "industrial production," which is featured prominently in all cases. The greater number of large industrial enterprises and industrial parks a township hosts, the higher its industrial production will be.

12. See chapter 6 for more in-depth analyses of case studies.

13. Those who score high take the front seats, and those who score low take the back seats. In addition, their ranking on these quantitative economic indicators are also included in the cadre target responsibility booklet the county distributes to townships in the following year.

14. This rudimentary investment attitude may not characterize the urban towns in Beijing or Shanghai municipality that tend to specialize in a particular sector, such as semi-conductors or fiber optics.

15. This is no different from corporate executives being driven by quarterly corporate earnings rather than focusing on devising strategies that are in the long-term interests of the corporation. In addition, there is a debate in the U.S. education system as to whether linking teachers' pay with students' test scores may discourage creative thinking, intellectual curiosity, and other qualities not explicitly captured by test scores. See Bengt Holmstrom and J. Tirole, "Multitask Principal-Agent Analyses: Incentive Contracts, Asset Ownership, and Job Design," *Journal of Law Economics & Organization* 7 (1991): 24–52.

16. Interview no. 84.

17. Interviews no. 74 and 116. Also mentioned in Shukai Zhao, "Accountability System of Township Governments (*Xiangzhen zhengfu de wenze tixi*)," *China Reform (Zhongguo Gaige)* 2 (2005).

18. c.f. Huang, "Managing Chinese Bureaucrats," which argues that rotation serves a useful purpose for preventing local political alliances.

19. Interview no. 116.

20. There was a heated scholarly and policy debate in the early 1990s about the possible disintegration of China as the country underwent significant fiscal decentralization resulting in the central government's declining share of revenue vis-à-vis the provinces. There were concerns that wealthy provinces, such as Guangdong and Zhejiang, may disobey the center's policies and ultimately break away from Beijing.

21. This distinction was pointed out by Jie Gao in "Governing by Goals and Numbers: A Case Study in the Use of Performance Measurement to Build State Capacity in China," *Public Administration and Development* 29 (2009): 21–31.

22. Huang, *Inflation and Investment Controls in China*. Huang, "Managing Chinese Bureaucrats." Landry, *Decentralized Authoritarianism in China*.

23. For more information on the performance measurement systems of major Western countries, see OECD, *Performance Management in Government: Performance Management and Results-Oriented Management* (Paris: Author, 1994). R. MacAdam and T. Walker,

"Evaluating the Best Value Framework in UK Local Government Services," *Public Administration and Development* 24, no. 3 (2004): 183–96. I. Proeller, "Outcome-orientation in Performance Contracts: Empirical Evidence from Swiss Local Governments," *International Review of Administrative Sciences* 73, no. 1 (2007): 95–111. C. Hood, "Gaming in Targetworld: The Target Approach to Managing British Public Services," *Public Administration Review* 66, no. 94 (2006): 515–21.

24. Christine Wong, "Central-local Relations Revisited: The 1994 Tax-Sharing Reform and Public Expenditure Management in China," *China Perspectives* 31 (2000): 52–63.

25. Susan L. Shirk, *The Political Logic of Economic Reform in China* (Berkeley: University of California Press, 1993). Under the pre-reform unified fiscal system, local governments had poor incentives for tax collection since most taxes collected locally were turned over to the central coffers and were subsequently distributed by an interregional transfer system to meet local expenditure needs.

26. Christine Wong, "Fiscal Reform and Local Industrialization: The Problematic Sequencing of Reform in Post-Mao China," *Modern China* 18, no. 2 (April 1992): 197–227. Christine Wong, "Can the Retreat from Equality Be Reversed? An Assessment of Redistributive Fiscal Policies from Deng Xiaoping to Wen Jiabao," in *Paying for Progress in China?: Public Finance, Human Welfare and Changing Patterns of Inequality*, ed. Vivienne Shue and Christine Wong (London: Routledge, 2007).

27. Oi, "Fiscal Reform and the Economic Foundations of Local State Corporatism in China." Whiting, *Power and Wealth in Rural China*.

28. These official figures account for recorded budgetary and extrabudgetary revenue. As this chapter later illustrates, unrecorded land-related revenue can be very substantial and help finance local-government expenditures. The official figures are from Anwar Shah and Chunli Shen, "The Reform of the Intergovernmental Transfer System to Achieve a Harmonious Society and a Level Playing Field for Regional Development in China," *World Bank Policy Research Working Paper 4100* (2006).

29. World Bank, *National Development and Sub-national Finance—A Review of Provincial Expenditures* (Beijing: Poverty Reduction and Economic Management Unit, East Asia and Pacific Region, The World Bank, 2002).

30. Albert Park et al., "Distributional Consequences of Reforming Local Finance in China," *China Quarterly* 147 (September 1996): 751–78.

31. James Kung, Chenggang Xu, and Feizhou Zhou, "From Industrialization to Urbanization: The Social Consequences of Changing Fiscal Incentives on Local Governments' Behavior," in *Institutional Design for China's Evolving Market Economy* (Oxford: Oxford University Press, forthcoming).

32. Shah and Shen, "The Reform of the Intergovernmental Transfer System to Achieve a Harmonious Society and a Level Playing Field for Regional Development in China," 3.

33. Author's calculation from data provided in ibid., 6.

34. Era Dabla-Norris, "Issues in Intergovernmental Fiscal Relations in China," *IMF Working Paper* WP/05/30 (2005): 3.

35. Author's calculation from data provided in Shah and Shen, "The Reform of the Intergovernmental Transfer System to Achieve a Harmonious Society and a Level Playing Field for Regional Development in China," 6.

36. Wong, "Central-local Relations Revisited."

37. Achim Fock and Christine Wong, *China: Improving Rural Public Finance for the Harmonious Society* (Beijing: World Bank, 2007), 8.

38. An exception to this rule is in the seven provinces (Anhui, Fujian, Heilongjiang, Hainan, Hubei, Ningxia, and Zhejiang), four municipalities (Beijing, Shanghai, Tianjin, and Chongqing) and five cities (Dalian, Qingdao, Shenzhen, Xiamen, and Ningbo) where these administrations bypass the prefectures to deal directly with the counties. See Shah

and Shen, "The Reform of the Intergovernmental Transfer System to Achieve a Harmonious Society and a Level Playing Field for Regional Development in China," 3.

39. Ibid., 29.

40. This observation is also made in Shukai Zhao, "The Burdens of Township Government Debts—A Survey of 20 Townships in 10 Provinces," *China Reform (Zhongguo Gaige)* 7 (2005).

41. Unlike in industrialized countries, the personal income tax is not a major source of revenue for any level of government in China.

42. John James Kennedy, "From the Tax-for-Fee Reform to the Abolition of Agricultural Taxes: The Impact on Township Governments in North-west China," *China Quarterly* 189 (March 2007): 43–59.

43. Ray Yep, "Can 'Tax-for-Fee' Reform Reduce Rural Tension in China? The Process, Progress and Limitations," *China Quarterly* 177 (2004): 42–70.

44. Feizhou Zhou, "Shengcai Youdao: Tudikaifa he Zhuanran zhong de Zhengfu he Nongmin," *Sociological Research (Shehuixue Yanjiu)* 1 (2007).

45. Kung, Xu, and Zhou, "From Industrialization to Urbanization."

5. DIVERGING PATHWAYS TO PROSPERITY

1. Peter Nolan and Fureng Dong, *Market Forces in China: Competition and Small Business The Wenzhou Debate* (London: Zed Books, 1989). Liu, "The 'Wenzhou Model' of Development and China's Modernization." Liu, "Reform from Below." For a more recent study of the factors contributing to successful industrialization in Wenzhou, see Calvin Chen, *Some Assembly Required: Work, Community and Politics in China's Rural Enterprises* (Cambridge, MA: Harvard University Asia Center, 2008).

2. Wenling county annal.

3. Jinchuan Shi, Wang Wei, and Qian Tao, *Private Economy and Institutional Innovation: Analyses of the "Taizhou Phenomena" (minying jingji yu zhidu chuangxin: taizhou xianxiang yanjiu)* (Hangzhou: Zhejiang Daxue Chubanshe, 2004), 4–5.

4. By historical record, the household responsibility system was first experimented—without the knowledge of the central government—in Sichuan since the people in the densely populated province had suffered, more than those in other provinces, from the disastrous effect of falling agricultural output from collective farming. For further information, see for instance Frank Dikötter, *Mao's Great Famine: The History of China's Most Devastating Catastrophe, 1958–62* (New York: Walker, 2010). Dali L. Yang, *Calamity and Reform in China: State, Rural Society, and Institutional Change since the Great Leap Famine* (Stanford, CA: Stanford University Press, 1996).

5. Zouping and Wenling county annals.

6. This is also mentioned in Whiting, *Power and Wealth in Rural China.*

7. Shi, Wei, and Tao, *Private Economy and Institutional Innovation.*

8. Wenling County Annals, p. 283. Production teams are the lowest denominator in agricultural collective units, consisting of tens of households.

9. This phenomenon is well documented: Tsai, *Back-Alley Banking.* Kristen Parris, "Local Initiative and National Reform: The Wenzhou Model of Development," *China Quarterly* 134 (1993): 242–63.

10. Private ownership was not legally recognized by the government until the late 1990s, though some private enterprises existed for many years prior to their official recognition.

11. Urban credit cooperatives (UCCs) are the equivalent of RCCs in urban areas, sharing both the same institutional and the same ownership structure. UCCs underwent reform to become city banks in the late 1990s.

12. Interview with the Wenling RCB manager.

13. This is measured using the five-level classification of bad debts in accordance with the international standard instead of the four-level classification typically used in Chinese accounting. While the former is based on the risk of non-repayment, the latter is based on loan expiration dates.

14. Tsai, *Back-Alley Banking.*

15. The Wenling County Annals, p. 455. It mentions specifically high-interest informal lending (*gaolidai*) as being active before the establishment of RCCs in the 1950s, the rotating credit associations as borrowing from close friends and relatives, and fund-raising (*jizhi*) as a means of raising capital to finance enterprises.

16. Many of my interviewees, including senior credit managers and enterprise owners in Taizhou, have indicated to me that the informal credit sector has become less active compared to a decade or two ago. There is, however, no substantive evidence to corroborate these individuals' observations.

17. Interviews with two private enterprise owners in a township in Taizhou.

18. Interview with a Taizhou RCB manager.

19. Interviews with a Taizhou RCB manager and a township RCC manager.

20. Only government-owned or privately owned land titles can be used as bank security or otherwise traded.

21. This is different from a straightforward deposit guarantee scheme widely adopted by credit institutions in China. The traditional scheme requires borrowers to deposit savings, regardless of the amount or duration, with the banks as a form of guarantee.

22. Even though the law stipulates that the rights to trade land rest with the county but not township governments, Zen has struck a special deal with Wenling county to trade land on its behalf, since it repatriates a large proportion of its tax revenue to the county for redistributional purposes. Zen retains close to 90 percent of the income from land sales in the township. Source: Interview with Zen township finance bureau director (interview no. 118).

23. See Articles 10 and 63 of the Land Management Law.

24. The law was amended in 2008 to allow farmers to deal with private enterprises directly; in spite of that, local governments' voracious appetite for land-related income shows no sign of abating.

25. There are three types of compensation—land compensation (*tudi buchang*), resettlement allowance (*anzhi buchang*), and crop compensation fee (*qingmiao buzhufei*). Article 46 of the Land Management Law imposes a ceiling on the combined value of the compensation of thirty times the farmer's average annual production value of arable land in the past three years.

26. Sources of information on land sales were interviews with various land management bureaus in townships and counties (interviews no. 86 and 112).

27. Some local governments deliberately lower prices for industrial-use land in order to compete for industrial investment with neighboring jurisdictions. See Ran Tao, Fubing Su, Mingxing Liu, and Guangzhong Cao, "Land Leasing and Local Public Finance in China's Regional Development: Evidence from Prefecture-level Cities," *Urban Studies* 47, no. 10 (2010): 2217–36.

28. In fairness, it should be pointed out that local governments have to allocate some expenditures on building infrastructure on newly acquired farmland, such as building roads and laying telecommunication cables, before it is sold to private developers or enterprises. Therefore, local governments do not pocket the entire land-sale proceeds; a proportion of which is usually invested in infrastructure development.

29. Michael Wines and Jonathan Ansfield, "Trampled in a Land Rush, Chinese Resist," *New York Times*, May 26, 2010.

30. The national averages are for 2005, obtained from the *China Statistical Yearbook 2006*.

31. For more details on the Sunan model, see Philip C. C. Huang, *The Peasant Family and Rural Development in the Yangzi Delta, 1350–1988* (Stanford, CA: Stanford University Press, 1990). Hsiao-Tung Fei, *Rural Development in China: Prospect and Retrospect* (Chicago: University of Chicago Press, 1989).

32. Andrew G. Walder, "Zouping in Perspective," in *Zouping in Transition: The Process of Reform in Rural North China*, ed. Andrew G. Walder (Cambridge, MA: Harvard University Press, 1998).

33. For political explanations for why asset stripping has occurred, see Lynette H. Ong, "Between Developmental and Clientelist States: Local State-Business Relationships in China,", *Comparative Politics*, 44, no. 2 (2012): 191–209.

34. Zouping County Yearbook, p. 304.

35. National taxes are known as *guoshui*, which are shared among the central, provincial, and county governments. The main compositions of national taxes were value-added tax (*zengzhishui*) and enterprise income tax. Source: Interview with Zouping National Tax Bureau.

36. Tiffany Zhu, "Zouping: A Town of Cotton Spinning," *Journal for Asia on Textile and Apparel*, December 2006.

37. Interview no. 100, the company's information on irasia.com, and the company's website.

38. Walder, "Zouping in Perspective."

39. Zouping Yearbook (1986–95), pp. 304–5.

40. Author's calculation from data provided by the Zouping county government website.

41. Interview with the ABC manager (interview no. 87).

42. Ibid.

43. Interview with the RCC manager in Zouping county (interview no. 95).

44. The Agricultural Bank of China floats base lending rate by 50 percent for small enterprise borrowers, but by only 30 percent for large enterprises. In Han, the RCC charges about 7 percent interest for loans to agricultural households and individual household business, but close to 11 percent for enterprise borrowers.

45. Of course, the size of the economy in the two localities differs, but even if that is taken into consideration, there remains a large gap in the power of grassroots loan officers in loan approvals.

46. Interviews with Han's RCC manager and Zouping RCC union.

47. Interview no. 100.

48. For more on how enormous gains from land transactions have encouraged local governments to convert land from agricultural to commercial uses, see chapter 4.

49. Aside from this reason officially provided by an interviewee from the county land management bureaus (interview no. 86), one can attribute the local government's generous behavior to its rapidly growing tax base, which reduces its need to take from the share that rightly belongs to farmers. Alternatively, farmers could have refused to sell their lands unless higher compensation was given. The actual reason of this higher compensation is unknown. The reason given in the text is what has been informed by the county bureau.

50. "Surplus labor" is an economists' term to denote excess farm labor that does not contribute to marginal production. For instance, if five people work on a farm to produce *x* amount of wheat, but the same could be produced by only three people, two are considered "surplus labor."

51. Zouping Yearbook (1986–95), p. 455.

6. THE LOCAL GOVERNMENT–LED PATH TO RURAL DECAY

1. These pseudonyms are given to protect the identities of my interviewees.

2. James Kung and Yi-Min Lin, "The Decline of Township-and-Village Enterprises in China's Economic Transition," *World Development* 35, no. 4 (2007): 569–84. For further analyses on the factors leading to the downfall of the collective enterprises, see Barry J. Naughton, *The Chinese Economy: Transitions & Growth* (Cambridge, MA: MIT Press, 2007), chap. 12.

3. Peter Ping Li, "The Puzzle of China's Township-Village Enterprises: The Paradox of Local Corporatism in a Dual-Track Economic Transition," *Management and Organization Review* 1, no. 2 (2005): 197–224.

4. Li and Rozelle, "Privatizing Rural China." Dong, Bowles, and Ho, "The Determinants of Employee Ownership in China's Privatized Rural Industry." Kung and Lin, "The Decline of Township-and-Village Enterprises in China's Economic Transition."

5. Interview no. 26.

6. Ministry of Agriculture TVE Management Bureau, "Development of Township and Village Enterprises in 1995," *Township and Village Enterprise Yearbook* (1996): 9.

7. This rudimentary investment attitude may not characterize the urban towns in Beijing or Shanghai municipality that tend to specialize in a particular sector, such as biotechnology and other high-tech industries.

8. Unless indicated otherwise, current data for the field sites in this chapter pertain to the time field studies were conducted, in 2005–6.

9. Interview with Cheng township party secretary (interview no. 37).

10. Interview with the managing director of Xiao Enterprise Private Limited (interview no. 28).

11. Interviews with Zhang and Zhou township party secretaries (interviews no. 48 and 51).

12. The county is the birthplace of one of the national revolutionary leaders of the CCP, and some have speculated that this has entitled it to special attention and treatment by the central government not enjoyed by other similarly poor counties.

13. RCCs in some locales were forced to take over the assets and loans of the local credit foundations.

14. Interview no. 74.

15. Xiao has a range of mineral resources; mining brings some income to the local government. For Cheng, being a county seat that is mostly service-oriented, sales tax as opposed to agricultural tax accounts for the bulk of its revenue.

16. Interviews with township finance bureaus. This point has also been raised in Kennedy, "From the Tax-for-Fee Reform to the Abolition of Agricultural Taxes."

17. The most heart-wrenching aspect of this reality is the fact that these children left to be looked after by their grandparents get to see their parents only once every few years. For numerous children I met, their only impression or memory of their parents came from photos and occasional long-distance phone calls.

18. For the general "push" and "pull" factors for internal migration in China, see Hein Mallee, "Migration, Hukou and Resistance in Reform China," in *Chinese Society: Change, Conflict and Resistance*, vol. 2, ed. Elizabeth J. Perry and Mark Selden (London: RoutledgeCurzon, 2003). Rachel Murphy, *How Migrant Labor Is Changing Rural China* (Cambridge: Cambridge University Press, 2002). Dorothy Solinger, "China's Floating Population," in *The Paradox of China's Post-Mao Reforms*, ed. Merle Goldman and Roderick MacFarquhar (Cambridge, MA: Harvard University Press, 1999), 220–40.

19. Interview no. 46.

20. Kennedy ("From the Tax-for-Fee Reform to the Abolition of Agricultural Taxes") has found similar phenomena in the townships in northwestern China, though we disagree on the exact cause of the phenomena.

21. For the entire survey, cropping and setting up of private business were the most common reasons for getting a loans from an RCC, accounting for 23 percent and 19 percent, respectively.

22. Nine-year compulsory education covers six years of primary schooling and three years of junior high school education.

23. Interview no. 36. When I conducted my fieldwork in 2004, SC1 county had just started paying teachers' basic salaries.

24. Fock and Wong, *China.*

25. World Bank, *China's Health Sector—Why Reform is Needed*, Rural Health in China: Briefing Notes Series, April 2005.

26. The other commonly cited problem with the new scheme is the voluntary nature of membership, which gives rise to "moral hazard"—that is, those who opt to join are more likely to develop or have had major illness, while healthy people are likely to opt out.

27. You-tien Hsing, *The Great Urban Transformation: Politics of Land and Property in China* (New York: Oxford University Press, 2010).

28. To a certain degree, local government's illicit and irregular conduct of land trade can simply be seen as corruption, which has been explored elsewhere; for instance, see Ting Gong, "Corruption and Local Governance: The Double Identity of Chinese Local Governments in Market Reform," *Pacific Review* 19, no. 1 (March 2006): 85–102. However, there are systemic causes for such local-government misconduct, which is the focus of the present study.

29. The other five perished townships were still largely agricultural and remote. As a result, there was not even demand for commercial-use land in these townships.

30. The negative sentiment was so overwhelming that they requested that I help report the case to the provincial government, with the explicit knowledge that I was a foreign scholar and the assumption that I might be able to attract attention from higher-level governments that they could not.

31. Scholars have used different terms to describe this phenomenon: Oi and Zhao (2007) termed it the "hollowing out" of township government, while Kennedy (2007) described the government as merely "administrative shells." Jean Oi and Zhao Shukai, "Fiscal Crisis in China's Townships: Causes and Consequences," in *Grassroots Political Reform in Contemporary China*, ed. Elizabeth J. Perry and Merle Goldman (Cambridge, MA: Harvard University Press, 2007), 75–96.

32. For studies on corruption of local officials, please see Xiaobo Lü, *Cadres and Corruption* (Stanford, CA: Stanford University Press, 2000). Sun, *Corruption and Market in Contemporary China.*

33. For an analytical piece on the transformation of the Sunan model, see Lynette Ong, "Between Development and Clientelist States: Local State-Business Relationships in China," *Comparative Politics* 44, no. 2 (2012): 191–209.

34. Notably, see Ethan Michelson, "Public Goods and State-Society Relations: An Impact Study of Rural Stimulus," Working Paper No.4 (Indiana University, IL: Research Center for Chinese Politics and Business, 2011).

35. Chris Buckley, "Special Report: Is Wen's 'New Socialist Countryside' Working?" Reuters, February 22, 2011. http://www.reuters.com/article/2011/02/22/us-china-labour-rural-idUSTRE71L1EN20110222.

CONCLUSION

1. Zhou, "The Central Bank's Role in the Rural Credit Cooperatives' Reforms." The estimates were based on an old classification of nonperforming loans that was based on loan expiration dates rather than on the risk of nonrepayment, as in the current classification.

2. Yu, "Reforms of the RCCs Should Be Pushed Forward."

3. For further information on TBTF and bank bailouts, see Stern and Feldman, *Too Big to Fail.*

4. Gretchen Morgenson, "The Fannie and Freddie Fallout," *New York Times*, July 13, 2008.

5. Xie, "Reforms of China's Rural Credit Cooperatives and Policy Options," 438. As Xie notes, *no* deposit insurance scheme exists in China to provide legal protection for depositors.

6. This is estimated to have cost the RCCs about 400 million yuan in 1989, 40 percent of their financial loss in that year. Source: Xu et al., *Reform and Development of Rural Finance in China*, 72.

7. RCCs bear an uncanny resemblance to the government-sponsored enterprises (GSEs) of the U.S. home mortgage giants Fannie Mae and Freddie Mac and the former Student Loan Marketing Association, Sallie Mae. Some observers sounded warning bells about the need for stricter regulations of GSEs as early as 1990 in the aftermath of the savings and loan crisis. GSEs are granted implicit guarantees by the federal government for performing certain public-policy objectives, namely increasing affordable housing and expanding low-cost education. In the cases of Fannie and Freddie Mac, they purchase home mortgages from banks and package them as securities that are sold to Wall Street investors. With federal guarantees behind them, the enterprises are able to trade the securities as if they are backed by the full faith of the U.S. government, though in fact federal authorities have no legal obligation to rescue the enterprises or GSEs in times of financial difficulties. They are also able to borrow on more favorable terms, and hence the federal guarantees help them secure capital at lower cost. Although the directors of a majority of the enterprises are elected by the shareholders, and the enterprises' profits are largely passed on to their shareholders, there is still an expectation of bailout by the government in times of trouble. Moreover, these corporations are not subject to the costly filing requirements of the Securities and Exchange Commission like other listed corporations. For further information, see Charles F. Bingman, "Review: The Hidden Power of GSEs," *Public Administration Review* 52, no. 5 (2008): 522–24. Thomas H. Stanton, *A State of Risk: Will Government-Sponsored Enterprises Be the Next Financial Crisis?* (New York: Harper Collins, 1991).

8. From the late 1990s to the early 2000s, the nonperforming loans of the state-owned banks were transferred three times, totaled 2.45 trillion yuan, to the Asset Management Companies (AMCs). The Asset Management Companies are expected to recover the value of some of the nonperforming assets. In addition, the PBoC injected US$60 billion out of its foreign reserves into the Big Four banks in 2003.

9. RCCs also get to keep the bad assets (though they have been written off the books) and retain any profit from recovering the assets.

10. Anonymous, "2003 Rural Credit Cooperative Reform," *Caijing (Finance and Economics)*, November 3, 2008.

11. For further information on the corporate governance structure of post-reform RCCs, see Ong, "Communist Party and Financial Institutions."

12. Lynette Ong, "Multiple Principals and Collective Action: China's Rural Credit Cooperatives and Poor Households' Access to Credit," *Journal of East Asian Studies* 6, no. 2 (August 2006): 177–204.

13. A survey by Xie et al. (2006) of post-reform RCCs finds an even higher number of shareholders: the average number for 48 post-reform banks surveys was 27,898.

14. Interviews no. 63, 67, and 79, conducted in Jiangsu and Zhejiang provinces.

15. These incidents were widely reported in the Chinese-language media: Anonymous, "Hunan RCCs' Interest Rates Exceed 6%, and 'Miraculous' Equity of 3 Billion Yuan," *Xinhua Daily News*, January 19, 2005. Qei Meng and Zhiyun Cheng, "New Problems in 'Buy-

ing Good Incentives' Policy," *Economic Observer (Jinji Guanchabao)*, June 25, 2006. These phenomena have also been observed in Xie, Zhong, and Shen, *RCC Reforms: What Have We Done? What Do We Still Need to Do?* 19.

16. Fa Tian and Chenying Zhou, "To Reconstruct Financial Relations among Local Governments (*Chonggou difang zhengfu jian caizheng guanxi*)," *Gaige (Reform)*, no. 2 (2004).

17. Fock and Wong, *China*.

18. The debt problem was also not restricted to Sichuan province and was likely even worse in other provinces. Indeed, among the five provinces surveyed in the 2007 World Bank report, Sichuan was the least indebted, behind Shaanxi, Jilin, Hebei, and Jiangsu.

19. Anonymous, "Hunan RCCs' Interest Rates Exceed 6%, and 'Miraculous' Equity of 3 Billion Yuan."

20. Official statistics and information on the fiscal stimulus package are extremely scarce, but 30 percent of 4 trillion yuan means that the average financing share of each province is about 46 billion yuan. This average amount is tremendous compared to the size of the regional economies. Guangdong, the province with the largest GDP, has an economy of 3,600 billion yuan, while Tibet, the province with the smallest GDP, has an economy of only 39 billion yuan. This remains staggering even once we take into account the likely possibility that richer provinces may have to pick up a bigger share of the tab.

21. Wu Chen, "China's Stimulus Package: A Six-Month Report Card," *Economist Intelligence Unit* (2009): 13.

22. In the first quarter of 2009, total loan growth was 4.6 trillion yuan, an amount exceeding the magnitude of the fiscal stimulus package. Even if we take into consideration the fact that a proportion of the loan growth is for the normal needs of a growing economy, credit growth in the first quarter was 10 percent of GDP in excess of the average credit expansion in the previous ten years. For more information, see Barry Naughton, "Understanding the Chinese Stimulus Package," *China Leadership Monitor* 28, no. 5 (2009).

23. Many RCCs, including those with negative capital adequacy ratios, have drummed up their lending since the announcement of the stimulus package in late 2008. For further information, see Yuzhe Zhang and Huilei Fang, "Loan Surge Sows Risk at Rural Credit Cooperatives," *Caijing*, October 21, 2009.

24. Kong Ho Chua and Shidong Zhang, "China Record Loans Diverted to Stocks, Shenyin Says," *Bloomberg*, February 17, 2009. Malcolm Moore, "Chinese Stimulus Cash Is Inflating New Stock Market Bubble, Officials Warn," *Telegraph*, June 30, 2009.

25. For a contrary view, see Andrew Batson and Janet Zhang, "The Magic Mountain: China's Public Debt" (GaveKalDragonomics, April 20, 2011). Ibid. They argue that local-government debt is under control, despite its non-transparent nature.

26. Kan Huo and Changyong Wang, "Peering into a Black Hole of Government Debt," *Caixin*, March 9, 2011, http://english.caing.com/englishNews.jsp?id=100234187&time=2011-03-09&cl=111&page=all.

27. National Audit Office, *Audit Report (Shenji jieguo baogao)*, 2011, http://www.audit.gov.cn/n1992130/n1992150/n1992500/2752208.html.

28. Victor Shih, "Local Government Debt: Big Rock-Candy Mountain," *China Economic Quarterly* (June 2010): 26–32.

29. Tom Holland, "The Hole in Beijing's Budget Is Bigger Than You Think," *South China Morning Post*, November 6, 2009.

30. Walder, "Zouping in Perspective."

31. Duckett, *The Entrepreneurial State in China*.

32. Blecher and Shue, *Tethered Deer*.

33. Oi, *Rural China Takes Off*. Oi, "The Role of the Local State in China's Transitional Economy."

34. Bernstein and Lü, *Taxation without Representation in Contemporary Rural China*. Xiaobo Lü, "Booty Capitalism, Bureau-preneurs, and the State in Transition: Organizational Corruption in China," *Comparative Politics* 32, no. 3 (2000): 272–94.

35. Ong, "Between Development and Clientelist States."

36. Minnie Chan, "Intercepting Petitioners is a Thriving Business," *South China Morning Post*, April 3, 2010.

37. A new study finds that variation in the death tolls was related to the political incentives of the Communist Party system. Those provincial leaders who had more incentives to climb the political ladder contributed more in grain procurement, which led to the famine in their respective provinces. See James Kung and Shuo Chen, "The Tragedy of the Nomenklatura: Career Incentives and Political Radicalism during China's Great Leap Famine," *American Political Science Review* 105, no. 1 (2011): 27–45.

38. Dikötter, *Mao's Great Famine*. Yang, *Calamity and Reform in China*.

39. Montinola, Qian, and Weingast, "Federalism, Chinese Style: The Political Basis for Economic Success." C.f. Aseema Sinha, "Political Foundations of Market-Enhancing Federalism: Theoretical Lessons from India and China," *Comparative Politics* 37, no. 2 (April 2005).

40. For further elaboration on this argument, see Lynette Ong, "Fiscal Federalism and Soft Budget Constraints: The Case of China," *International Political Science Review* forthcoming (2012).

41. Though only one of the BRI's twenty-three divisions, it is nonetheless responsible for the lion's share of its profits. In 2008, it boasted a savings portfolio of US$5.9 billion and loan portfolio of US$3.9 billion. The other divisions include small credit and cooperative loans, products and marketing, treasury, and commercial and corporate loans.

42. Hans Dieter Seibel and Agus Rachmadi, "Growth and Resilience of Savings-Based Microfinance Institutions: The Case of the Microbanking Units of Bank Rakyat Indonesia," 2009, www.microfinancegateway.org/gm/document_1,9,41397/GrowthandResilience.pdf.

43. See Marguerite S. Robinson, *The Microfinance Revolution, Volume 2: Lessons from Indonesia* (Washington, DC: World Bank, 2002). Seibel and Rachmadi, "Growth and Resilience of Savings-Based Microfinance Institutions: The Case of the Microbanking Units of Bank Rakyat Indonesia."

44. China's rural population is nine hundred million, compared to Indonesia's one hundred fourteen million.

45. Since the fiscal policy has been intensely debated elsewhere, it will not be discussed further here. For further discussion, see An Chen, "The 1994 Tax Reform and Its Impact on China's Rural Fiscal Structure," *Modern China* 34, no. 3 (July 2008): 303–43. Le-Yin Zhang, "Chinese Central-Provincial Fiscal Relationships, Budgetary Decline and the Impact of the 1994 Fiscal Reform: An Evaluation," *China Quarterly* 157 (1999): 115–41.

46. Jonathan Rodden, *Hamilton's Paradox: The Promise and Peril of Fiscal Federalism* (New York: Cambridge University Press, 2006). C.f. Stuti Khemani, "Party Politics and Fiscal Discipline in a Federation: Evidence from the States of India," *Comparative Political Studies* 40, no. 6 (2007): 691–712.

47. Jonathan A. Rodden and Gunnar S. Eskeland, "Lessons and Conclusions," in *Fiscal Decentralization and the Challenge of Hard Budget Constraints*, ed. Jonathan Rodden, Gunnar S. Eskeland, and Jennie Litvack (Cambridge, MA: MIT Press, 2003), 431–62.

48. Alternatively, the audit commission could assess and report on the magnitude of debt. However, to do so for all levels of local governments on a regular basis would be a monumental task.

49. One could argue that with more economic growth and more tax revenue, the government can clean up the rivers and address environmental pollution as it can with bailing out banks. But the focus here is not on remedies, but the first part of the issue, which is promoting environmentally friendly industries instead of all taxpaying industries and achieving local economic growth through use of local resources.

Glossary of Chinese Terms

Pinyin	Chinese	English
anzhi buchang	安置补偿	resettlement allowance
bianzhi	编制	ordinary cadre personnel management system
caizheng	财政	public finance
chuji	处级	an administrative rank, usually for county leaders
dangwei	党委	party committee
dianshui	垫税	to cover fiscal shortfalls
difang caizheng shouru	地方财政收入	local tax receipts
difang rongzi pingtai	地方融资平台	local government financing vehicles
fenshuizhi	分税制	Tax Sharing System
fupin daikuan	扶贫贷款	poverty alleviation loans
fu keji	副科级	an administrative rank, usually for deputy township leaders
gangwei zerenzhi	岗位责任制	cadre responsibility system
getihu or geti	个体户/个体工商户	micro-enterprises or small commercial establishments
gongshanghu	商户	
gongye yongdi	工业用地	industrial-use land
guoshui shouru	国税收入	central-government tax receipts
huiyuan daibiao dahui	会员代表大会	members' representative meeting
jiaoyu fujia fei	教育附加费	additional education fees
jiexin huanjiu	借新换旧	obtain a new loan to repay an old loan
jilv jiancha weiyuan	纪律检查委员	discipline inspection committee member
jilv jiancha weiyuanhui	纪律检查委员会	discipline inspection committee
jinrong	金融	finance
jiti qiye	集体企业	collective enterprise
jiti zijin	集体资金	collective funds
jiucheng gaizao	旧城改造	old town refurbishment
kaohe zhibiao	考核指标	evaluation criteria
keji	科级	an administrative rank, usually for township leaders
kuai	块	area or horizontal accountability
mu	亩	one-sixth of an acre, or 6.5% of a hectare
nomenklatura	官僚	leading cadre personnel management system
nongcun hezuo jijinhui	农村合作基金会	rural cooperative foundations

pinkunxian	贫困县	officially designated "poor counties"
qingmiao buzhufei	青苗补助费	crop compensation fee
renshibu	人事部	personnel bureau
rugu huiyuan	入股委员	fee-paying members
sannong wenti	三农	the problem of the "three agricultures," referring to farmers, villages, and the agricultural sector
shangye yongdi	商业用地	commercial-use land
shehui zhuyi xinnongcun	社会主义新农村	New Socialist Countryside
shengji pinkunxian	省级贫困县	a poor county by provincial standards
siying qiye	私营企业	private enterprise
tiao	条	vertical or industry accountability
tudi buchang	土地补偿	land compensation
tudi churangjin	土地出让金	land conversion income
tudi guanlifa	土地管理法	Land Management Law
xiangcun jiti jingji zuzhi	乡村集体经济组织	township and village economic organizations
xiaoe daikuan	小额贷款	micro-credit
xingzheng jiguan	行政机关	administrative bureaus
yiban zhibiao	一般指标	ordinary targets
yibashou	一把手	the most powerful leader
yidaoqie	一刀切	one-size-fits-all
ying zhibiao	硬指标	"hard targets"
yipiao foujue	一票否决	veto power
yongren	用人	utilization of human resources
yongqian	用钱	utilization of financial resources
yusuanfa	预算法	Budget Law
zheng keji	正科级	an administrative rank, usually for township leaders
zhengji	政绩	political achievements
zhinong zaidaikuan	支农再贷款	agricultural on-lending
zhuandai	转贷	"rolling over" loans
zhuanxiang daikuan	专项贷款	earmarked central bank loans
zhuanxiang piaoju	专项票据	debt-for-bills swaps
zhuren	主任	director or manager
zibudizhai	资不抵债	liabilities-in-excess-of-assets value
zichou zijin	自筹资金	self-raised funds
zifuyingkui	自负盈亏	responsible for profits and losses independently
ziranren gu	自然人股	"natural person" share

Index

Page numbers followed by *f* refer to figures, by *t* to tables, and by *n* to notes.